Crime, Justice, and Defoe

Costerus New Series

STUDIES IN ENGLISH WORLDWIDE

Editors

Theo D'haen (*Leiden University, The Netherlands/
Leuven University, Belgium*)
Raphaël Ingelbien (*Leuven University, Belgium*)
Birgit Neumann (*Heinrich-Heine-Universität Düsseldorf, Germany*)
Carmen Birkle (*Philipps-Universität Marburg, Germany*)

VOLUME 238

The titles published in this series are listed at *brill.com/cos*

(1)

THE
PROCEEDINGS
ON THE
KINGs Commission of the Peace,
AND

Oyer and *Terminer*, and *Goal-Delivery* of *Newgate*, held for the CITY of *London*, and COUNTY of *Middlesex*, at *Justice-Hall* in the *Old Bayly*:

ON

Friday, Saturday, Monday and *Wednesday*, being the 12th, 13th, 15th, and 17th, of *January*, 1721. in the Eighth Year of His MAJESTY's Reign.

BEFORE the Right Honourable Sir WILLIAM STEWART, Kt. Lord Mayor of the City of *London*; the Rt. Honourable the Lord Chief Baron *Bury*; the Honourable Mr. Justice *Dormer*; Sir *William Thompson*, Kt. Recorder; *John Raby*, Esq; Deputy-Recorder; with several of His Majesty's Justices of the Peace for the City of *London* and County of *Middlesex*.

London Jury.	Middlesex Jury.
Alexander Masters,	*Edward Boswell,*
James Horton,	*Joseph Spencer,*
Benjamin Turbat,	*John Ford,*
Joseph Winsmore,	*John Prater,*
John Burdett,	*Isaac Fielding,*
James Mackall,	*Edward Livnoy,*
Theophilus Joyner,	*John Parsons,*
William Hunt,	*Joseph Watson,*
Peter Taylor,	*Francis Geuge,*
Robert Burton,	*Thomas Richmond,*
Thomas Robinson,	*Henry Newton,*
John Edden.	*Henry Goddard.*

Hannah Perkins, alias **Elizabeth Ellison**, of St. *Andrew Holbourn*, was indicted for feloniously stealing out of the Dwelling-House of *Joshua Perry*, a Camblet Ridinghood, value 15 s. and other Things; and 14 s. in Money, the Goods and Money of *Joshua Perry*, on the 9th of *December* last. It appeared the prisoner was a Servant to the Prosecutor, and stole the Goods, which she confest when apprehended, and told them where to find them. At the Bar the said nothing in her Defence, and the Jury found her guilty to the value of 39 s.

Jane Pearse, of St. *Sepulchres*, was indicted for privately stealing from the Person of *John Grevit*, a Gold Ring, value 18 s. the Goods of the said *John Grevit*, on the 8th of *December* last. *John Grevit* depos'd, that going along *Fleet-lane*, about Eleven at Night, he met the prisoner, who took him by the Hand, and wrench'd the Ring off his Finger; upon which he held her fast, and bid her give it him again; but she told him she had not got it, but if he'd look upon the Ground he might find it. He then call'd the Watch, with whose Lanthorn he search'd on the Ground for his Ring, but to no purpose, upon which they secured the prisoner. The prisoner in her Defence said, that the Prosecutor coming out of an Alehouse, and seeing her, ask'd her to drink a Glass of Wine, which she refusing, he charg'd her with taking off his Ring; she answered, I know nothing of it. He then call'd the Watch, and desired him to lend him his Lanthorn, for he believed he had dropt his Ring; but not finding it, he charg'd her with taking it from him, upon which she was carried to the Compter. The Jury found her Guilty to the value of 10 d.

Susan Jackson and **Mary Sharp**, of St. *Ann Black Fryers*, were indicted for privately stealing from the Person of *Will. Price*, a pair of Silver Buckles, value 10 s. 2 Gold Rings, 18 s. a Handkerchief, 2 s. a Hat, 10 s. a Peruque, a pair of Stockings, a Moidore, a Guinea, and 17 Shillings in Silver, the Goods and Money of *William Price*, on the 6th of this Instant *January*. *William Price* depos'd, that between 3 and 4 in the Afternoon, having landed at *Black Fryers* Stairs, and coming up *New-street*, he saw the prisoner (*Jackson*) running with a Chair on her Head, and the People crying out, stop her; he stopt her accordingly, but being soon after told she was Crazy, he offer'd to give her a Pint of Beer, which she accepted. They went to the *Bur Bear* in *New-street*, and after they had drank one Pint, the prisoner *Jackson* said, since you have been so kind as to give me one Pint, I'll give you another, and so call'd for it in. When they had emptied that, *Jackson* desired him to carry the Chair up stairs into her Room, which he did, and she followed him. They being both sat down, she said, now if you will but give me one pint of Wine, I shall be easy; he consented, she call'd up *Sharp*, and sent her for the Wine. When the Wine was brought, he drank one Glass, and fell fast asleep, and slept about 4 Hours; and when he awaked, the Prisoner, and his Cloaths, and Money were missing; but finding *Jackson* about 11 the same Night, she gave him the Hat and Wig from under her Ridinghood, saying, she did not design to rob him. The Constable depos'd, that he saw *Jackson* deliver the Hat and Wig, which were produc'd, and sworn to in Court by the Prosecutor; and that afterwards going to *Jackson* in the Compter, one of the Prisoners there told him, that the 2 Rings were pawned at the Bar. *Jackson* in her Defence, own'd the Circumstances of the Prosecutor's meeting her with a Chair, and of their going to drink together; but *she* said, he was drunk, and would needs carry the Chair up Stairs, and then vomited in her Room. That he gave her a piece of Gold to be rude with her, but she refus'd it, and desir'd him to go home. He said he would not, for he'd lie there all Night, and with that he stript himself, lay down on the Table, and fell fast asleep, and there she left him. An Evidence for *Jackson* depos'd, that she had been Lunatick, us'd to run about the Streets with her Hair loose; that she had been three

Old Bailey Proceedings 12–17 January 1721[/1722]. London: printed for Benj. Motte. Sold by J. Roberts, [1722]. This image is reproduced by permission of Harvard University Law School Library, Historical and Special Collections Repository.

Crime, Justice, and Defoe

Law Enforcement Reported and Imagined in Eighteenth-Century England

By

Jeanne Clegg

BRILL

LEIDEN | BOSTON

Cover illustration: Title page Moll Flanders, 1722, courtesy of the William Andrews Clark Library, University of California Los Angeles.

Library of Congress Cataloging-in-Publication Data

Names: Clegg, Jeanne author http://id.loc.gov/authorities/names/n82248540
   http://id.loc.gov/rwo/agents/n82248540
Title: Crime, justice, and Defoe : law enforcement reported and imagined in
   eighteenth-century England / by Jeanne Clegg.
Description: Leiden ; Boston : Brill, 2025. | Series: Costerus new series,
   0165-9618 ; 238 | Includes bibliographical references and index.
Identifiers: LCCN 2025020948 (print) | LCCN 2025020949 (ebook) | ISBN
   9789004734494 hardback | ISBN 9789004734517 pdf
Subjects: LCSH: Defoe, Daniel, 1661?-1731--Criticism and interpretation |
   Crime in literature http://id.loc.gov/authorities/subjects/sh94004444 |
   Law enforcement in literature
   http://id.loc.gov/authorities/subjects/sh2005005585 | Criminal law in
   literature http://id.loc.gov/authorities/subjects/sh2016002632 |
   Literature and society--England--History--18th century
   http://id.loc.gov/authorities/subjects/sh2008106899
Classification: LCC PR3408.C76 C54 2025 (print) | LCC PR3408.C76 (ebook)
   | DDC 823.5--DC23/eng/20250514
LC record available at https://lccn.loc.gov/2025020948
LC ebook record available at https://lccn.loc.gov/2025020949

Typeface for the Latin, Greek, and Cyrillic scripts: "Brill". See and download: brill.com/brill-typeface.

ISSN 0165-9618
ISBN 978-90-04-73449-4 (hardback)
ISBN 978-90-04-73451-7 (e-book)
DOI 10.1163/9789004734517

Copyright 2025 by Koninklijke Brill BV, Plantijnstraat 2, 2321 JC Leiden, The Netherlands.
Koninklijke Brill BV incorporates the imprints Brill, Brill Nijhoff, Brill Schöningh, Brill Fink, Brill mentis, Brill Wageningen Academic, Vandenhoeck & Ruprecht, Böhlau and V&R unipress.
All rights reserved. No part of this publication may be reproduced, translated, stored in a retrieval system, or transmitted in any form or by any means, electronic, mechanical, photocopying, recording or otherwise, without prior written permission from the publisher. Requests for re-use and/or translations must be addressed to Koninklijke Brill BV via brill.com or copyright.com.
For more information: info@brill.com.

This book is printed on acid-free paper and produced in a sustainable manner.

*In memory of Beppe Colasanti
one of a kind in research and in life*

Contents

Preface XIII
Abbreviations XV

1 **Introduction** 1
   1   Other Subjectivities 1
   2   Sergeants to Take Thieves 4
   3   Old Bailey Stories 10

PART 1
Catching Thieves in Fact and Fiction: Detecting and Apprehending

2 **At the Scene of the Crime I: Catching Pickpockets** 17
   1   Introduction 17
   2   Catching Women Pickpockets 1720–1722 18
   3   Moll Flanders Advises 20
        3.1   *A Gentleman Very Rich* 20
        3.2   *A Key to the Clue* 22
   4   Catching Male Pickpockets 1720–1722 26
   5   Colonel Jack's Apprenticeship 29
        5.1   *The Hands of the Mobb* 29
        5.2   *In the Customs House* 32
   6   Conclusion 34

3 **At the Scene of the Crime II: Minding the Shop** 36
   1   Introduction 36
   2   Shoplifters Apprehended 1720–1722 39
   3   Apprehending Moll Flanders 44
        3.1   *Hawks E-y'd Journeymen* 44
        3.2   *Two Mis-takes* 47
        3.3   *The Black Part of This Story* 50
   4   Conclusion 52

4 After the Fact I: A Market for My Goods   53
- 1 Introduction   53
- 2 Criminal Disposal 1720–1722   54
  - 2.1 *Stopped Offering for Sale*   54
  - 2.2 *Receivers Prosecuted*   57
- 3 Moll Flanders' Super-fence   60
- 4 Brokers 1720–1722   63
- 5 Private Compositions   67
  - 5.1 *Moll's Governess Makes a Booty*   67
  - 5.2 *Colonel Jack's Errand of Consequence*   69
- 6 Conclusion   73

5 After the Fact II: Thieves Discovering Thieves   76
- 1 Introduction   76
- 2 Thieves Discovering Thieves 1720–1722   78
  - 2.1 *Shoplifters Discovered*   78
  - 2.2 *Street Robbers Discovered*   80
- 3 Fear of Witnesses   84
  - 3.1 *Moll's Joyful News*   84
  - 3.2 *Will's Brave Gang*   89
- 4 Conclusion   94

PART 2
The Intricacies of Office

6 What It Is to Be a Constable   99
- 1 Introduction   100
- 2 An Insupportable Hardship   101
- 3 Constables in the *Proceedings*, 1720–1722   105
- 4 Moll's Constables   110
  - 4.1 *The Hue and Cry after Jemy*   110
  - 4.2 *Rules for Searching*   112
  - 4.3 *A Good Substantial Kind of Man*   114
- 5 A Faithful Officer Humiliated   118
- 6 Conclusion   122

CONTENTS

7 **Before the Justice** 125
   1   Introduction 125
   2   Justicing Business 125
   3   London Magistrates at Work, 1720–1722 131
   4   Justices in *Moll Flanders* 137
       4.1   *A Justice Satisfied* 137
       4.2   *Trifling with Justice* 139
       4.3   *An Ancient Gentleman in Bloomsbury* 141
       4.4   *A Full Hearing in Foster Lane* 144
       4.5   *Fix'd Indeed* 148
   5   Conclusion 149

PART 3
Proper Places of the Law: Newgate, the Old Bailey and Beyond

8 **Newgate: From Committal to Indictment** 153
   1   Introduction 153
   2   Newgate Traffic 155
   3   Indictment 159
   4   Preventing Trial in *Moll Flanders* 163
       4.1   *Tampering with Witnesses* 163
       4.2   *Jemy in the Press Yard* 167
   5   Conclusion 169

9 **The Old Bailey** 171
   1   Introduction 171
   2   Arraignment 173
       2.1   *Arraignments 1720–1722* 173
       2.2   *Arraign'd, as They Call'd It* 174
   3   Altercation 175
       3.1   *Burglary Trials 1720–1722* 175
       3.2   *Courage for My Tryal* 184
   4   Verdict 187
       4.1   *Burglary Verdicts 1720–1722* 187
       4.2   *Small Comfort* 192
   5   *Allocutus* 193
       5.1   *Sentencing 1720–1722* 193
       5.2   *The Dreadful Sentence* 196
   6   Conclusion 198

10 **Punishing and Pardoning** 200
    1   Introduction 200
    2   Pardoning Procedures 201
    3   Avoiding the Rope in *Moll Flanders* 204
        3.1   *The Favour of Being Transported* 204
        3.2   *Jemy and Friends* 209
    4   Avoiding the Rope in *Colonel Jack* 213
        4.1   *The Value of a Pardon* 213
        4.2   *The Wonders of Providence* 217
    5   Conclusion 220

Epilogue 222

Bibliography 227
Index of Participants in Old Bailey Trials, J.P.s' Hearings and Related Names 242
Author and Subject Index 249

Preface

This book has taken such a very long time to write that I have accumulated a huge number of debts. It grew out of the notion, conceived in the early 1990s, that early English novels were related to testimony given in common law trials, an idea which I partially tested in conversations with friends and in essays on Defoe's favourite type of narrator, the eyewitness, on Swift's sermon denouncing false witness, and on informers, their roles and reputations over the long eighteenth century. Over the years that followed old loves (John Ruskin especially), and passing infatuations (monsters, servants, actors) occupied much of my research time, and first the Iraq war, then Covid and its pestilential predecessor, the plague, clamoured for attention. In the meantime, however, I had become well and truly hooked on reading Defoe's criminal fictions alongside the *Old Bailey Proceedings*, thankfully freely accessible and searchable online. Based on this wonderful source of information (and misinformation) on what went on in London's most important criminal court, one with which many of Defoe's early readers would have been familiar, are a series of conference papers and essays which laid the foundations of this book and have been partly re-used here.[1] I am immensely grateful to the organisers of and participants in the conferences of the Defoe Society, of the British, Italian and International Societies for Eighteenth-Century Studies, and to the editors of the periodicals and volumes in which the essays appeared. I owe no less to the anonymous reviewers of those essays and of a late draft of this book; their generous and detailed comments have stimulated, encouraged and helped enormously

---

1 In particular, my 2015 essay and that of 2019b focused on the procedures and practices which this book as a whole tries to illuminate, but their treatment of the trial itself was seriously flawed by failure to notice that Defoe's Moll Flanders is not charged with shoplifting but burglary; Chapter 9 rectifies that here. Chapter 3 is based on ideas floated at the Defoe Society Conference in Bath in 2015 and developed in my 2016 essay on street robbery. Chapter 6 re-uses a great deal of the 2021 essay on constables. Chapter 5 grew out of a paper on friends and enemies given at the 2017 BSECS conference in Oxford. At the Defoe Society Conference in New Haven in 2017 I focused on the 'alternative stories' Moll and her Governess use to convince J.P.s to let them go, a theme developed in other contexts at the 2018 BSECS conference, one that recurs in this book. Finally, I tried out a few conclusions at the 2019 ISECS conference in Edinburgh; one or two survive in the Introduction and Epilogue, both of which benefited from exchanges on the reception of the ideas of Cesare Beccaria at a seminar held at the University of Rome La Sapienza, the proceedings of which were published in 2019.

with revision. Conversations with others, some of whom read proposals and early versions of chapters have been invaluable I would like to mention with special gratitude Rosa Maria Colombo, Bill Dodd, Roberto De Romanis, Katherine Ellison, Barbara Gunnell, Mark Knights, Rosamaria Loretelli, Giacomo Mannironi, Paola Pugliatti, David Robey, Robert Shoemaker and Shelley Tickell. Many thanks also to my students at Ca' Foscari University Venice who took, like ducks to water, to investigating the reporting and imagining of law enforcement in eighteenth-century London, contributing Wikipedia articles on obscure pamphlets and bringing fun to our classes.

Crime, Justice and Defoe would never have been finished, however, if I had not been able to set aside teaching and spend long periods of study in England and the United States. I was given sabbatical leaves by all three of the universities I taught at during the 1990s and since (Pisa, L'Aquila, and Ca' Foscari Venice), periods of absence made possible by colleagues who took over my classes and administrative duties. More encouragement came in the form of three short-term fellowships from the William Andrews Clark Library in Los Angeles; these offered, in addition to time to read rare books in peace and in delightful surroundings, opportunities to meet and learn from those who direct, look after and frequent that scholar-friendly haven of sanity, knowledge and pleasure. The Clark librarians, especially Scott Jacobs, and those of the Bodleian and British Libraries deserve many thanks, as do my sister, Moira, in Los Angeles and the dear friends in London and Oxford of whose warm hospitality I took – and continue to take – advantage. For their generous moral support, advice and affection over the years, I am grateful to Alfonso Berardinelli, Tito Bianchi, Alide Cagidemetrio, Sabrina De Carlo, Maria Grossmann, Geraldine Ludbrook, Margherita Malanga, Niki Mozillo, Amneris Roselli, Emma Sdegno, Jean Tilog and Enrica Villari. I can only thank in memory my good friend Folger Mac Fadden, my ever-optimistic mother, Edna, and Beppe Colasanti, much missed.

In spite of all this help, the book would never have made it into print had I not landed in the lap of Brill. Masja Horn and her colleagues have been infinitely cheerful and reassuring over several years of patiently waiting for me to stop revising. I cannot thank them enough for giving me a deadline, for helping find a sensible title, and for seeing it through the press and out into the world. Last but not at all least, many thanks to Jeremy Carden for making sure that my typescript got from Rome to Leiden in good shape, and Ishwarya Mathavan for dealing patiently with my many pentimenti. It goes without saying that the mistakes that remain are my own.

Abbreviations

Car.	*Charles*
CJ	*Colonel Jack*
Geo.	*George*
JP	Justice of the Peace
LL	*London Lives* (www.londonlives.org). Subsequent text indicates the document reference number.
MF	*Moll Flanders*
OA	*Ordinary of Newgate's Account.* Subsequent text indicates the date of issue.
OBO	*Old Bailey Proceedings Online* (www.oldbaileyonline.org). Subsequent text indicates the trial reference number.
Phil. & Mar.	Philip and Mary
Wm. & M.	William and Mary

CHAPTER 1

Introduction

1   Other Subjectivities

Three years after the death of her fifth husband, Moll Flanders has run out of money and lost the charms that have so far stood her in such good economic stead. In 'want of Friends and want of Bread … made Desperate by Distress', she is prompted by a spirit to dress well and go down to the commercial heart of the City of London, where 'the Devil brought me to be sure to the place'. Her equivalent to the high place in the desert where Satan tempts Christ (Matthew 4:1) is the threshold of a Leadenhall Street apothecary's shop, from which she sees

> lye on a Stool just before the Counter a little Bundle wrapt in a white Cloth; beyond it, stood a Maid Servant with her Back to it, looking up towards the top of the Shop, where the Apothecary's Apprentice, as I suppose, was standing up on the Counter, with his Back also to the Door, and a Candle in his Hand, looking and reaching up to the upper Shelf for something he wanted, so that both were engag'd mighty earnestly, and no Body else in the Shop.[1]
>
> MF, 151

Registering for us the positions and spatial relationships of objects, fixtures and people, Moll also maps the psychological relations that criss-cross the room, noting what others see – and more importantly what they do not see – and sizing up the scene's potential, both in terms of opportunity and of risk. That 'little Bundle wrapt in a white Cloth', so humble yet so mysterious and desirable, is between doorway and counter, and therefore visible to the hungry woman at the threshold, but not to the maid, who has her back turned and her eyes fixed on the supposed apprentice. Like her, he has his back to the door, and is standing precariously on the counter, while 'looking and reaching up … for something he wanted' and holding onto his candle. Being otherwise 'engag'd mighty earnestly', the two fail to keep watch on the perimeter of the

---

1   All references to the text of *Moll Flanders* (MF) are to the Norton Critical Edition edited by Albert J. Rivero, 2004.

shop, from where Moll steps into their blind spot, reaches behind her back for the bundle, and goes 'off with it, the Maid or the Fellow not perceiving me, or any one else' (*MF*, 151).

The telling of Moll's first theft is fraught with tension, an awareness that things might easily have turned out differently. Her body language, her entering backwards in order to suggest an innocent motive, the *litotes* 'not perceiving', imply that at the last moment the maid might have turned around, or the apprentice looked down, or indeed that 'any one else' – the apothecary, a customer, the owner of the forgotten bundle – might have come onto the scene, noticed that hand groping blindly back, and grabbed her. Moll leaves without knowing where she is going, twisting and turning to escape imaginary pursuers, and running all the faster, 'the farther I was out of Danger' (*MF*, 152). Back in her lodgings and for now 'perfectly safe', she is overtaken by her new identity and the thought of what will inevitably follow: 'Lord, *said I*, what am I now? a Thief!' why I shall be taken next time and be carry'd to *Newgate* and be Try'd for my Life!' (*MF*, 152). Shifting from present to future tense and on to unlikely conditional mode, she momentarily contemplates returning her prize: 'as poor as I was. if I had durst for fear, I would certainly have carried the things back again'. Back where and to whom, we might wonder. Out of the contents of the bundle – some 'very good and almost new' child's bed linen, fine lace, small silver treasures and a bit of money – Moll conjures up an image of her victim, endows her with a past and with hopes for the future which can now no longer be realised: 'may be some poor Widow like me, that had pack'd up these Goods to go and sell them for a little Bread for herself and a poor Child, and are now starving and breaking their Hearts, for want of that little they would have fetch'd, and this Thought tormented me worse than all the rest, for three or four Days time' (*MF*, 152).

Like several repentances to come, this one wears off. Moll Flanders never carries anything back, but neither is she is taken 'next time' or for many times after this one. Nor will Colonel Jack ever actually be 'carry'd to *Newgate* and be Try'd for ... [his] Life', although at one point he is certain that he will be (*CJ*, 128),[2] and at another fears a death even more gruesome than hanging (*CJ*, 303). In both novels, mothers, brothers, teachers, pupils, comrades and other doubles are taken, committed to gaol, tried and punished, so that their stories remind us of what could/may/should happen to Defoe's narrators. Even in accounts of successful getaways, such as that from the apothecary's shop,

---

[2] All references to the text of *Colonel Jack* are to the Broadview edition edited by Gabriel Cervantes and Geoffrey Sill (2016).

INTRODUCTION

fear of the law runs like an electric current through the narrative. We are told what 'really' happens in the indicative mood and simple past tense, but also, through the use of various forms of *irrealis*, what would have happened if 'other subjectivities' had prevailed.[3] I borrow the expression from Lincoln B. Faller (1993, 56), who has shown how, in *Moll Flanders* and *Colonel Jack*, narrating voices convey their own intense subjectivity through verbs of perception and sensation, but in debating with themselves make us aware of 'a variousness of consciousness ... alternative, more "normal" points of view' (93). Faller attributes this sense of multiplicity to Defoe's use of dialogue, 'trialogue' and reported speech, of which there is a great deal. Yet speech is not really needed to produce these effects: neither the apothecary's apprentice nor his maid says a word, yet we enter into their consciousnesses nonetheless, and indeed into those of others who – like the poor widow – are merely figments of Moll's imagination. Likewise with the tavern server, whom she tricks out of a silver tankard and of whom we wonder:

> What will happen to him when his mistress finds he overlooked the tankard? Or how will the woman at the burning house – so effusive in her thanks for Moll's help – feel when she realizes that she has entrusted her children to a thief, and that, though safe, they've been parked uninvited at a neighbor's? And then, all her most precious possessions, gone! How are we to feel about Moll's outsmarting these and other honest people, when such people could just as well be us, our friends, clients, patrons, employees, or relatives? The fact that Moll's victims come from all levels of society means that practically everyone who could afford the price of the book would have been in a position to ask such questions. All these episodes ... involve great dangers for Moll, but readers would have seen these dangers in a context complicated by their awareness of her victims' viewpoints, some of which would have been all too easy to share.
>
> FALLER, 1993, 148

---

3   *Irrealis* moods are grammatical moods that indicate that a certain situation or action is not known to have happened at the moment the speaker is talking. They include conditionals, subjunctives, optatives, hypotheticals, potentials, interrogatives and prescriptives. As we shall see, Defoe is a master of the hypothetical, a notion explored in depth by Katherine Ellison (2023) in her inquiry into the relation between AI large language models, such as ChatGBT, and fiction.

Not all of those outsmarted by Defoe's thieves are as poor, honest or trusting as the tavern boy and the woman in the fire. Some are too rich, careless and/or eager to display their wealth for us not to enjoy seeing them relieved of some of it, others too officious, overbearing or plain stupid for us not to be glad to see them outwitted by their predators. They are all, in any case, not merely victims but potential – and sometimes actual – detectors, captors, prosecutors and witnesses.[4] This is something eighteenth-century readers of *Moll Flanders* and *Colonel Jack* would have taken for granted, but to which we are now culturally blind.[5] It can only be understood in the light of the ways in which the judicial system of Defoe's time differed from our own.[6]

2   Sergeants to Take Thieves

The aphorism of the Elizabethan classicist, diplomat and jurist Sir Thomas Smith, according to which 'everie English man is a sergiant to take the theefe' (1981 [1583], 90) sounds strange to modern ears. Our expectations about law enforcement are framed largely in terms of professional roles and closely regulated procedures. In fiction as in life, amateurs are interesting because they are anomalous; the norm we assume is that a criminal will be discovered and pursued by a police officer, a private eye, an investigative journalist or a team of forensic experts, the evidence gathered and a prosecution case organised by

---

[4] In Defoe's lifetime they would never have described themselves or been described as 'victims'; Cox, Shoemaker and Shore (2023) trace the marginalisation of the private prosecutor as the work of detecting, gathering evidence and organising a court case was taken over first by the police, and later by the state. In the eighteenth century, 'victim' is, on the contrary, a term sometimes applied by the condemned to themselves; George Watson, for instance, spoke of himself as having fallen a 'Victim to Justice' (*OA*, 17360705), and James Hall described himself as soon 'to fall a Victim to public Justice' (*OA*, 17410914).

[5] As Beth Swan has shown (1997, 12), novelists from Defoe to Godwin assume their readers to have a great deal of legal knowledge and to be deeply interested in the justice system, an assumption that long remained 'one of the most important blind spots in literary criticism'. Swan's main interest is in matters of marital law and women's understanding of the legal system, but she discusses aspects of fiction in relation to criminal law in Chapter 4 of her book and again in her essay of 1998, where she focuses mainly on Moll's trial and the events that follow.

[6] Many of these differences were drawn to the reader's attention by G.A. Starr in his invaluable notes to the World's Classics edition of 1976 (not all of which survive in Starr and Bree's 2011 edition). In her contribution to the *Oxford Handbook of Daniel Defoe* (2023) Kate Loveman discusses the differences systematically, and offers a penetrating discussion of Defoe's representation of 'law in action' which at several points anticipates my own.

an investigating magistrate or state prosecution service, then presented in court by professional lawyers following strict procedures and rules of evidence overseen by trained judges.

To us, therefore

> the most striking feature of the system used in early modern England to identify, capture and secure suspects is its broad participatory base. The private individual was the most important law enforcing officer in the community. Public obligation intruded on private life repeatedly. Residents drifted easily between official and private status. At no point in the early stages of accusation did private individuals or public officials completely control the legal process. Private initiative dovetailed with the powers allotted to public officials ... Each actor retained the power to play his part as he saw fit. Each was inspired by his own desires but also constrained by the behavior of every other actor.
> HERRUP 1989, 91–92

The importance of the private element is most evident during the early stages of law enforcement. In theory, constables and headboroughs chosen annually by local residents from among themselves were responsible for uncovering crimes and seeking out suspects, but in practice these men rarely took initiatives. More typically someone would realise that something was missing, or notice suspicious behaviour and, perhaps with the help of relatives and neighbours, set about catching the culprit. They might call on officers to help detain and accompany suspects before justices of the peace, but usually only after they had caught them and only if they intended to prosecute. Many preferred to take back the goods, accept an apology and perhaps some material compensation, and/or apply some informal method of punishment, such as ducking, holding under a pump, or beating.

Those determined to go down the institutional route would have had to make other difficult decisions, and to interact with the officials and clerks who formalised indictments. How harshly a charge was framed would determine whether a case was heard by a single magistrate or two, or went to quarter sessions or to the assizes, each of which could apply a different range of procedures and punishments. According to statutes dating from the sixteenth century, justices of the peace were meant only to draw up charges, bind over witnesses and commit suspects (Langbein 2005, 42–43), but in practice they often sought alternatives to prosecution, encouraging parties to conflicts to reach compromises for the sake of peace in the community (Shoemaker 1991, Ch. 4; King 2000, 92–93). Prosecutors who persisted would have to collect the evidence themselves and persuade their witnesses to go first before a grand jury, then a petty jury. Both were time-consuming and expensive procedures, so much so that Henry Fielding was famously to remark that 'a very poor person, already plundered by the thief ... must be a miracle of public spirit if he doth not chuse to conceal the felony and sit down contented with his present loss' (1751, 170).

Once in court, other decision-makers enter the frame. According to the traditional 'altercation' or 'accused speaks' format, the court heard both sides speak publicly, usually without the aid of lawyers, who could assist the prosecution but were forbidden to speak for the defence (Langbein 2005, 48–61). Juries could acquit, convict or mitigate the effects of laws by finding a defendant guilty on a lesser charge or downgrading the value of the goods stolen. Judges, the only legally trained participants, could influence verdicts, and exercise a degree of discretion in choosing a punishment, and in reprieving or recommending a pardon, which could be absolute or conditional. Even after sentencing, friends, family, neighbours and patrons could petition for remissions or discharges. Formally it was the monarch who determined whether a convicted felon would go free or be punished, but that decision was only the final step in a 'complex and participatory process' (Herrup, 1989, 95).

Peter King (2000, 1–2) uses a helpful analogy to describe the process as a whole:

> Although the formal criminal law and legal handbooks sometimes appeared rigid and inflexible, in reality the administration of the eighteenth-century justice system created several interconnected spheres of contested judicial space in each of which deeply discretionary choices were made. Those accused of property offences in the eighteenth century found themselves propelled on an often bewildering journey along a route which can best be compared to a corridor of connected rooms or stage sets. From each room one door led on towards eventual criminalization, conviction and punishment, but every room also had other exits. Each had doors indicating legally accepted ways in which the accused could get away from the arms of the law, while some rooms also had illegal tunnels though which the accused could sometimes be smuggled to safety. Each room was also populated by a different and socially diverse group of men and women, whose assumptions, actions, and interactions, both with each other, and with the accused, determined whether or not he or she was shown to an exit or thrust on up the corridor.

This 'corridor' offers a useful image of the structure of this book,[7] which follows Defoe's protagonists along their unplanned journeys from detection and arrest to pre-trial, trial and beyond. In tracing their progress, we shall see with whom their creator chooses to have them meet and negotiate, with what outcomes, and how behaviour at one stage affects what happens next – and vice versa, for each decision would be influenced by expectations about how it would affect future ones. We shall also notice how often it is suggested that things might have gone differently, the possibilities being various but not infinite in number. As a writer of fictions claiming to be true, Defoe needed to take account of the limitations imposed by his early readers' assumptions about who might do what, when and how at any given stage of law enforcement. Do his novels at certain points violate those expectations, or elaborate on them in order to entertain, shock or suggest different ways of enforcing the law? Does he show marked preferences for certain types of interaction and outcome, while underplaying or ignoring others? Which, if any, of his narrative choices carry persuasive force? Do they consolidate and reinforce the validity of current practices, or question them and promote innovation—or have it both ways?

These are matters of historical interest because during Defoe's time and the following decades the parameters and the practice of law enforcement were changing in important ways. Much of the impetus for change came from outside the state: from interest groups, local government and voluntary societies who promoted measures to be implemented by parliament, which during the reigns of William and Anne met on a much more regular basis than it had earlier. Other changes took place without public debate and by way of *de facto* adjustments to policing and to judicial practice. They were for the most part 'piecemeal, uncoordinated, *ad hoc*', they were subject to reversals and sometimes, as in the case of the Transportation Acts (Rubin 2012), produced effects quite other than those intended. Yet taken together, according to John Beattie, they anticipated the better known reforms of the late eighteenth and nineteenth centuries, and resonated with Cesare Beccaria's insistence on 'the need to persuade offenders that if they broke the law they would be caught, if caught they would be brought to trial and convicted, and if convicted, punished' (2001, 475; see also Clegg 2021). At the level of detection, the introduction of city street lighting and of a paid night watch, increased numbers of paid deputy constables, the legitimation of entrepreneurial thief-taking and the development of systematic gathering and dissemination of information, all

---

7 As King acknowledges, this simile had been used earlier by Stephen Box (1981, 158).

contributed to the displacement of amateur, 'community' policing by more professional practices, and pointed in the direction of greater state intervention (Beattie 2001, Chapters 3–5; Wales 2000). Further on up the procedural chain, pre-trial hearings by justices of the peace evolved – in spite of the statutory limitations – into full scale investigations (Beattie 2001, Chapter 2), while the development of a crown witness system and the introduction of massive statutory rewards for convicting accomplices stimulated prosecution and conviction rates (Langbein 2005, 148–165; Clayton and Shoemaker 2022). As for the trial itself, although it was not until 1838 that defendants could claim a legal right to counsel, a change which allowed lawyers to definitively dominate hearings and gave birth to the 'adversarial' trial familiar to us from English and American films and television, in practice lawyers were assisting both sides in courts from the 1730s, and attorneys were often present at magistrates' hearings from before then (Langbein 2005, 167–177).

It was in modifying punishments that the state intervened most directly – in two different ways. One series of statutes extended the availability of benefit of clergy (a legal fiction that allowed the literate to claim exemption from prosecution in secular courts) to include women and the illiterate, while another, the series that came to be known as the 'Bloody Code', hugely extended the number of capital offences by excluding many offences from benefit of clergy (Beattie 1986, 141–179). Transportation to the colonies, publicly subsided from 1720, became a standard punishment for non-violent theft, largely replacing the whippings and brandings of the past, and to a smaller extent the death penalty (Beattie 2001, Chapter 9). In the meantime, the press had come to offer new spaces for the multi-faceted business of crime publication, providing later Stuart and Georgian England with a huge and regular diet of news which affected public perceptions of crime and justice (Harris 1982; Snell 2007; Shoemaker 2008a; Lemmings 2012; Ward 2014).

Defoe was no detached onlooker on all of this. As dissenters, his family and their associates had been persecuted in the Restoration period. As a young man he was appointed to a petty jury (Novak 2001, 75), but later was imprisoned for debt, tried, imprisoned and pilloried for seditious libel, accused of horse theft and pursued by civil suits that forced him to spend the last days of his life in hiding, experiences that would have given him a 'special sensitivity to injustice' (Backsheider 1990, 3). To a projector, polemicist, spy and journalist closely attentive to current events and deeply concerned with political, economic and moral issues of his day, the workings of the law could not in any case have been a matter for indifference. We may never know precisely and for sure how much Defoe contributed to the flourishing crime literature of his time; scholars have become more cautious than they once were about attributing anonymously published writings.[8] Yet he probably contributed articles on the behaviour of pickpockets and highwaymen to *Appleby's Original Weekly Journal* (Novak 2012) and, wrote the most interesting of the many lives of Jonathan Wild (Novak 1996, 101–102; Clegg 2003), although not two pamphlets on street robbery and how to deal with it once thought to be his (Bond 1971; Sill 1976). In any case, questions concerning regarding crime prevention and the administration of justice crop up again and again in works certainly attributable to him, from the early *Reformation of Manners* satires, the *Essay on Projects* and *A Poor Man's Plea* to his articles for the *Review*, the later conduct manuals and the polemics published under the pseudonym 'Andrew Moreton'. The views expressed in them are sometimes extreme, which is not to say that they are unambiguous and, because of 'Defoe's inveterate tendency to impersonate', it is not always clear who is expressing them (Damrosch 1973, 159).[9] In his fictions, experiments in a genre which was taking over and developing didactic functions from conduct manuals, criminal and spiritual biographies and other ideologically oriented narratives (Hunter 1990, Part 1), we are offered many reflections and instructions, but it is even less easy to trace a consistent line of argument. Yet it seems worth seeing how far one can get. One of the aims of this book is to try to understand where *Moll Flanders* and *Colonel Jack* work to naturalise and consolidate the innovations in law enforcement coming into effect in the eighteenth century, where they encourage the preservation of customary ways of dealing with crime, and where they would have it both – or several – ways. We may not be able to identify in either novel 'a coherent ideological effect', for, as Gabriel Cervantes suggests, the novels are 'rife with incoherence, static and confusion connected to specific historical difficulties and impasses' (2011–2012, 251–252). If this study throws light on the difficulties and impasses concerning the workings of justice as perceived in the early 1720s, it will have gone a long way to fulfilling its purpose.

---

8 In *The Canonisation of Daniel Defoe* (1981) and *Defoe De-Attributions* (1994), F.N. Furbank and W.R. Owens contested the attribution to Defoe of many titles ascribed to him in the nineteenth and early twentieth centuries, and more recently even his authorship of *Moll Flanders* and *Roxana* has been questioned (Marshall 2010), although not that of *Colonel Jack*. I do not intend to enter the ongoing debate on this matter, but my reading of the two novels does depend on their being by the same author.

9 Damrosch's essay concludes with the observation that 'a survey of Defoe's views on any given subject can be no more than the sum of its parts, and … a quite remarkable number of those parts turn out to be full of contradictions or ambiguities …The more one looks at any single piece, the less one is certain what conclusions to draw from it.'

3 Old Bailey Stories

My reading of *Moll Flanders* and *Colonel Jack* from a law enforcement perspective depends heavily on the work of the social historians who have done so much over the past fifty years to show how the law was administered and experienced in the England of the long eighteenth century. Those so far cited are only a few of the many studies which have helped bring to the surface assumptions embedded in Defoe's fictions. This book is also indebted to studies in the cultural history of representation, a field which has developed rapidly since the late twentieth century, but in which Richard Ward has identified three important issues as needing more adequate discussion:

> First of all, previous research has tended to analyse single genres of seventeenth- and eighteenth-century printed crime literature in isolation, going against what was the more likely contemporary practice of reading a range of genres together … Londoners read a variety of different publications each of which offered unique – sometimes distinctly contradictory – images of crime and justice … Secondly, there has been little attempt in previous work to analyse eighteenth-century crime literature within the context of actual judicial practice … Studies of printed crime reporting have largely ignored the social context in which texts were consumed … Thirdly … [m]ost scholars who have written on the subject, particularly the genres of criminal biography and last dying speeches, have concentrated on the more Universalist messages of those publications … it should also be noted that beneath this enduring fascination with Universalist messages ran shifting currents of interest in the changing level of criminal activity.
>
> WARD 2014, 11–13

With the caveats that this study focusses more on justice than on crime, and that it does not attempt to tackle anything like the whole range of genres one would ideally read alongside each other, it does aim to contribute to the interdisciplinary discussions in which Ward and others are engaged.

The kinds of early eighteenth-century text I make dialogue with Defoe's criminal fictions, a selection of conduct books and a large number of trial reports, have been chosen for the light they shed on the theory and the practice of law enforcement. Prescriptive manuals, such as those intended to guide constables through their tricky tasks, but also those written for justices, jurors and prosecutors, help us understand the difficulties faced by people without legal training in carrying out their civic and official duties. Most important for my purposes have been the commercial-cum-official reports that from the late seventeenth century on regularly provided readers with massive amounts of information about prosecuted offences. The *Old Bailey Proceedings* (or *Sessions Papers*, as they are sometimes called), which were published shortly after the end of each of the eight sessions held at London's principal criminal court, is thankfully freely accessible in searchable digital form. Priced relatively cheaply (in the 1720s they cost 3 or 4 pence per issue), the *Proceedings* enjoyed great popularity throughout the early to mid-eighteenth century, testifying to a market not just for the sensational and salacious stories of murders, rapes and violent robberies that dominated broadsides, ballads and newspapers, but also for soberly presented information on run-of-the-mill property crimes of the kind that interested Defoe, and on more or less successful ways of dealing with them. Like the novels, they were destined mainly for the middling sort – people who would have appreciated hints on arresting, prosecuting and giving evidence, although they were thought by some to have been read by offenders and attorneys for suggestions on how to prepare defences. These, as well as the Newgate chaplains' (Ordinaries') *Accounts* of the lives and last days of the condemned, would have been known to many of Defoe's early readers,[10] and would have helped form their expectations about how actual thieves might be caught, consigned to justice and formally prosecuted.

By no means do the *Proceedings* tell the whole story of Old Bailey trials, for journalists' notes were heavily pruned for publication, and in such a way as to show 'that crime was a significant problem, but the courts did their best, while

---

10   Anyone who could have afforded *Moll Flanders* (priced at five shillings) would have been able to afford at least one issue of the *Proceedings*, although not necessarily vice versa. That the novel was aimed at the same readership as bought the Ordinary's *Account*, which was at this time being published by Defoe's associate, John Applebee, is confirmed by advertisements for *Moll Flanders* that appeared in the issues for 8 and 18 July 1722; *Colonel Jack* was advertised in the *Account* dated 31 December 1722 (*OA*, 17221231). *Moll Flanders* was also advertised in the *Proceedings* for 28 February 1722, 4 April 1722 and 16 January 1723. The novel is also mentioned in two trial reports. When 1732 John Powel prosecuted his servant, Catherine Bennet, for stealing items that included a bible and a copy of *MF*, he valued the two books at one shilling each (*OBO*, t17320906-14). An utterly ghastly story in which *Moll* features briefly is that of the torture and starving to death of Anne Williamson by her truly monstrous husband (*OBO*, t17670115-24).

ensuring trials were conducted fairly, to punish the guilty' (Shoemaker 2008a, 573). Even so, Shoemaker continues (578),

> Because every trial has two sides and the *Proceedings* had to provide both where possible in order to demonstrate that there had been a fair trial, there were often at least two stories competing for the readers' attention, and so the readers could choose to identify with the defendant rather than the prosecution. As Hal Gladfelder has argued, printed trial accounts possessed a 'resistance to closure,' which allowed the points of view of defendants to be inconclusively juxtaposed with those of their accusers.

This brings us conveniently to what I believe to be the only literary study which has fully recognised the cultural and formal debt of the genre of the novel to the trial report. On the one hand, Hal Gladfelder (2001, 66–68) points out that

> the early sessions papers from the Old Bailey ... often foregrounded cultural antagonisms – conflicts over the role of the police, for example, or over the prerogatives of social rank or the laws' encroachment on customary rights – which had no other form of expression. And, because of the criminal law's disproportionate concern with the propertyless, trial reports describe the material conditions and everyday life of the urban poor especially, with a fullness of detail available in no other form of writing until Defoe fabricated the autobiographies of Colonel Jack and Moll Flanders in the 1720s ... trial narratives opened up the field of cultural representation, recounting the histories of those who would otherwise have remained beneath the threshold of social visibility.

On the other, by gradually incorporating verbatim records of testimony and deploying empirical detail as a means to persuade and authenticate, trial reports pioneered new narrative techniques that were to be adopted in realistic fiction:

> The peculiar endlessness of circumstantial realism ... its relentless amassing of facts that could count as evidence – endlessly opens the narrative to discordant meanings, contradictory plots. It is this formal resistance to closure which I see as the most *productive* legacy of the criminal trial to the fictions of Defoe and Fielding – and, through

them, to what would become the canon of the novel over the later eighteenth and nineteenth centuries.[11]

2001, 71

In referring to the propertyless, Gladfelder is thinking of the accused, yet if it were not for trial reports the fairly ordinary people – admittedly most of them male and propertied – who caught, prosecuted and witnessed against thieves, would also 'have remained below the threshold of social visibility'. Modern readers have understandably paid more attention to the complicated lawbreakers Defoe chose as his narrators than to those of the anonymous and often flatly characterised law enforcers who come briefly to the front of the stage, say a few words, and disappear into the wings. Yet it is the real equivalents of these minor characters who are addressed by the editor of *Moll Flanders* when he offers readers 'Instruction' of a very practical kind:

> ALL the Exploits of this Lady of Fame, in her Depredations upon Mankind stand as so many warnings to honest People to beware of them, intimating by them by what Methods innocent People are drawn in, plunder'd and robb'd, and by Consequence how to avoid them.[12]
>
> MF, 5

The 'honest People' among Defoe's early readers may well have been pleased to make use of these warnings, especially if they had themselves been victims of pickpockets and shoplifters, and/or had heard tell of, read in newspapers or in the *Proceedings* about, the 'Depredations' actually committed on the streets of London. They may also have taken up hints – some of them very heavy ones – on how to catch a thief, how to carry out a search safely, how to engage with officers of the law and settle disputes, how to frame an indictment or give evidence in court and, last but not least, how and why one should show mercy to the guilty or seek a pardon on her or his behalf.

---

11   Trial reports are not the only kinds of crime writing to offer multiple points of view. As Andrea McKenzie (2007, 124, 149–151) has shown, the Ordinaries' *Accounts* also stage struggles for the truth, but, being mainly concerned with divine justice, give secular voices limited space. King (2009) notes that later in the century newspapers give voice to victims' points of view, if only because they report crime as it happens and usually before anyone has been accused.

12   As G.A. Starr noted (1976, 359), this is 'the conventional justification of rogue biography' – but it does not follow that it was not meant to be taken seriously.

This book aims to bring Defoe's victim/prosecutors, and those who help them, out of the shadows, but not, of course, to push his more interesting, garrulous protagonists off stage, even if that were possible. We may, however, better understand what Moll and Jack have to tell us if we listen as carefully as they do to their antagonists: the shopkeepers, servants, apprentices, neighbours and anonymous passers-by who, with varying degrees of success, run after, catch and sometimes prosecute them, or whose presences are observed or imagined in such spaces as the Leadenhall Street apothecary's shop where Moll Flanders begins her career as a thief.

PART 1

*Catching Thieves in Fact and Fiction:
Detecting and Apprehending*

∴

CHAPTER 2

At the Scene of the Crime 1: Catching Pickpockets

1   Introduction

Moll Flanders' theft from the apothecary's shop is the first of a series of miscellaneous opportunity thefts during which she feels she is in danger of being seized by those at or near the scene of the crime. She will become expert in avoiding capture during her on-the-job training in the two varieties of property crime with which this chapter and the next are concerned: picking pockets and shoplifting. In narrating Moll's professional career, Defoe repeatedly drives home the message that a victim's best chance of detecting and catching a thief is by observing closely and acting before she or he can get away. This is also where the young Major Jack and his gang of pickpockets, and later Colonel Jack and his teacher, Will, are most vulnerable. It is also where, in a country lacking a detective police force, most actual thieves were taken if at all,[1] and where readers of the *Proceedings* would expect them to be caught. Before turning to the novels, therefore, we briefly survey the evidence provided by reports on pickpocketing trials held at the Old Bailey between January 1720 and December 1722, discussing accounts of trials of women separately from those of men and boys. As Diedre Palk (2006, 81) has shown in her study of the years 1780–1820, the circumstances in which women stole privately from the person were quite distinct from those favoured by and available to men:

> Apparently the same crime was being committed, but in varying environments, and demonstrating different behaviours between men and women. This difference is evident in what was stolen and from whom; in what is known about the defendants and how they operate – and, most significantly, where they operated … in the method and location of the crime, the differences are most striking.

---

1   King (2000, 21) concluded that in nearly 26.4% of all the larceny cases that went before the Essex Quarter Sessions in 1748–1800, the accused had been seen in the act of theft, and that another 13.4% had been seen in the area.

2 Catching Women Pickpockets 1720–1722

Stealing 'privately' from the person – that is without the victim realising what is happening – goods worth one shilling or more was one of the first forms of theft for which benefit of clergy was disallowed, making it a capital offence. Passed in 1565 and not repealed until 1808, the relevant statute specified in its preamble the type of thief it was aimed at:

> A certain kind of evil-disposed person ... [who] do confer together, making among themselves as it were a brotherhood or fraternity of an art or mystery, to live idly by the secret spoil of the good and true subjects of this realm ... at time of service or common prayer, in churches, chapels, closets and Oratories ... also in the Prince's palace, house, yea and presence, and at the places and courts of justice ... and in fairs and markets, and other assemblies, and ... at ... [the] executions of such as had been attainted of any murder, felony or other criminal causes, ordained for the terror and example of evildoers ... under the cloak of honesty of their outward appearance, countenance and behaviour, subtilly, privily, craftily ... to the utter undoing and impoverishing of many.
>
>   8 Eliz. c.4, s.2, 1565, cit. in PALK 2006, 69

In reality, organised 'fraternities' of pickpockets were probably quite rare,[2] and the majority of those caught and tried under the statute were not men who operated in the open, public spaces listed here and in daylight hours, but women who stole in enclosed, private spaces – lodgings, brothels, taverns, alleys, park gateways and so on – almost always at night, usually after plying their victims with drink and 'as an adjunct to sexual activity or "treats"' (Palk 2006, 83, 86). In court 'judges commonly made it clear that they thought the victims of such crimes not worth much sympathy' (Beattie 1986, 180), and the acquittal rate for such women was high; many potential prosecutors must have preferred not to bring charges.

---

[2] The belief that criminals of various kinds habitually organised themselves into combinations seems to have gained credence over the seventeenth century. Tim Wales (2000, 71) sees official preoccupations with criminal gangs as linked to anxieties about political conspiracy and Geoffrey Sill (1983, 124) notes that by the 1720s 'the State was taking an increasingly active role in the prosecution of offences which indicated the presence of collective or systematic criminal activity'.

The one hundred and forty pickpocketing cases that were brought to the Old Bailey between January 1720 and December 1722 fit Palk's picture. Eighty-four of the defendants were women, and in only nine of these was the prosecutor also identified as female; at least seventy-one of those indicted were women accused by men.[3] In reporting testimony, the *Proceedings* were generous with salacious details. The account of Bartholomew Huggins's prosecution of Barbara Useley for privately stealing half a guinea from his person is typical:

> The Prosecutor deposed, that going up Drury-Lane between 8 and 9 at Night with a Friend, they met the Prisoner and another Woman, who ask'd them to drink; that they went into Newtoners-Lane together. The Prisoner went up Stairs with his Friend and the other Woman and he staid below, that when she came down, she ask'd if he (the Prosecutor) was pleased, and was answer'd yes; that he had paid for what he had, and was going, but the Prisoner said, come let him have another touch for Good-will, and while he was busy with her, he felt her Hand in his Pocket, got up and mist his Money. The Prisoner in her Defence said, that the Prosecutor was on the Bed with the other Woman with her Coats up, and would afterwards have lain with her self, but she refusing him, he charged her with this Fact. The Jury considering the whole matter, Acquitted her.
>
> OBO, t17200427-53

Huggins was one of forty-three pickpocketing prosecutions of women that failed. In eleven no evidence was presented, suggesting that between the drawing up of the indictments and the trial date the victims thought better of exposing themselves to public shame and ridicule. There must have been others who did not manage to make an arrest: the women would have been on their home territory, where their clients could not always expect help from those present. Gilbert Kean testified that when, in 'a House' in Hanging Sword

---

3 The genders of two prosecutors are not apparent from the trial reports. The one hundred and forty total for a mere three years seems high compared to the one hundred and twenty-three women indicted in the seventeen years studied by Palk (2006, Table 9). Did the Societies for the Reformation of Manners, which were actively prosecuting 'lewd and disorderly' women in the early years of the eighteenth century, help boost indictments of women for pickpocketing? Tim Wales (2000, 72–73) observes how the 'campaign for moral reformation ... merged with concerns about rising London crime' and that the first of the societies, that for Tower Hamlets, included 'two men who later became leading thief-takers'.

Court to which he had gone with Elizabeth Gilbert, he charged her with taking his silver watch and a guinea, upon which

> Elizabeth Jesson and Tabitha Ellis came up, and said she was an Honest Woman and would not rob him; that they endeavouring to get between him and the Prisoner in order to give her an Opportunity to get off, he shut the Door and kept his Hand on it; then they put out the Candle, and pull'd him down backward by his Turnover, that he cry'd out Murder, and the Watchmen came to his Assistance, otherwise he believed they would have murder'd him.
>
> OBO, t17200712-11; see also t17211000301-50

Watchmen were called in to help with at least thirteen arrests, and constables in at least twenty-nine, and even they sometimes found it difficult to apprehend suspects. Robert Hoe claimed to have been 'carried ... out of the Way' by Sarah Wells, alias Calicoe Sarah, to Rosemary Lane, where he missed his watch and money and charged her: 'she put his Watch into his Hand again; however he kept her, and would have had her before a Justice, but she cry'd out Everett Everett! who came, fell upon the Prosecutor and beat him. That the High Constable was denied Entrance for an Hour' (OBO, t17200115-47).[4]

Defoe's Moll does not frequent the sleazy districts of Drury Lane with its theatres and brothels, or Rosemary Lane with its 'Rag Fair', and neither does she associate with riff-raff like Sarah Wells and her protector Everett. She does venture once into sexploitation, but her pick up is of a different class from the men who usually prosecuted at the Old Bailey.

3 Moll Flanders Advises

3.1 *A Gentleman Very Rich*

It is 'a Merry time of the Year, and *Bartholomew Fair* was begun', Moll tells us, adding quickly that she 'had never made any Walks that Way, nor was the common Part of the Fair of much Advantage to me'. Instead, she takes a turn in the more socially mixed Cloisters, where she enters a raffling shop and is singled out by a 'Gentleman extreamly well Dress'd, and very Rich'. He

---

[4] Wells had been in Newgate at the same time as Moll King, whom Defoe may have visited and who, Howson suggests (1970, 162), 'gave him the kernel of the idea' for *Moll Flanders*.

wins her a prize – 'I think it was a Feather Muff' – and carries her in his coach to the Knightsbridge pleasure gardens, where he treats her 'very handsomely' and continues to drink 'very freely'. It is by now near ten o'clock, and he takes her to 'a House where it seems he was acquainted, and where they made no scruple to show us up Stairs into a Room with a Bed in it' (*MF*, 177). Having had his way with Moll, the 'Gentleman' brings her away in the coach, where he falls into a befuddled sleep, leaving her to take 'this opportunity to search him to a Nicety' and net what, for a pickpocket of the 1720s, would have been a huge haul: 'a gold Watch, with a silk Purse of Gold, his fine full bottom Perrewig, and silver fring'd Gloves, his Sword, and fine Snuff-box'. Moll then prepares her getaway:

> gently opening the Coach-door, [I] stood ready to jump out while the Coach was going on; but the Coach stopping in the narrow street beyond *Temple-Bar* to let another Coach pass, I got softly out, fasten'd the Door again, and gave my Gentleman and the Coach the slip both together, and never heard more of them.
>
> *MF*, 178

It is not true that Moll 'never ... [hears] more' of her fine gentleman,[5] but as we shall see in Chapter 4, when contact is re-established, nothing is further from his mind than the thought of apprehending and prosecuting her. Defoe adheres to reality in this. Palk (2006, 81–82) concludes from her sample that 'the men who tangled with prostitutes, and who were prepared to indict them for a capital offence' came not from among the very rich and upper class but from a 'cross-section of the less financially flourishing members of male society':

> The cases brought against pickpockets were not often brought by victims in a higher station in life. The gentry and successful middling sort were presumably wise enough not to find themselves in the areas of London where such misfortune could befall them. If they should be so unwise, then they would avoid becoming involved in prosecutions, which could easily damage their reputations and family standing. Their loss would not be sufficiently significant to them. The stage was left to ordinary tradesmen, artisans and other working men.

---

5 G.A. Starr (1976, 393) notes that the last phrase was omitted in the second edition, an indication that Defoe 'had not yet planned the remainder of the episode'.

In making Moll's client 'very Rich' and, as she repeatedly reminds us, a 'Gentleman' – he turns out to be 'no less than a Baronet, and of a very good Family' (*MF*, 180) – Defoe chooses to differentiate him socially from those who appear in the *Old Bailey Proceedings* as prosecutors of female pickpockets, but heaps all the more blame on him for that.[6] In one of the most emphatically didactic passages in the novel, Moll delivers a long tirade on the sins of the flesh of which this is only a small part:

> There is nothing so absurd, so surfeiting, so ridiculous as a Man heated with Wine in his Head, and a wicked Gust in his Inclination together; he is in the possession of two Devils at once, and can no more govern himself by his Reason than a Mill can Grind without water ... such a Man is worse than a Lunatick; promoted by his vicious corrupted Head he knows no more what he is doing, than this Wretch of mine knew when I pick'd his Pocket of his Watch and his Purse of Gold.
>
> *MF*, 178

This message would have found favour with readers of a reforming inclination. Later in the century a court ruling established that the stipulation that theft from the person had to be committed privately for it to count as pickpocketing did not apply to victims who 'by intoxication had exposed themselves to depredation' (Radzinowicsz, cited in Palk 2006, 70). Defoe's story of Moll and her gentleman 'Lunatick' anticipates this change and may have helped prepare public opinion to endorse it.

3.2   A Key to the Clue

The victims Moll Flanders usually steals privately from, though surely just as rich and of as high a station as her baronet, are strictly of her own sex. Her speciality is in the narrowly defined one of 'taking off Gold Watches from Ladies sides'. Ladies wealthy enough to wear gold watches would not have been roaming the streets of London on foot, unprotected and at night; to steal from them, Moll must learn how to operate undetected in daylight and in spaces frequented by people who, unlike habitués of brothels, public houses and dark alleyways, would be all too ready to warn of pickpockets at work and help apprehend them. Her 'environment' of pickpocketing will therefore resemble more closely the public and well-lit areas frequented by

---

6   On middling-sort perceptions of the aristocracy as licentious as well as idle, see Hunt 1996, 69.

male pickpockets (Palk 2006, 84). However, in confining her attentions to ladies and to watches, and gold ones at that, Moll differs from actual male pickpockets of the early 1720s who, as we shall see, stole mainly from men and whose pickings were usually more modest. To accomplish their very specific variety of stealing from the person, she and her comrade/teacher will need to pass themselves off as ladies like their victims, and to this end closely emulate their victims' dress code: 'on these Adventures we always went very well Dress'd, and I had very good Cloaths on, and a Gold Watch by my side, as like a Lady as other Folks' (*MF*, 167).

Moll's account of her trial run is an instructive cautionary tale for these 'other Folks'. Her teacher picks out 'a Prize':

> and this was a young Lady big with Child who had a charming Watch, the thing was to be done as she came out of Church; she goes on one side of the Lady, and pretends, just as she came to the Steps, to fall, and fell against the Lady with so much violence as put her into a great fright, and both cry'd out terribly; in the very moment that she jostl'd the lady, I had hold of the Watch, and holding it the right way, the start she gave drew the Hook out and she never felt it; I made off immediately, and left my Schoolmistress to come out of her pretended Fright gradually, and the Lady too; and presently the Watch was miss'd; ay, *says my Comrade*, then it was those Rogues that thrust me down, I warrant ye, I wonder the Gentlewoman did not miss her Watch before, that we might have taken them.
>
> *MF*, 159

Defoe offers us several stories in one here. At the surface level there is the account of the fake fall, Moll's dextrous unhooking of the watch and her getaway, narrated in the simple past indicative. At a second level there is her schoolmistress's cover story of 'Rogues' having 'thrust ... [her] down', reported in direct speech to the credulous, pregnant lady. The third version of events is expressed as an unrealised conditional: had the pregnant lady been quicker to miss her watch, 'we' – the lady and her 'helper' – might have taken the phantom rogues.

This scenario, or something like it, will be replayed so many times that Moll grows 'audacious to the last degree':

> the more so, because I had carried it on so long, and had never been taken; for in a word, my new Partner in Wickedness *and I* went on together for so long, without ever being detected, that we not only

grew Bold, but we grew Rich, and we had at one time One and Twenty Gold Watches in our Hands.

MF, 160

Even as she boasts about having so often evaded capture, a series of *litotes* – 'never ... taken', 'without ever being detected' – conjures up the possibility of opposite outcomes. Each of those 'One and Twenty Gold Watches' represents a failure in law enforcement.

Defoe makes Moll spell out what would have made for success in telling of another attempt on a 'Gentle-woman', again 'in a Crowd', and again near a place of worship – this time a dissenters' meeting house. Places of worship would have attracted pickpockets because crowded with well-to-do people in their Sunday best and assumed to have their thoughts on higher matters.[7] Sarah Wells, whom we have already met (Section 2.2), had been convicted under the name Mary Goulston for stealing a gold watch from Mrs. Ann Earnly on her way out of church (*OBO*, t17181205-199). In the meeting house episode Moll comes 'in very great Danger of being taken' (*MF*, 166) because the lady on whom she sets her sights has fastened her watch securely; the thief has to tug hard to get it loose, and this alarms her victim into giving the traditional alerting cry of '*Pick-pocket*'. One jump ahead as usual, Moll has pre-emptively deflected suspicion by projecting the presence of other thieves in the vicinity, and by herself assuming the part of intended target: 'I ... cried out as if I had been kill'd, that some body had Trod upon my Foot, and that there were certainly *Pick-pockets* there; for some body or other had given a pull at my Watch'. Stopping short against the forward movement of the crowd, Moll allows others to come between her and her target, and is further aided by the presence of an unwitting decoy:

---

[7] Stealing from churchgoers was topical in these years; twice in 1721, Thomas Purney, then Ordinary of Newgate, discussed the ethics of targeting them with prisoners. Questioned as to whether he had 'rob'd a Person in a Chaise during Divine Service, who was awatering his Horse before the Church Door?', John Winshipp retorted that 'he suppos'd that Action was the same wherever it was done, and at what time soevr' (*OA*, 17210728). Purney found a more receptive subject in Philip Story, a robber who 'enquired of me, whether Picking of Pockets in a Church was Sacrilegde or not? He was answer'd, that it was one sort of Sacriledge; and might perhaps be more Offensive in the sight of God, than what was generally so, as it may deter some from frequenting the Temple of God, as it may make those who are there Uneasy and Cautious and take their Thoughts off from Heaven, which stealing Plate, &c. from a Church does not; and also, as it must be the greatest Affront to God, for any one to interrupt those who are taking to him by Prayer.' (*OA*, 17211023).

> AT that very instant, a little farther in the Crowd, and very Luckily too, they cried out *a Pickpocket* again, and really seiz'd a young Fellow in the very Fact. This, tho' unhappy for the Wretch was very opportunely for my Case, tho' I had carried it off handsomely enough before, but now it was out of Doubt, and all the loose part of the Crowd run that way, and the poor Boy was deliver'd up to the Rage of the Street
>
> MF, 167

The diversion fortunately provided by this 'Wretch' is only one of the 'great many concurring Circumstances in this Adventure, which assisted to my Escape', and not the principal one:

> the chief was, that the Woman whose Watch I had pull'd at was a Fool; that is to say, she was Ignorant of the nature of the Attempt, which one would have thought she should not have been, seeing She was wise enough to fasten her Watch, so, that it could not be slipt up; but she was in such a Fright, that she had no thought about her proper for the Discovery; for she, when she felt the pull, scream'd out, and push'd herself forward, and put all the People about her into disorder, but said not a Word of her Watch, or of a *Pick-pocket*, for at least two Minutes time; which was time enough for me, and to spare; for as I had cried out behind her, *as I have said*, and bore myself back in the Crowd as she bore forward; there were several People, at least seven or eight, the Throng begin still moving on that were got between me and her in that time, and then I crying out *a Pick-pocket*, rather sooner than she, or at least as soon, she might as well be the Person suspected as I, and the People were confus'd in their Enquiry; whereas, had she with a Presence of Mind needful on such an Occasion, as soon as she felt the pull, not skream'd out as she did, but turn'd immediately round, and seiz'd the next Body that was behind her, she had infallibly taken me.
>
> MF, 167–168

In this passage *litotes* ('Ignorant', 'no thought ... proper for the Discovery', 'said not a Word') are reinforced by a hypothetical ('might as well be the Person') and unrealised conditionals ('one would have thought she should not have been' ... 'had she ... not skream'd out ... but turned around'), all working together to generate an alternative scenario in which 'she had infallibly taken me'. The lesson is heavily glossed: 'THIS is a Direction not of the kindest Sort to the Fraternity; but 'tis certainly a Key to the Clue of a *Pick-pockets* Motions, and whoever can follow it, will as certainly catch the Thief as he will be sure to miss it if he does not' (*MF*, 168).

More clues are offered in the last of Moll's thefts from the person, an episode Lee Kahan (2009, 36–37) takes as illustrating her 'ability to gather intelligence and then use it to create plausible fictions that she constructs through the accumulation of circumstantial detail'. She has set her sights on the 'fine gold Watch ... and ... good Necklace of Pearl' of a 'Little Miss' walking with her younger sister in St James's Park. They have a liveried footman to guard them, but this 'Fool of a Fellow' spills enough information about the young ladies, their titled parents and their household for Moll, who is 'very well dress'd', to be able to get close and introduce herself as a family friend (*MF*, 202–203). Then, in the confusion caused by the passing of the King, she takes 'care to convey the gold Watch so clean away from the Lady *Betty*, that she never felt it, nor miss'd it, till all the Crowd was gone, and she was gotten into the middle of the *Mall* among the other Ladies'. By this time the thief too has gone, taking her leave 'as if in haste', and allowing the crowd to 'as it were Thrust me way from her, and that I was oblig'd unwillingly to take my leave.' (*MF*, 203).

In a sense Moll *is* unwilling to take her leave. In a coda to the episode, she imagines for us two versions of what might have taken place if she had stayed until Lady Betty missed her watch. In the first, Moll would have assumed her favourite policing role and helped make 'a great Out-cry about it with her', then accompanied her home and purloined her necklace at least. On the other hand, 'when I consider'd that tho' the Child would not perhaps have suspected me, other People might, and if I was search'd I should be discover'd; I thought it was best to go off with what I had got, and be satisfy'd' (*MF*, 204). Once again, against the narration of successful theft and getaway is set a hypothetical version of events that could have ended in a search, discovery – and then what?

4   Catching Male Pickpockets 1720–1722

In choosing to steal privately in public spaces and daylight hours, Moll resembles not so much the actual women indicted at the Old Bailey for pickpocketing in 1720–1722 as the sixty-one males (five of them 'boys') prosecuted on that charge. There the resemblance ends for, with only five exceptions,[8] the

---

8   Martha Dower (*OBO*, t17200427-12); Elizabeth Cole (t17201012-5); Sarah Socket (*OBO*, t17210525-1); Sarah Evans (*OBO*, t17220704-69) and Mary Leak (*OBO*, t17220907-52).

victims of these male defendants were also male, and most of their pickings were of comparatively small value. A few of the same items said to have been stolen by female defendants – pocket books, sums of money, watches, rings and snuff boxes – are listed in indictments of males, but in a full thirty-four cases, more than half of the total, the only goods stolen were handkerchiefs, usually valued at two or three shillings each and always down-charged by juries to ten pence.[9] As for the 'environment of pickpocketing', a few men were robbed at night and while sleeping off a drinking session in a tavern (Thomas Barr, *OBO*, t17200907-5), on a market stall (William Howard, *OBO*, t17210113-5) or a dunghill (John Dace, *OBO*, t17221010-3), but most testified to having had their pockets picked as they walked the streets of London.

These prosecutors had evidently been quick to apprehend their suspects. Zachary Polock 'going by Lombard-street... felt a Hand in his Pocket, whereupon he turn'd short, and seized the Prisoner with his Handkerchief in his Hand' (*OBO*, t17200907-13). Similar testimony was given by Richard Coxsell (*OBO*, t17200303-6), Samuel Illidge (*OBO*, t17200602-2), James Glover (*OBO*, t17200427-18) and Henry Farren (*OBO*, t17210712-4). Others undertook a degree of detective work. John Holloway followed and took William Witherel, 'the Handkerchief by him' (*OBO*, t17200303-1); James Cooper grew suspicious of Michael Vine, followed and 'feeling of him draw his Handkerchief out of his Pocket at the end of Bow-Lane, took him by the Collar and found it in his Hand-before he could put it up' (*OBO*, t17200907-1). Thomas Cook, 'seeing the Prisoner and another Lad lurking about under the Piazza, suspected them, searcht the Prisoner, and found his Handkerchief and 4 more in a private Pocket behind him' (*OBO*, t17210301-4).

Unlike Moll's victims, these men seem to have been of middling or lower sort,[10] and may have been engrossed in matters of business or trade when robbed. Thomas Brook was 'talking against the Royal-Exchange' when a 'Mr. Mitten' saw Philip Jersey take his exceptionally expensive silk handkerchief, searched and secured the thief (*OBO*, t17210712-1). Richard Hilliard was hearing a cause at the Court of Common Pleas in the Guildhall when his 'remarkable' snuffbox was taken (*OBO*, t17210712-17). Other victims, the *Proceedings* makes clear, had allowed themselves to be distracted by street entertainments, and yet managed to catch hold of their thieves. James Barber

---

9   Handkerchiefs would have been attractive to thieves because, besides being easily portable and less identifiable than watches and other valuables that were often engraved with owners' and makers' names, they were among the 'goods that were in greatest demand, less conspicuous and most easily negotiable in the communities to which they [the thieves] belonged' (Tickell 2018, 95).
10   Only one, John Hill, is labelled 'Gent.' (*OBO*, t17220510-23).

had been standing in Leicester Fields 'to hear 4 Boys play on the Violin' 'last Execution day at night' when he secured Abel Wild in the act of pulling his handkerchief out of his pocket (*OBO*, t17221010-27). Benjamin Forward missed his 'as he stood at the Ring in Moorfields', but promptly followed Joseph Booth, who obligingly 'gave it him without asking, and said he'd do so no more' (*OBO*, t17220704-6). Forward prosecuted nevertheless, as did Barnard Dixon, who had been standing 'to see them play at Cudgels in Smithfield' when 'a little Boy' tipped him off to the theft of his handkerchief by another 'Boy' (*OBO*, t17210712-6).

Churchgoers would have been able to count on fellow members of their congregations to warn and help take suspects. Sarah Rainbow was one of the few female victims to prosecute for pickpocketing in the early 1720s. Described in the *Proceedings* as 'Lame', Rainbow was being helped into a chair after evening sermon at St James's Chapel when 'she felt something press against her side, and clapping her Hand to feel for her Watch, it was gone'; she quickly laid her hand on Sarah Fox who, with Susanna Jones, was 'apprehended, and immediately search'd in the Vestry' (*OBO*, t17221205-9). More typical prosecutors are Richard Storey, who caught John Clare sliding his handkerchief out of his pocket while in Stepney Church (*OBO*, t17200427-30), John Higgs, who missed his on leaving St Andrews Holborn and apprehended William Blewit (*OBO*, t17220404-1), Robert Street, who missed his bible, followed John Green and found it on him (*OBO*, t17210830-53) and John Stevens, who seized Robert Colthorp in the choir of Westminster Abbey (*OBO*, t17220404-42).[11] Philip Gascoign (*OBO*, t17220907-19) and Charles Winckworth had been attending funerals when their pockets were picked (*OBO*, t17201012-9).

Several prosecutors were aided by passers-by who had no apparent connection with them. Joseph Bryan was seen taking Richard Stockwell's silk handkerchief 'by another Person, who told the Prosecutor of it, they secur'd him' (*OBO*, t17200115-5). Thomas Husbands watched Thomas Bostock twice try for Thomas Bedford's handkerchief and, when he succeeded, 'seized him so quick that he had not an Opportunity to drop it' (*OBO*, t17201012-2). Humphrey Holloway saw Robert Sutton take William Elliot's and give it to John Pomeroy, on whom they found several others (*OBO*, t17220907-59); similar evidence was given by Thomas Wyser against John Alston and Thomas

---

11 Colthorp was acquitted but must have resented his arrest and detention: the next day he was convicted for assaulting his prosecutor.

Williams (*OBO*, t17221010-8). William Bull happened to be looking out of a window when he saw John Glover snatch Jeremiah Hemyn's handkerchief, whereupon he 'ran down Stairs and inform'd the Prosecutor, who pursued, and took the prisoner' (*OBO*, t17220704-18). A woman selling fruit in Cheapside recognised the two pickpockets following Isaac Tilliard and told a Mr. Holland, who 'made haste after them' and took one by the collar (*OBO*, t17201012-7). When John Prior saw John Wood take his handkerchief, he 'laid him on with his Cane, [and] cry'd out a Pickpocket', but at the trial it was William Burridge who claimed 'that he took the Prisoner, and found the Handkerchiefs upon him' (*OBO*, t17210113-1).

It is possible that Mr. Holland, like the Richard Greening who secured and searched John Edwards (*OBO*, t17210113-6), was a constable or watchman, and that William Burridge was a thief-taker (see Chapter 5). Even so, enough men and boys were detected and apprehended on the streets of London by casual passers-by to impress readers of the *Proceedings* with their fellow citizens' willingness to help catch thieves and mount a successful court case. Whereas less than half the women indicted for stealing privately from the person in our three years were convicted, forty-eight out of the sixty males accused, including all five 'boys', were found guilty. The message to be gleaned from Defoe's second crime fiction would have been less encouraging to would-be prosecutors.

5 Colonel Jack's Apprenticeship

5.1 *The Hands of the Mobb*

Unlike most of the male pickpockets who stood trial at the Old Bailey in 1720–1722, the pickpockets in *Colonel Jack* are *all* young boys, a difference that would have reinforced contemporary anxieties about criminal children on the streets of London (Gollapudi 2017). At about twelve years old the narrator's easy-going elder brother, the Major, is recruited by a pair of older boys to carry away their pickings from Bartholomew Fair so that, if caught, they will not be found with the goods on them. The Colonel records their prizes in a 'List of their Purchase the first Night', attaching micronarratives which, like Moll's revelations of her *modus operandi*, offer 'a Key to the Clue to a Pickpockets' motions'. The first three are:

> 1. A white Handkerchief from a Country Wench, as she was staring up at a *Jackpudding*, there was 3s 6d and a Row of Pins, tyed up in one End of it.

II. A colour'd Handkerchief, out of a young Country Fellow's Pocket as he was buying a *China* Orange.

III. A Ribband purse with 11s. 3d. and a Silver Thimble in it, out of a young Woman's Pocket, just as a Fellow offer'd to pick her up.

NB. She mist her Purse presently, but not seeing the Thief, charg'd the Man with it, that would have pick'd her up, and cry'd out a Pick-Pocket, and he fell into the Hands of the Mobb, but being known in the Street, he got off with great Difficulty.

CJ, 71

As Gladfelder (2001, 103) notes, the list imitates 'the form of criminal deposition and newspaper advertisements of stolen goods':

> The descriptions have almost a clairvoyant lucidity, Colonel Jack remembering some forty years later not only the exact amount stolen from each person but the value of each coin and sketching a vividly tactile and kinesthetic memory of the circumstances of each theft, even though he was not there nor at the later division of the spoils. The details are recollected in imagination, not directly witnessed, but they are recorded in the format of prosecutorial evidence, asserting their material exhaustiveness as a marker of truth.

Defoe here imitates language that might have been used by witnesses deploying reference to material circumstances in their efforts to convince juries of the guilt of those they accuse.[12] No one will prosecute these boys, however, and the only suspect taken, the man who had tried to pick up the young woman with the ribband purse, turns out to be locally known and is let go.

It is not likely, in any case, that the 'Fellow' would have been prosecuted formally; he would at worst have been subjected, like the 'poor Boy' in the meeting house episode in *Moll Flanders*, 'to the Rage of the Street, which is a Cruelty I need not describe' (*MF*, 167). Cruel as that rage may be, Moll explains, it is a fate thieves prefer to being 'sent to *Newgate*, where they lie a long time, till they are almost perish'd, and sometimes they are hang'd, and the best they can look for, if they are Convicted, is to be Transported'. Of the legally sanc-

---

12   On the development of judicial thinking about circumstantial evidence, see Welsh 1992, Chapter 1, and on evidence in general in *Colonel Jack*, Clegg 1998.

tioned procedure, the young Jack knows nothing, for he has no judicial understanding of his mode of getting by:

> as to the Nature of the Thing, I was perfectly a Stranger to it I knew indeed what at first I did not, for it was a good while before I understood the thing, as an Offence: I look'd on picking pockets as a kind of Trade, and I thought I was to go Apprentice to it ... only a thing for which if we were catch'd, we run the Risque of being Duck'd or Pump'd, which we called Soaking, and then all was over; and we made nothing of having our Raggs wetted a little; but I never understood, till a great while after, that the Crime was Capital, and that we might be sent to *Newgate* for it, till a great Fellow, almost a Man, one of our Society was hang'd for it and then I was terribly frighted, as you shall hear by and by.
>
> CJ, 76

Coming near the end of a leisurely, rambling sentence which invites readers to infer that traditional community punishments are poor deterrents, the flat statement that one overgrown lad 'was hang'd for it' comes as a shock. Did Defoe wish to remind both potential thieves and potential catchers of thieves of the sentence that, until the Transportation Act of 1718, was mandatory for convicted pickpockets, and was still being passed on convicts in the early 1720s? A full twenty-five of the eighty-four men, women and children found guilty of privately stealing from the person between January 1720 and December 1722 were condemned to die, and in at least three cases the sentences were carried out.[13] Of the rest, jury mitigation allowed one to be sentenced to a whipping and fifty-seven to be deported to the colonies. The early chapters of *Colonel Jack* contemplate no intermediate penalty, but later ones will present several years of hard labour overseas as more effective in reducing property crime than either beatings or the gallows. As Gabriel Cervantes observes (2011–2012, 264–265), the experiences of Major Jack and his 'Society' prepare

---

13   Martha Purdue (Purdew in the trial report) and Mary Granger appear in the Ordinary's *Account* for 26 October 1720 (*OA*, 17201026), Thomas Rogers, alias Cane, who had turned out to be a transportee returned before his time, in that for 5 July 1721 (*OA*, t17210705-1). Fourteen of the women certainly received conditional pardons, as the other seven may well have done, for they are not mentioned in issues of the Ordinary's *Account* for 1720–1722.

the reader to welcome transportation as the best punishment for non-violent property crime.[14]

5.2   *In the Customs House*

The type of pickpocketing in which Colonel Jack serves his own apprenticeship is far more ambitious than the Major's, and because it is committed in socially exclusive business environments, it carries greater risk of resulting in prosecution on a capital charge. Following a pattern we shall come across again in Chapter 4, Defoe has his protagonist come to his 'trade' only after a period on the 'economy of makeshift' (see Shore 2003). Having been 'turned loose to the World' after the death of their nurse, the three Jacks survive on the charity of their east London community 'without much begging' or troubling the parish. But while the Major soon takes to picking pockets and the Captain to kidnapping, the young Colonel supplements his income by running errands and guarding the shops of 'some of the poorer Shop-Keepers … 'till they were up to Dinner, or went over the Way to an Ale-house, and the like' (*CJ*, 65–66). Gradually, however, he, like Moll, is drawn in by the 'subtle Tempter', and is trained in thieving by an expert with pretensions: 'HE was above the little Fellows, who went about stealing Trifles, and Baubles in *Bartholomew-Fair,* and run the Risque of being Mobb'd for three or four Shillings; his aim was at higher things' (*CJ*, 75). Like Moll's teacher, Jack's instructor, Will, is 'very Dextrous at the Ladies Gold Watches' but, unlike her, he 'never that I know of, miss'd his Aim, or was catch'd in the Fact' (*CJ*, 99). Of greater topical interest in the early eighteenth century, especially to readers with commercial and banking interests, would have been his targeting of 'considerable Sums of Money, and Bills for more large sums of money and of credit notes'. As Beattie writes (2001, 250), pickpocketing was 'an old capital offence that took on a new character in an age in which increasing numbers of valuable documents were being carried by merchants and financiers in London'. Again like Moll's, these thefts would have had to be carried out in business hours and in the presence of people who would willingly intervene to help a victim, if alerted promptly. On the other hand, as Jack explains in recounting his first solo attempt, the worries

---

14   Ian Bell (2020, 148) calls attention to the dynamic role of Augustan satire in centralising and standardising the 'polyphony of social punishments' which 'was slowly being replaced by the virtually exclusive arbitration of the rule of law and its accredited agents'.

to which high-flying businessmen were subject render them vulnerable to thieves:[15]

> the Gentlemen are in great Hurries, their Heads and Thoughts entirely taken up, and it is impossible they should be Guarded enough against such little Hawks Eyed Creatures, as we were; and therefore they ought either never to put their Pocket-books up at all, or to put them up more secure, or to put nothing of Value into them…
>
> CJ, 99

Will had earlier given his pupil a lesson in how to take advantage of the rush of business by taking him to the crowded new Customs House for the Port of London,[16] where no one notices Will purloining a letter case and handing it to Jack, who has camouflaged his presence by collecting pins from the floor. The pair are thus able to leave the building without drawing attention to themselves:

> He did not run, but shuffl'd along a pace thro' the Crowd, and went down not the great Stairs, which we came in at, but a little narrow Stair-Case at the other End of the Long Room; I follow'd, and he found I did, and so went on, not stopping below as I expected, nor speaking one Word to me, till thro' innumerable narrow Passages, Alleys and Dark ways, we were got up into *Fenchurch-street*, and thro' *Billiter lane* into *Leadenhall-street*, and from thence into *Leadenhall-Market*.
>
> CJ, 77

The boys can rely on their young legs and intimate knowledge of the back streets of the City to get quickly away, but the scene of the crime remains fraught with peril, as Will discovers when, next day, he rashly returns to the Customs House for a second pick at the cherry. He is recognised and 'immediately the whole Crowd of people gather'd about the Boy, and Charg'd him

---

15   Margaret Hunt (1996, 20–21) writes of the anxieties that beset the middling sort in the unstable conditions of eighteenth-century commerce and investment, especially during the South Sea crisis of 1720, when members of the 'big bourgeoisie' lost vast fortunes overnight.

16   Wren's Custom House had been destroyed by fire in 1714–1715 and rebuilt on a larger scale to accommodate the staff needed to deal with the duties needed to pay for the wars of this time.

point Blank!' After some roughing up, he is subjected to a process that closely resembles a magistrate's hearing:

> the Commissioners examined him; but all was one, he would own nothing, but *said he* walk'd up a thro' the Room only to see the Place both then, and the time before, for he had own'd he was there before; so as there was no proof against him, of any Fact, no, nor of any Circumstances relating to the Letter Case, they were forc'd at last to let him go; however, they made a show of carrying him to *Bridewell*, and they did carry him to the Gate, to see if they could make him confess any thing; but he would confess nothing, and they had no *Mittimus*; so they durst not carry him into the House, nor would the People have receiv'd him, I suppose, if they had, they having no Warrant for putting him in Prison.
> CJ, 85

Defoe clearly expected his readers to be familiar with the procedure followed by the commissioners. They question Will in the hope of obtaining some 'proof against him, of any Fact', or at least 'Circumstances relating to the Letter Case', and know that they cannot consign him to the City's house of correction without a *mittimus,* a document that only a justice of the peace could provide. Luckily for Will, he has none of the booty about him, and enough legal knowhow to be able to meet his interrogators on their own terms: he refuses to be frightened into confessing and provides a plausible reason for his presence in the Customs House. As we shall see in future chapters, such know-how will also prove vital to Jack and Moll as they brush with a justice system potentially far more dangerous to them than the informal, plebeian one practiced on the street.

6 Conclusion

In the eighteenth century most thieves were taken, if taken at all, by people at or near the scenes of their crimes. In a case of theft from the person performed 'privately', that would either be the victim, if he or she detected the thief in time, or someone in the vicinity who is observant and ready to intervene quickly. The 'environments' in which pockets were picked would have varied greatly, but in early modern England were strictly gendered. In the *Proceedings* for the early 1720s we read of large numbers of women accused by men of stealing their valuables in dark, enclosed spaces and while drinking and/or having sex, and of large numbers of men and boys stealing usually quite modest 'goods', often handkerchiefs, from men on the streets of London. Many prosecutors in the first group clearly did not find it easy to bring their thieves to justice, and many more men despoiled in such circumstances surely never did. Moll Flanders gets away successfully from her one and only venture in sexploitation because her victim is too drunk to realise what is going on at the time and, unlike the men who actually prosecuted, too socially superior to expose himself to a public process of law when, some days later, he is given a chance to get her arrested. Most of those from whose persons Moll steals are of his class, but of her own sex. Specialising narrowly in taking only 'gold watches from Ladies' sides', she must operate in the open, in daylight and in public places, environments far more conducive to catching pickpockets if only because those present are more than ready to help. Although never herself taken, she is made to recount her adventures in such a way as to pass on, through hypothetical versions of what might have taken place at the crime scene, instruction in how to catch thieves like herself.

Major Jack and the other boys who raid the pockets of country people at the fairs of London closely resemble the younger members of the cohort of handkerchief thieves that would have been familiar to readers of the *Proceedings* in the 1720s. However, Defoe is surely truer to life in having those that get caught dealt with by the mob on the street rather than being handed over to formal process of law, a process which, he reminds us, involved a spell in London's most notorious prison and could end in a hanging or transportation. Colonel Jack and his tutor Will run that risk when they prey on merchants and financiers, victims more likely to undertake a prosecution – but for the fact that, as we shall see in Chapter 4, their need to recover their fabulously valuable credit notes and bills outweighs their allegiance to the judicial system.

CHAPTER 3

At the Scene of the Crime II: Minding the Shop

1   Introduction

When Defoe made Moll Flanders carry out her first theft in a shop, and later sent her to train professionally under an expert shoplifter, he would have been nourishing his own and many of his readers' intense interest in all things commercial. His first crime fiction casts bright light on the cultural history of what Shelley Tickell (2008, 2) calls 'the most emblematic of eighteenth-century crimes'. Stealing from shops was a by-product of the consumer revolution that made a new range of goods available to the English and led to fixed retail outlets with inviting displays taking the places of market stalls, fairs and hawkers (Mui and Mui 1989, 27). It had come to be categorised as a discrete form of theft by the 1660s, and by the 1690s was a focus of mounting anxiety about immorality and crime, particularly by women, who accounted for 77% of those indicted for shoplifting at the Old Bailey during that decade. In 1691 benefit of clergy was extended to women convicts on the same basis as for men, a change which was intended to boost prosecutions, but which also made shoplifting 'one of the most accessible, remunerative and least rigorously punished offences' (Tickell 2018, 146). It would have been all the more attractive compared to other forms of property crime, such as housebreaking and pickpocketing, because shoplifters could select their booty from a wide range of new fashion items for which they would have found ready markets (Lemire 1988 and 1990, cited in Tickell 2018, 9).

It was in this 'fertile climate' for shoplifting (Tickell 2018, 3) that the so-called 'Shoplifting Act' of 1699 was generated. Originating in a bill to 'encourage the Apprehending of House-breakers, Horse Stealers and other Felons', the measure was extended to cover 'burglary … or robbery in shops, warehouses, coach-houses or stables', and to promote not only apprehending but also prosecuting and punishing (Tickell 2018, 149). Like other components of the 'Bloody Code', this statute was the creation of cross-party backbenchers, men with commercial and metropolitan interests who would have shared the outrage expressed by the authors of *The Great Grievance of Traders and Shopkeepers*.[1]

---

1   Beattie (2001, 329) thought that the *Great Grievance*, which he dated spring 1699, was responsible for the addition of shoplifting to the list of felonies targeted, but Tickell

Thefts from shops and warehouses, the petitioners complained, had increased to the extent that they were now the 'daily experience' of London shopkeepers, the perpetrators being so well organised that 'strictest diligence cannot secure' against them:

> they personate all degrees of Buyers, in all their respective Qualification, having their Several Societies and Walks, their Cabals, Receivers, Solicitors, and even their Bullies to rescue them if taken, as some late Instances shew; as well as their combin'd Purses to defend themselves in their Villainy, with their repeated Threats, if prosecuted: and carry on the same, as if they were a Body-Politick or Corporate.

The 'Loss and Damage' sustained as a result, the pamphlet claimed,

> doth very much exceed in Value all other robberies within this Kingdom; a late Shop-lift before her execution confessed that she (in her Calling) had stolen to the Value of Twelve Thousand Pounds; by which Practice many Shopkeepers have been insensibly ruined, and all much prejudiced by their Loss of Goods, Time, and Charge in Prosecutions; by the Expense of keeping more servants for their Security, and sometimes by their falling as a Prey to their united malice and Revenge for adhering to Prosecute.

To the difficulty and expense of prosecuting, the lightness of the punishments handed out by the courts and the attractions of compounding for the return of stolen goods, the pamphlet attributed the fact that 'few Offenders are taken; when taken, not one in Ten is prosecuted; when prosecuted not one in Ten but either is cleared by Whipping, or by Burning in the Hands; and if condemned, usually Transportation is granted which is much to be feared hath not its intended Effect'.

As Tickell (2018, 40) shows from her analysis of trials held at the Old Bailey in the eighteenth century, the claims put forward in the *Great Grievance* were largely unfounded. Only about 4,000 shoplifting cases were brought to the Old Bailey over the hundred years 1715–1815, so it was hardly a 'daily Experience', and since no more than 20% of shop thieves were professionals, the woman who confessed to having 'stolen to the Value of Twelve Thousand Pounds'

(2018, 148) suggests that the bill had already been amended before the petition was presented.

would have been a rare bird. Mainly amateur, occasional and driven by need, eighteenth-century shoplifting was, like pickpocketing, 'an intermittent form of makeshift' for the poor, most of whom stole from shops within the outlying neighbourhoods they inhabited (Tickell 2018, 5). From these they took inconspicuous goods that satisfied the everyday needs of people not unlike themselves, and could be easily sold on: stockings, handkerchiefs, and the ribbons and printed cottons used to make clothing in fashion with working people. Theft would therefore have constituted a more serious economic problem for the humbler shopkeepers than for the owners of smarter, centrally located shops supplying the elite with luxury goods, although it would have been the latter who articulated resentment and pressured parliament to take action.

It was therefore on a 'false understanding' of the crime that the Shoplifting Act was based. Like so many of the statutes of the reigns of William and Anne, it aimed on the one hand at encouraging members of the public to undertake formal proceedings, on the other at inculcating terror in potential thieves. Two incentives to apprehending and prosecuting were provided for: a reward in the form of a certificate exempting those who succeeded in convicting from public office and guarantees of pardons to culprits who gave evidence against two or more associates. The certificate, known as a 'Tyburn ticket', was to prove attractive to London householders reluctant to lose time serving as constables and in other capacities; those to whom exemption was of no use, such as thief-takers but also, presumably, anyone who was not a householder in the parish, could make a tidy sum by getting such a ticket reassigned.[2] The pardoning provision was clearly intended to encourage members of the 'gangs' of shoplifters thought to be infesting London to give evidence against each other, and against receivers and other accessories.

In this chapter we shall come across a fair number of shoplifters denouncing their fences, and in Chapter 5 another group of 'discoverers' giving evidence against partners for whom they had stood watch or carried away the stolen goods. As for deterrents, the statutes shifted branding, a punishment available for clergyable offenses, from the hand to the cheek, a change that proved counter-productive and was reversed in 1706. Much longer-lived was the provision that made stealing privately from shops to the value of five shillings ineligible for benefit of clergy, and thus a capital offence, a status it maintained until 1823.

---

2   Beattie (2001, 330 and n.) found two 'Tyburn tickets' that, in 1719, earned their assignees–Jonathan Wild being one of them–£11 and £8.8s respectively.

Few accused shoplifters were actually hanged in the eighteenth century. As with pickpocketing, it was not easy to prove a crime committed 'privately' and, again as with pickpocketing, most of those found guilty were saved by juries who downgraded the value of goods stolen to bring the offence within clergy and thus make it possible for judges to sentence directly to branding, whipping or, after 1718, to transportation. Even so, the introduction of mandatory death sentences for private thefts of fairly valuable goods from shops conferred on this 'minor, non-violent crime ... conspicuous legal standing as a capital offence' (Tickell 2018, 2).

This surely made the crime itself and the enforcing of the law against it more interesting as narrative material, and ethically more problematic. The possibility that the arrest of a shoplifter may be the first step along the road to the gallows would have intensified the dramatic potential of the action itself and placed huge responsibilities on the actors involved. As we shall see, Defoe makes the most of that potential in narrating the taking, or attempted taking, of Moll Flanders and her kind; first, however, let us look at how her actual equivalents were caught and started on their grim journeys through prosecution procedure.

2 Shoplifters Apprehended 1720–1722

In eighteen of the seventy-five reports of shoplifting trials heard at the Old Bailey between January 1720 and December 1722 it is not at all clear how the defendants had been apprehended. Most of the rest were taken in one of three ways. Fourteen were stopped by those to whom they tried to sell the goods stolen, while nineteen were probably arrested on information supplied by accomplices who testified against them; these two groups will be discussed in Chapters 4 and 5. It is not surprising that the largest group of those accused, twenty-four, were apprehended in or near the shop by people who saw the theft take place or noticed that something was missing, and either seized the suspects themselves, or gave the alarm and were helped in stopping them by passers-by.[3]

---

[3] Thefts observed should not have been indictable under the Shoplifting Act and may have been treated by the court as larceny; the *Proceedings* do not usually specify under which statute a defendant had been indicted. It is not likely that many accused objected to the wording of their indictments; Thomas Knight is the only one in my shoplifter sample reported as having done so, and he was overruled (*OBO*, t17210113-9). Later in the century

The *Proceedings* are not always forthcoming about who grabbed those accused.[4] Among prosecutors who pursued and seized suspects directly, Arthur Greenhill followed Anne Wilkinson to Bow church yard, brought her back to his shop and took a pair of worsted stockings valued at 2s 6d out of her petticoat; one Henry Biggs testified to seeing him do so, and Wilkinson supplied further evidence of her guilt by falling on her knees to beg pardon (*OBO*, t17210525-3). John Smalwood, prosecuting Richard Hedgly for taking '5 pair of worsted Stockings, val. 17 s.', deposed in court 'that about 9 at Night he saw the prisoner put his Hand in at the Shop Window, and take the Goods, and stopt him with them. The prisoner own'd the Fact at the Bar, but said he did it out of meer necessity' (*OBO*, t17220404-4). Ruth Jones and Mary Yeomans seem to have operated as a pair, and may have been professionals; William Thorn accused them of stealing Moroccan leather valued at 6s, claiming 'that the Prisoners came into his Shop to cheapen Goods; that Jones pretended to go out to match some Silk while Yeomans bought the Leather, but going the contrary way, he suspected her and brought her back, and took the Skin from under her Petticoat' (*OBO*, t17210525-14).

Relatives, especially wives and daughters, were often left to mind shops, which would in many cases have been parts of dwelling houses. During Robert Fenwick's prosecution of Mary Hughes for stealing '11 Yards and Half of Stuff', his wife 'deposed that she being in her Parlour behind the Shop, saw the Prisoner take the Goods and immediately sent her Servant after her' (*OBO*, t17200115-40). At the trial of Edward Corder, indicted by John Jackson, Elizabeth Jackson deposed that she 'was sitting in a back Room, about 7 at Night' when she heard someone open a drawer containing 19 shillings, 'ran out and stopt the Prisoner in the Shop, with the Goods upon him, till some others came to her Assistance' (*OBO*, t17211206-6). Thomas Rice entered Samuel Elson's shop, haggled over the price of some lace, then 'took 1 piece, put it in his Bosom and ran away with it; but being seen to take it was followed and apprehended. Mrs. Elson was positive she saw him put it in his Bosom and run away with it, tho' it was not found upon him' (*OBO*, t17211011-5). Susan Kirton successfully challenged Sir Charles Burton, who had been bargaining over the price of seals in her father's shop and purloined 'a Cornelian Seal set in Gold,

---

more objections were raised and supported by lawyers, forcing prosecutors to resort to multiple indictments; see Tickell 2018, Chapter 6.

4 The *Proceedings* record that 'two Evidences' claimed to have seen Susannah Lloyd take a checked tablecloth off Nathaniel Clark's shop counter (*OBO*, t17200303-38). George Streight testified to having lost 2s 6d but it was 'Another' who claimed to have seen his next-door neighbour take the money off the counter (*OBO*, t17200602-5).

value 15 s': 'Mrs. Kirton missing a Seal, and observing a Handkerchief in his Hand, desired him to shake it, which he did, holding one corner of it fast; but she took it from him, and the Seal dropt out' (*OBO*, t17220907-23).[5]

Succinct though these reports are, they convey a clear sense of the scene as perceived by the shop guardian. Against Jane Short,

> Mary Hutton deposed that the Prisoner came into her Mother's Shop under pretence of buying Ribbon; that she reach'd her down 7 pieces, and she (the Prisoner) made bold with one of them; which this Evidence perceiving, let her go out of the Shop about 3 Doors, then had her brought back, and took the Ribbon out of her Breast.
>
> *OBO*, t17210419-4

If Hutton delayed acting until she could be sure that Short had actually stolen the ribbon, Mary Leighton was even more circumspect, making sure that she had witnesses to her discovery of thirteen yards of ribbon on Margaret Townley, and to the thief's begging pardon. In court Leighton deposed

> that the Prisoner came into her Mother's Shop to buy Ribbon, and that she saw her take the Goods mentioned in the Indictment, out of the Window; that she let her go out of the Shop a good way, and then sent to fetch her back again, that when she was brought back she searcht her, and took the Ribbon out of her Pocket, which was produc'd in Court and swore to; that she found other Pieces of Ribbon about her, but could not swear to them; that then the Prisoner fell down on her Knees and begg'd pardon. Two other Evidences deposed that they saw the Ribbon taken out of her Pocket, and that she fell down on her Knees and begg'd Pardon.
>
> *OBO*, t17200712-4

The *Old Bailey Proceedings* do not tell us who Mary Hutton, Mary Leighton and Mrs. Elson sent after their suspects, but they were probably employees. Eighteenth-century servants were widely suspected of stealing, and a few appear among early 1720s defendants in shoplifting cases,[6] but much more often

---

5 'Customers' of the middling and genteel sort were rarely suspected (Tickell 2018, 32). That of baronet Sir Charles Burton was one of the few shoplifting trials to earn a place in a compilation volume; see *Select Trials* 1742, I, 236–237.

6 After 'missing his Money several times' an unnamed prosecutor, with the help of William Barrow (probably a constable), 'had some markt, and put it into his Till', later finding some of the marked money on his servant, Owen Pritchard (*OBO*, t17210830-25). When John Hart

we find them telling the court how they had caught thieves, often on their own initiative. Defoe (1726, Chapter 5) was to denounce masters who left shops in the care of 'raw boys that mind nothing', with the result that 'there are more outcries of "Stop thief!" at their door and more constables fetched to that shop, than to all the shops in the row'. Belying this, Joseph Burton deposed that William Carl came into Joseph Marriot's shop to cheapen stockings, 'but he perceiving something under his Coat when he went out, followed and brought him back' (*OBO*, t17210525-11). The unnamed servant to Edward Hillior agreed with Alice Jones on 'a Hat of about 10s' to be collected later, 'but he perceiving she could hardly walk fetch her back again, and the Hat mentioned ... fell from between her Legs' (*OBO*, t17200427-2). John Smithers, alias Smithurst, indicted by Samuel Illidge for taking two volumes from his shop, was said to have been 'immediately followed by the Prosecutor's man (whom he struck with them on his Breast)' (*OBO*, t17210301-48).

I find no other mention of violence *by* suspects – perhaps more was used *against* them, if only because searches must have involved some manhandling. John Goodchild's servant was apparently determined to incriminate Katherine Crompton for taking some expensive muslin, but took the precaution of having a female witness present during his search: 'he perceiving her take the Muslin, called the Maid down Stairs, and searching her, took a piece of Striped Muslin from under her Ridinghood, then carried her backward and found four pieces more of plain Muslin' (*OBO*, t17200907-30). Joseph Lock, servant or apprentice to Samuel Wilson, caught thieves visiting his master's button shop on at least two occasions. In November 1721 he heard the glass case rattle, found it broken and missed a gross of buttons and a copper gilt watch chain, valued at a total of 14s; stopping John Scoon, he charged a constable with him and got Scoon to produce the chain from the waistband of his breeches (*OBO*, t17211206-3). A few months later, Jane Holms bought and paid for a penknife, but was followed by Lock, 'who found a Gross of Buttons in her Basket' (*OBO*, t17220704-1).

Among shops catering to more elite customers would have been that of mercer Thomas Fletcher, who prosecuted a woman 'of St. Vedast, alias Foster' for stealing '50 Yards of Silk Galloon, and 76 Yards of Silk Ferret'. Fletcher's servant John Sturges told the court that

---

missed silk stockings from his shop 'he examined the prisoner his Boy, who confest' (*OBO*, t17220907-43). On paranoia about servant theft, see Paula Humfrey, 2016 and, of course, Defoe's *Great Law of Subordination* (1728).

the Prisoner came into the Shop under pretence of buying some Galloon for her Ridinghood, that she being difficult in matching the Colour, he went to serve a Customer, and left another Servant to sell her, and observed her to take some pieces of Galloon and Ferret; that she bought 1 yard, went out of the Shop, turn'd back and bought another yard, when he saw her take 4 Pieces more; that he let her go out of the Shop, then fetcht her back and had her up Stairs in the Dining-Room, and found the Goods upon her. John Collier confirmed the finding the Goods upon her.

OBO, t17210419-17

In her defence 'alias Foster' made the unlikely claim that the silk (all 126 yards of it!) had fallen into her pinned up petticoat without her realising. She was, however, able to call several witnesses to her reputation and it was probably they who convinced the jury to value her huge haul at only ten pence, thus allowing the judges to let her off with a whipping.

Shop employees clearly carried a great deal of responsibility for security but, as we have seen in the case of male pickpockets, people who had no personal connection with victims were often ready to help. As Tickell writes (2018, 10), 'Court testimony advertises the remarkable level of interest and engagement shoplifting occasioned among the man and woman in the street. Their extensive collaboration with retailers in combating the crime is conspicuous'. The 'Mr. Neal' who 'hearing the Cry of Stop Thief behind him, turn'd back, and saw the Prisoner drop the Goods' (*OBO*, t17200115-40), may have been a constable, but there is nothing to suggest that whoever apprehended Arthur Hullerton when Mrs. Walker 'went out, [and] cry'd out to stop the Prisoner' was anyone other than a casual passer-by (*OBO*, t17221205-26). The same applies to the unidentified person who, alerted by the cry 'Stop Thief', seized William Spencer, whom Richard Hewet has seen reach over his counter and take a shirt and pair of stockings (*OBO*, t17220112-17). Even without being called upon, neighbours and passers-by intervened readily. Prosecutor Henry Baylis deposed against Mary North that he had seen her 'shuffle something under her Riding-Hood', but it was Joseph Austin, in whose doorway he found North sheltering, who 'brought her back again with the Goods in her lap'. When William Thatcher saw Thomas Tinsly take a shoe out of John Ward's shop, he 'stept to the door and took it upon him' (*OBO*, t17220907-50).

Were Neal, Austin and Thatcher hoping for a reward from the victims they assisted, or for a 'Tyburn ticket' from the parish? One wonders about the motives of Thomas Forster and Thomas Holden, both of whom claimed to have caught Thomas Pearce with a brass porridge pot taken from the window of

William Goodman's shop (*OBO*, t17210525-13). Were Forster and Holden competing with each other? Or were they collaborating, as Isaac Johnson and William Dunkley may have been in the capture of David Pritchard with twenty-eight yards of stolen crape:

> Isaac Johnson deposed, that he seeing the Prisoner loitering about the Prosecutor's Shop, watcht him; and when the Stationer's Door (which was next to the Prosecutor's) was shut, he saw the Prisoner put his Arm over the Grate and take the Goods; whereupon he ran up to him, and took him with the Goods under his Left Arm. William Dunkley deposed, that he seeing the former Evidence stand at the end of the Street, askt him what he staid there for; who told him that he had observed the Prisoner lurking about, and suspected that he had a Design against the Prosecutor's Shop: that he said he has done, and they ran to seize him; but a Coach running by, this Evidence did not come up till the former Evidence was scuffling with the Prisoner on the Ground with the Goods under him.
>
> *OBO*, t17210831o-18

Johnson's patient wait for Pritchard to make his move, the precision of his testimony – the thief had 'the Goods under his Left Arm' – and Dunkley's recognition of him, suggest that the two were habitual takers of thieves. As we shall see later, the likes of Johnson and Dunkley have no place in Defoe's fictions, but equivalents of the other zealous minders of shops feature frequently among those who on several occasions nearly apprehend Moll Flanders, and eventually do.

3 Apprehending Moll Flanders

3.1 *Hawks-Ey'd Journeymen*

Early eighteenth-century readers coming to Defoe from the *Proceedings* would have taken it for granted that anyone present at the scene of a theft from a shop, but especially shop employees, would make an effort to catch the thief. The maid and apprentice to the Leadenhall Street apothecary may not be very vigilant, but we are surely meant to assume that if they had noticed Moll taking the little white bundle they would have pursued her as she flees the scene of the crime. Not long afterwards, another lucky bundle comes her way:

> I was going thro' *Lombard-street* in the dusk of the Evening, just by the end of *Three King Court*, when on a sudden comes a Fellow running by me as swift as Lightning, and throws a Bundle that was in his Hand just behind me, as I stood up against the corner of the House at the turning into the Alley; just as he threw it in he said, God bless you Mistress let it lie there a little, and away he runs as swift as the Wind: After him comes two more, and immediately a young Fellow without his Hat, crying stop Thief, and after him two or three more, they pursued the two last Fellows so close, that they were forced to drop what they had got, and one of them was taken into the bargain, the other got off free.
>
> I STOOD stock still all this while till they came back, dragging the poor Fellow they had taken, and luging the things they had found, extremely well satisfied that they had recovered the Booty, and taken the Thief; and thus they pass'd by me, for I look'd only like one who stood up while the Crowd was gone.
>
> ONCE or twice I ask'd what was the matter, but the People neglected answering me, and I was not very importunate; but after the Crowd was wholly pass'd, I took my opportunity to turn about and take up what was behind me and walk away.
>
> MF, 154

The action here is simple, but the psychological dynamics are quite complex. Moll has chosen for her evening stroll an especially wealthy corner of the City, a court known for its bankers, goldsmiths and mercers (Starr 1976, 388). It is not wholly by chance, therefore, that she is on hand when thieves with a taste for fine textiles run past. Moll does indeed let the bundle lie, in effect accepting the thief's invitation to act as an accomplice, while for public purposes playing the part of curious passer-by. Only after the pursuers have returned with their captive and the crowd has dispersed does she take over from the 'real' thief and walk away with the bundle. From its contents, 'a Peice of fine black Lustring Silk, and a Peice of Velvet; the latter was but part of a Piece of about 11 Yards; the former was a whole Peice of near 50 Yards', reveal that 'it was a *Mercer's* shop that they had rifled', and evidently a large one, since these sixty odd yards of silk constitute only a small part of the 'considerable' goods stolen. As for the young man leading the chase, we may infer that he had been 'without his Hat' because he had been minding his master's shop when he noticed the theft and set off in pursuit without stopping to put it on. His alacrity has been rewarded, but only in part, for he and his helpers catch only one of the three thieves, and fail to notice the bundle Moll is standing in front of. Is Defoe suggesting that if they been more observant and less pleased with themselves, they might have recovered that also, and perhaps taken the two who get away?

Moll here seems to be laughing up her sleeve here, but she soon learns to fear the surveillance skills of London shopkeepers and their assistants. She has barely finished training in shoplifting when her teacher and another pupil, 'happening to be upon the hunt for Purchase ... made an attempt upon a Linnen-Draper in *Cheapside*, but were snapp'd by a Hawks-ey'd Journeyman, and seiz'd with two pieces of Cambrick, which were taken also upon them' (*MF*, 160-1). The older woman, 'having the brand of an old Offender', pays with her life, stirring in Moll memories of the death sentence her mother had received for 'borrowing three Pieces of fine *Holland*, of a certain Draper in *Cheapside*' (*MF*, 10).[7] This 'terrible Example' frights Moll 'heartily' and 'made me the more wary, and particularly I was very shie of Shoplifting, especially among the Mercers, and Drapers who are a Set of Fellows that have they Eyes very much about them' (*MF*, 164).

In the *Complete English Tradesman*, Defoe was to single out those in this branch of the retail trade as needing to be extra vigilant:

> Such is the slippery dealings of this age, especially in mercers and drapers business, that the shop-keeper ought never to turn his back towards his customers; and this is the reason why the mercers and drapers in particular are oblig'd to keep so many journey-men, and so many apprentices in their shops, which were it not for the danger of shop-lifting, wou'd be a needless, as it is a heavy expense to them.
>
> 1 [Supplement], 44, cited in FALLER 2008, 152

In the 1690s the Mercers' Company had agreed to pay the wages of six extra watchmen to patrol the area around the Royal Exchange (Beattie 2001, 179), so it is credible that some of their members employed staff for policing purposes. Defoe has two such 'Messengers' play security roles in an episode which has dire consequences for Moll's partner, and nearly for Moll herself:[8]

---

7 Cheapside was another street known for its 'great dealers'; Starr 1976, 389.
8 'Messengers' whose official function was to carry diplomatic mail 'were also sent to arrest suspects in cases of interest to the Crown' (Beattie 2001, 243).

> I had made a Prize of a Piece of very good Damask in a *Mercers* Shop, and went clear off myself, but had convey'd the Peice to this Companion of mine, when we went out of the Shop; and she went one way, and I went another: We had not been long out of the Shop but the *Mercer* mist his Peice of Stuff, and sent his Messengers, one, one way, and one another, and they presently seiz'd her that had the Peice, with the Damask upon her; as for me, I had very Luckily step'd into a House where there was a Lace Chamber, up one Pair of Stairs, and had the Satisfaction, or the Terror indeed of looking out of the Window upon the Noise they made, and seeing the poor Creature drag'd away in Triumph to the Justice, who immediately committed her to *Newgate*.
> MF, 174

In sending his employees 'one, one way, and one another', this canny shopkeeper anticipates the escape tactics used by his thieves and catches one. But might he have taken both if Moll had remained at street level rather than, 'very Luckily', entering a house with an upstairs lace chamber where she may mingle inconspicuously with customers? Or if his messengers had looked up and seen Moll at the window, rather than making all that noise and dragging off the first 'poor Creature' they come upon? In the two episodes we now turn to, Defoe shows that in enforcing the law, prudence as well as zeal and speed is called for if 'mistakes', in the now obsolete sense of taking 'improperly, wrongfully, or in error' (*Oxford English Dictionary* 2024), are to be avoided.

3.2   Two Mis-takes

As Lincoln Faller shows (2008, 146–147), the episode of the Covent Garden mercer is a particularly complex one:

> Moll is not the only attention-seeking, attitude-defining 'other' at hand … it is possible also to consider and judge the roles of various other individuals, as well as fragments of the great social mass.
>
> Dialogue (or, to be more exact, reported speech), plays an important role in generating these additional possibilities. Here as elsewhere, it establishes a dense and complex context for the protagonist's monologue, keeping the reader's relation to the text dynamic and alive … readers are suddenly, if briefly, freed from the narrator's point of view. They hear a 'window' opening to an outside world, onto normal lives and normal concerns … As the text shifts from straight forward narration (monologue) to dialogue and back again, it forces readers to shift gears continually, to keep up an ongoing readjustment of the various

'ratios' they would otherwise tend to establish between themselves and his criminals.

It is not only our attitudes to criminals that we are repeatedly forced to readjust: we have often also to change the 'ratio' of our relationship to those who catch thieves and try to consign them to the law. In the first scene of the episode, Moll is wandering through Covent Garden in 'the Disguise of a Widow's Dress',[9] when

> there was a great Cry of stop Thief, stop Thief; some Artists had it seems put a trick upon a Shop-keeper, and being pursued, some of them fled one way, and some another; and one of them was, they said, dress'd up in Widow's Weeds, upon which the Mob gathered about me, and some said I was the Person, others said no, immediately came the Mercer's Journe[y]-man, and he swore aloud I was the Person, and so seiz'd on me; however, when I was brought back by the Mob to the Mercer's Shop, the Master of the House said freely that I was not the Woman that was in his Shop, and would have let me go immediately; but another Fellow said gravely, pray stay till Mr. ---, *meaning the Journeyman* comes back, for he knows her, so they kept me by force near half an Hour...
> MF, 190

Already we have five different and contrasting points of view. The mob is divided between two diametrically opposed opinions, the journeyman is adamant in his identification of Moll as 'the Person' while the mercer exonerates her, and another 'Fellow' gravely gives advice that results in Moll being forcibly detained by a constable. As they wait, other servants 'us'd me saucily' and the master hardens in his attitude, obstinately refusing to let his captive go even while admitting that he cannot identify her. More voices will be heard when the first journeyman returns, lays hands on Moll in an attempt to search her, and is contested by two more journeymen, William and Anthony, who triumphantly drag in the 'true Widow', on whom they have found the stolen goods. Running through the whole episode is a three-way debate – to which we shall return in Chapter 6 – between

---

9 Covent Garden was another elite shopping district (Tickell 2016, 51), but also known for its brothels and gambling dens; see below, Chapter 6.

Moll, the mercer and the constable on the duties proper to officers of the law. Eventually polyphony collapses into chaos, culminating in a violent affray and the initial situation being turned on its head. The would-be law enforcers, 'the Master and Man, and all his Servants' are arrested for breaking the peace, pelted with mud, taken before a justice and made to pay heavily for their 'mistaking' of Moll, while 'the Woman they had taken, who was really the Thief, made off, and got clear away in the Crowd; and two others that they had stop'd also, whether they were really Guilty or not, that I can say nothing to' (*MF*, 194).

Moll's doubt as to whether the 'two others ... were really Guilty or not' invites us to wonder whether the mercer's journeymen had not made two more wrongful arrests in addition to that of Moll, about which we are certain – or are we? Moll had been seized before she had stolen anything, but as she tells us at the beginning of the episode, she had been 'only waiting for any thing that might offer, as I often did' (*MF*, 190). In the event she profits handsomely from what does 'offer': no mere length of silk but, as we shall see, a lucrative chance to sue for false arrest. Moll's Governess speaks more truly than she intends when she observes 'that a Theif being a Creature that Watches the Advantages of other Peoples mistakes, 'tis impossible but that to one that is vigilant and industrious many Opportunities must happen' (*MF*, 211).

The next 'mis-taking' of Moll yields less in material terms, but offers the reader another lesson in the need for patience and prudence in catching thieves. It is the evening of Christmas Day and she has gone abroad

> to see what might offer in my way; when going by a Working Silver-Smiths in *Foster-lane* I saw a tempting Bait indeed, and not to be resisted by one of my Occupation; for the Shop had no Body in it, as I could see, and great deal of loose Plate lay in the Window; and at the Seat of the Man, who usually as I suppose Work'd at one side of the Shop.
>
> I WENT boldly in and was just going to lay my Hand upon a peice of Plate, and might have done it, and carried it clear off, for any care that the Men who belong'd to the Shop had taken of it; but an officious Fellow in a House, not a Shop, on the other side of the Way, seeing me go in, and observing that there was no Body in the Shop, comes running over the Street, and into the Shop, and without asking me what I was, or who, seizes upon me, and cries out for the People of the House.
>
> *MF*, 211–212

Moll has touched nothing and, having glimpsed someone running over, had the presence of mind to knock on the floor and call out, so that she can now claim to have entered in order to buy spoons:

> The Fellow laugh'd at that Part, and put such a value upon the Service that he had done his Neighbour, that he would have it that I came not to buy, but to steal, and raising a great Crowd, I said to the Master of the Shop, who by this time was fetch'd Home from some Neighbouring Place, that it was vain to make Noise, and enter into Talk there of the Case; the Fellow had insisted, that I came to steal, and he must prove it, and I desir'd we might go before a Magistrate without any more Words; for I began to see I should be too hard for the Man that seiz'd me.
>
> THE Master and Mistress of the Shop were really not so violent as the Man from tother side of the Way, and the Man said, Mistress you might come into the Shop with a good Design for ought I know, but it seem'd a dangerous thing for you to come into such a Shop as mine is, when you see no Body there, and I cannot do Justice to my Neighbour, who was so kind to me, as not to acknowledge he had reason in his Side; tho' upon the whole I do not find you attempt'd to take anything, and I really know not what to in it;
>
> MF, 212

Trapped between his concerned neighbour and an indignant 'customer', forced to decide who to believe in full view of the ever present 'great Crowd', Defoe's silversmith is indeed in a quandary of a kind that many victims must have been beset by. Luckily for him and for Moll, the alderman of the ward happens by and agrees to arbitrate. In the impromptu 'full Hearing' that follows – to which we shall return in Chapter 7 – the impatient neighbour's failure to wait for the thief to actually take hold of any of the plate is turned against him and Moll is discharged, only to be successfully caught and consigned to justice, a mere three days later, by neither a canny mercer, a 'Hawks-ey'd Journeyman' nor an officious neighbour, but by two members of that most humble and reviled class of eighteenth-century employees: that of maid servants.

3.3   *The Black Part of This Story*

The episode begins with Moll confidently entering through an open door a building which is 'not a Mercers Shop, nor a Warehouse of a Mercer, but look'd like a private Dwelling-House, and was it seems Inhabited, by a Man that sold Goods for the Weavers to the Mercers, like a Broker or a Factor'. She is choosily furnishing herself with some particularly lovely, flowered silk when she is rudely interrupted:

> THAT I may make short of this black Part of this Story, I was attack'd by two Wenches that came open Mouth'd at me just as I was going out at the Door, and one of them pull' me back into the Room, while the other shut the Door upon me; I would have given them good Words, but there was no room for it; two fiery Dragons cou'd not have been more furious than they were; they tore my Cloths, bully'd and roar'd as if they would have murther'd me; the Mistress of the House came next, and then the Master, and all outrageous, for a while especially.
>
> MF, 214

Defoe's choice of two maids to capture Moll would not have surprised readers coming to the novel from the *Old Bailey Proceedings*, where they would have read of many servants catching thieves on behalf of their employers. They might, however, have been puzzled to understand why these subaltern women are allowed to take the initiative in starting formal judicial process:

> I GAVE the Master very good words, told him the Door was open, and things were a Temptation to me, that I was poor, and distress'd, and Poverty was what many could not resist, and beg'd him with Tears to have pity on me, the Mistress of the House was mov'd with Compassion, and enclin'd to have let me go, and had almost perswaded her Husband to it also, but the sawcy Wenches were run even before they were sent, and had fetch'd a Constable, and then the Master said, he could not go back, I must go before a Justice, and answer'd his Wife that he might come into Trouble himself if he should let me go.
>
> MF, 214

As we learn from the *Proceedings*, many actual thieves pleaded with their victims for mercy, and many more of whom we know nothing must have done so successfully. Far from being 'a unified interest group with a common attitude and agenda', Shelley Tickell shows that actual eighteenth-century retailers were driven by different 'business temperaments', and when faced with thieves manifested 'a range of attitudes from passive acceptance to virulent rage' (2016, 139–142). Defoe has his fictional equivalents reflect this diversity, placing the Covent Garden mercer and his men at the 'virulent rage' end of the scale, this broker and his wife among those, probably the majority, who preferred not go to the expense and trouble of a prosecution, or risk sending a woman to the gallows for a theft she had failed to conclude successfully. If the master rejects Moll's plea, it is out of fear of the legal consequences of allowing an escape, for, as we shall see in Chapter 6, by calling the constable, his maids have forced him, as well as Moll, into the hands of the law.

4 Conclusion

Shoplifting may have been, as Shelley Tickell claims, 'the emblematic crime' of the eighteenth century, yet the prominence Defoe gives it in his fiction is remarkable in that it occupied a lowly position in other crime literature of his time: only four shoplifters earned themselves places in the extended, 1719 edition of Alexander Smith's *History of the Lives and Robberies of the Most Notorious Highwaymen, Footpads, Shoplifts, and Cheats* (Tickell 2018, 170). The parts played by tradesmen, their employees, customers and neighbours in catching thieves at the scene of a crime are recorded in the *Proceedings* amply, but flatly and mechanically according to their function in obtaining a verdict. Defoe's hatless young man, his 'Hawks-ey'd' (but sometimes rash) journeymen and other servants who hurtle through the streets after thieves or grab them as they are about to make off with their masters' or neighbours' goods, are given individuality, temperament, sometimes even a personal history. Varied also are the shopkeepers who must decide what to do with a taken suspect: hang onto her and have her searched, rush her off to a justice, make a deal and let her go, ask for guidance from a passing alderman? They are responsibilities, difficulties and quandaries inevitably created by the deeply discretionary judicial system of his time, all part and parcel of the complex task of minding a shop in eighteenth-century London.

CHAPTER 4

After the Fact 1: A Market for My Goods

1 Introduction

Moll Flanders prepares us for her first theft by telling of her fear that the money left to her by her late husband 'would not support me long ... I fancied every Sixpence that I paid but for a Loaf of Bread, was the last that I had in the World, and that To-morrow I was to fast, and be starv'd to Death' (*MF*, 150). The bundle impulsively snatched from the apothecary's shop turns out to contain little of any immediate use to a woman on the brink of starvation:

> a Suit of Child-bed Linnen in it, very good and almost new, the Lace very fine; there was a Silver Porringer of a Pint, a small Silver Mug and Six Spoons, some other Linnen, a good Smock, and Three Silk Handkerchiefs, and in the Mug, wrap'd up in a Paper Eighteen Shillings and Sixpence in Money.
>
> *MF*, 152

Lucky that money 'wrap'd up in a Paper'; everything else Moll will need to sell if she is to keep the wolf from the door. How easily will she able to do this without being detected, apprehended and hauled before a justice? In the absence of a detective police force, the people early eighteenth-century thieves had to fear most, next to those present at the scene of the crime, fall into one of two categories: those to whom they tried to sell their stolen goods – the focus of this chapter – and their partners in crime, the focus of the next. Both the marketing of stolen goods and the roles of accomplices were the objects of public concern and of innovative legislation in Defoe's time.

We begin (Section 2.1) with traders who testified to having stopped thieves offering stolen goods for sale and speculate about their motives for passing up the chance of a cheap purchase. While most no doubt acted out of solidarity with fellow retailers, some may have been motivated by fear of being charged with receiving. Section 2.2 draws on the *Proceedings* for examples of prosecutions of receivers in 1720–1722 and relates them to parliamentary efforts to criminalise the commerce in stolen goods. In Section 3 we see how Moll Flanders differs from her actual counterparts in that she lands herself a reliable and efficient professional receiver. Section 4 looks into compounding, the selling back of stolen goods to their rightful owners, an alternative means of disposing of them and one attractive to thieves, victims and brokers. Section 5 discusses the long compounding episodes in *Moll Flanders* and *Colonel Jack* and suggests that in the 1720s they would have been read as supporting the government's recent attempt to crack down on the practice.

2 Criminal Disposal 1720–1722

2.1 *Stopped Offering for Sale*

In eighteenth-century England the trade in second-hand goods was a vibrant one, and included modes of exchange no longer familiar to the western world. It was still usual for people to buy from stall-holders, hawkers, relatives, friends, 'brokers of old Goods'. In his *Humble Proposal to Prevent the Beginning of Theft* (cited in Beattie 2001, 39), J.D. blamed such brokers, 'of whom there are many in all the Out-Parts of the Town', for initiating children into thieving by buying their pickings. Beattie (1986, 189) writes of

> the ease with which almost any object could find a buyer or be pawned. A piece of soap, an old blanket, a pewter plate, candle ends, rags, a few scraps of paper or iron virtually anything could be turned to account, and it seems clear that many shop keepers and publicans as well as pawnbrokers and street traders were willing to accept goods without asking too many questions.

Shelley Tickell (2018, 119) suggests that criminal disposal might have been 'completely integrated into and indistinguishable from the routines of borrowing, exchange and pawning', constituting a 'fluid area between makeshift and crime'.

Most of this traffic would never come to light, but occasional traces are to be found in the *Old Bailey Proceedings* for 1720–1722. When John Hart missed stockings and gloves from his shop he examined his boy, William Pitway, and learned that he had sold most of them to shoe-blacker Samuel Mires, who was also a 'little Boy'. To Ann Manson, 'an Apple Woman', Pitway had sold '2 odd Silk Stockings and 1 pair of Worsted', and the rest to Joan Humphris, 'a Curd and Whey Woman, both in Stocks Market' (*OBO*, t17220907-43). During his examination by Justice Lade, Thomas Yeomans told how Reynolds Winter had sold the clothes they had stolen 'to a woman in the mint', and some of the bath metal rings taken from John Syddall's shop 'to a Doctor that uses the mint and that the Doctors name is Clifford' (*LL*, LMSLPS150330027). Ann Nichols confessed before Justice Sir John Fryer to stealing ribbon and ferrett from three separate shops over two days, and to having sold 'to one Mr. Beachcroft a Slop Seller near Billinggate 3 peices of Ribbonring for which he gave her 8s.9d' (*LL*, LMSLPS150320101). When she was tried a week later (as Ann Nicholls) she added that this dealer in cheap, ready-made clothing (here named Beachcrest) 'bid her bring any thing she could get to him, and he would give her Money for it' (*OBO*, t17211206-2).

Of the contents of Moll Flanders' little white bundle, the child's linen and smock could probably have been sold to traders like Manson and Beach-crest, but to convert the fine lace, silver porringer, mug and spoons into ready money, she would have needed to contact either a professional receiver or an established retailer. In approaching the latter, thieves exposed themselves to the scrutiny of specialists who would be familiar with the values of goods and sometimes recognised their provenance. Out of thirty-four shoplifters apprehended between January 1720 and December 1722 a third were taken while trying to make a sale, or soon after having made one. Samuel Dickens had not even noticed that 'a Camblet Riding-Hood and 14 Yards of Persian Silk' had gone missing from his shop until he was given notice by a suspicious pawnbroker who had stopped Elizabeth Pool when she offered her the silk, but in trying to explain its provenance mistook its measurements (*OBO*, t17200115-34). William Hilton, who took twenty-four leather soles from the shop of Benjamin Parry, 'was discovered by offering it to sale at an under price' (*OBO*, t17220907-25). William Knight's master became suspicious when John Cauthrey was willing to take fifteen shillings for a wig and sent 'to enquire after his Character' (*OBO*, t17210525-28). Edward Preston, 'taken offering ... to Sale' two perriwigs and twelve ounces of human hair stolen from the shop of his master, may have made a similar mistake (*OBO*, t17200907-29). Bookseller Mr. Baker deduced, from the titles pasted onto the three books James Codner had sold him, that they could have come from one Gustavus Hacker, and sent to 'to know if they had lost such Books' (*OBO*, t17201207-12). At the trial of James Sparry and Edward Raymund (or Raymond), Thomas Ackersly told how he had been knocked down and robbed of a hautboy, a flageolet and six pence on a Saturday evening. News of this mugging must have spread around dealers in musical instruments like wildfire, for servant John Stanly deposed that on the Monday Raymund 'came to his Master (Wright's) Shop, and offered the Hautboy to sale, Sparry at the same time standing at the Window. Stanly pretending to call his Master, fetch Ackersly and a Constable, who apprehended them' (*OBO*, t17220907-63).

Goldsmiths could surely count on word getting around quickly. At the trial of Thomas Knight, accused of breaking into William Deard's shop (or stall) and taking jewellery and other valuables to the tune of £666 5s, 'Mr. Moittier deposed, that the Prisoner came to sell a parcel of broken Gold Toys; but he having heard that the Prosecutor had been robb'd stopt the Prisoner, and sent for the Prosecutor, who owned them' (*OBO*, t17210113-9). Moittier may have heard of the robbery on the grapevine, but by the 1720s printed handbills and newspaper advertisements were also being used to warn that stolen goods might be offered for sale (Styles 1989). When John Body's jewellery shop on London Bridge was rob'd in the Night, he 'distributed Advertisements among the Goldsmiths' and got an excellent response (*OBO*, t17220704-45).

Silver tankards were a special case. Valued in my sample at somewhere between £6 and £10 each, they were perhaps the most valuable objects to have passed regularly through the hands of plebeian Londoners, and were often stolen (Beattie 2001, 34). Yet they would have been difficult to sell because they could be identified by hallmarks and were sometimes engraved with owners' initials, as was the one Elizabeth Eves took from the house of her employer (*OBO*, t17201012-6). When charwoman Hannah Graham alias Grimes brought a silver tankard to Isaac Bowman's shop, she

> said it was her own, but being askt what Letters were upon it, she named the wrong; then she said it was her Mothers; whereupon he kept the Tankard and sent a Porter with her to enquire whether it was or no; and also to enquire after her Character in the Neighbourhood.
>
> *OBO*, t17210712-30

Hannah Conner took a silver mug to goldsmith John Braithwait and asked him to weigh it, but he questioned her until 'at last [she] owned she stole it out of the Prosecutor's Shop in Canon Street' (*LL*, LMSLPS150310116; t17201207-6). Sarah Herbert dismembered the one she had stolen from the Yorkshire Gray Tavern before offering some of the pieces for sale, but the missing ones were recovered and, like Graham and Connor, she was convicted and sentenced to death (*OBO*, t17211206-65).

Many shopkeepers dealing in less valuable commodities must have resigned themselves to letting an occasional loss go at that, but some went to great lengths to track a culprit across multiple transactions and get convictions. Recurrent pilfering of twist from his shop provoked John Everingham into tracing Alice Jones, alias Evans back from the shop of a Mr. Crouch to a Mr. Hall, and from Hall to 'Mr. Rawlinstone a Broker the back side of St. Clements'; at Jones's trial he brought 'one Manwaring' and Sarah Camfield to identify as his property the twist Jones had been found trying to sell to the broker (*OBO*, t17200303-4).

Manwaring and Camfield were presumably outworkers and would have felt obliged to collaborate, but how easy had Everingham found it to convince Crouch, Hall and Rawlinstone to help him? Were all the traders we have seen stopping and testifying against thieves motivated solely by their sense of civic duty and of solidarity with the business community? We turn now to the possibility that some may have acted out of fear of finding themselves on the wrong side of the law.

2.2   Receivers Prosecuted

Transactions involving stolen goods put buyers as well as sellers at risk of prosecution. Between 1720 and 1722, fifty-seven men and thirty-four women were indicted at the Old Bailey for having knowingly bought stolen goods. Nearly half were found guilty, usually on the evidence of the thieves who had supplied them. Hugh Mattison, who kept a book stall in Lincoln's Inn Fields, was convicted of receiving books which had been in the custody of William Bowyer and been supplied by Bowyer's journeyman, Thomas Peacock, and another servant (*OBO*, t17220704-44). Peacock himself deposed against Mattison, and in the same sessions also against Long Acre bookseller, Thomas Green (*OBO*, t17220704-66). Interestingly, Green was acquitted on the evidence of two fellow booksellers and a beadle, who testified that in the past he had 'detect[ed] Several Persons, that offer'd stoln Books to sale' (*OBO*, t17220704-66). Servant Elizabeth Eves told of selling her employer's marked tankard and other silver to William Reynolds, who was indicted for receiving and called upon to explain recent file marks on some silver plate discovered behind a shutter in his shop and the low price he had paid for the tankard (*OBO*, t17201012-6). Eves, who had confessed and 'owned the Fact on her Tryal' received a death sentence (*LL*, LMSLPS150310095), while Reynolds, a member of the governing body of the Goldsmiths' Company, was acquitted as a result of testimonials to his good character from colleagues.

At the lower end of the market, Susan Coats, who tried to sell to a Mr. Wass some of the bath metal rings stolen by her husband, was indicted for receiving (*OBO*, t17220228-8). Both the little boy Samuel Mires and the apple seller Anne Manson were indicted as accessories for receiving stockings and gloves stolen by William Pitway (*OBO*, t17220907-43), Ann and Mary Alexander for receiving clothes and candles taken by apprentice Elizabeth Alexander, presumably a relative (*OBO*, t17200602-19), and Jane Baine for receiving a short, blue silk apron given to her by James Allen – perhaps a sweetheart? (*OBO*, t17201012-12).

These last few items may well have been intended as gifts for the recipients' own use; none of those indicted sound like professional receivers. Mary

Wright may have been a borderline case: her son, Edward, was reported to have said that 'he was drawn in by his Mother, who would not let him alone till he was Hang'd'. Prosecutor Joseph Walker went to a great deal of trouble to entrap the boy and succeeded in getting him sentenced to death and his mother transported (*OBO*, t17200907-34). Among those who probably made their livings by dealing in stolen goods, Katharine Pars, alias Smith, and her husband, John Faires, alias Robert Smith, were said to have kept Elizabeth Askew and three other children to 'go a Thieving' with their own three offspring (*OBO*, t17210301-29 and t17210419-49). According to church burglar Henry Bishop, Alexander Parish had given him the key to a padlock so that he could 'carry Goods into his Shed at any Hour of the Night', so Parish too may have been a professional (*OBO*, t17200907-42). Nathaniel Glanister, indicted in May 1722 (*OBO*, t17220510-37) and his father, Thomas, in October, were evidently among 'the major receivers who provided capital and support and a fencing network for the large-scale criminal confederacies' (Beattie 1986, 189). Under cross-examination, the Holborn neighbours whom the Glanisters had called to court to testify to their good reputation, 'with much ado, were brought to acknowledge, that he [Thomas] was a Man of a very ill Character, and notorious for buying of stolen Goods'. This no doubt clinched the case against both Glanisters and got them transported, but it was probably Christopher Leonard, one of the burglars who supplied them, that was responsible for their arrest. In court he deposed

> That himself, Richard Trantum (not yet taken) and Mary D'arbieau broke open the House of Mr. Folwell in the Night, and took from thence the Goods mention'd in the indictment; which they sold the Prisoner in Holborn (his Son Nathaniel being then present and assisting ...) The Plate was mark'd, and this Evidence ask'd him if he could dispose of it: O! says he, I could safely dispose of the King's Crown if I had it.
>
> *OBO*, t17221010-29

Leonard clearly resented the hard bargain driven by Glanister: he told the court that the receiver 'gave them 4 s. 6 d. an Ounce for the Plate, by his own Weights, which were none of the heaviest, and 12 l. 10 s. for the Silk, which was worth 70 l. and threw them a Guinea over in the whole'. If this was so, the burglars had been paid less than 10% of the value of the silk, much less than the one third to a half of stock value they might have expected to make from their theft (Tickell 2018, 122).

As with all the prosecutions mentioned so far, indictments for receiving were laid by the ordinary members of the public. However, like the other thieves we have heard testifying against their fences, Christopher Leonard would have been encouraged to turn his in by the justice of the peace before whom prosecutor John Folwell accused them. Already in the reigns of William and Anne, Beattie (2001, 250) found

> strong suggestions in the examinations of suspects by London magistrates ... that receivers were being targeted as instigators of crime. In case after case, accused thieves – and especially shoplifters and pilfering servants – were routinely induced to name their receivers. And at the same time, attempts were made to strengthen the law in ways that would make the conviction of receivers more certain and their punishment more serious.

Before the Glorious Revolution magistrates would have been able to do little or nothing to suppress receiving, which had been considered merely a misdemeanour at common law. This changed in 1691, when the 'Benefit of Clergy Act' made receivers accessories to felonies, and therefore punishable as felons if the thieves were convicted. The law was tightened further in 1702, when receivers of stolen goods were classed as accessories even if the thief had been admitted to clergy or pardoned, and again in 1706, when it became possible to convict a receiver of a misdemeanour even if the thief were not taken (Beattie 2001, 250–251, 317). Finally, the Transportation Act of 1718 included a provision doubling the penalty for knowingly buying stolen goods. Apart from measures directed explicitly at receivers, encouragements to give evidence against accomplices built into the Shoplifting Act 'were at least in part aimed at uncovering and prosecuting receivers, and at limiting theft in shops by deterring those suspected of encouraging it'. Similarly, the statute that in 1713 made theft from houses over forty shillings a capital offence and promised pardons to those who confessed seems to have been aimed at servants in league with receivers (Beattie 2001, 39).

How effective was this legislation? In 1725 Defoe wrote, à propos of Jonathan Wild, that the 1691 statute had transformed the market in stolen goods:

> There was a time, indeed, when there were brokers and receivers whose business it was to take everything off of their [thieves'] hands as soon as they had gotten it, and a young shoplifter or housebreaker

had no sooner got a booty but he knew where to go and carry it, as to a warehouse or repository, where he was sure to have money for it, and that something near the value of it too ...

But there being an Act passed in the reign of the late King William, making it a felony to buy or receive any stolen goods, knowing them to be stolen, and one or two bold people having suffered on that very account, the receiving trade was spoiled all at once; and when the poor adventurer had, at the hazard of his neck, gotten any purchase, he must run all that hazard over again to turn it into money.

It is true, after some time, the temptation being strong and the profits great, there were persons frequently found again that did help the adventurers, and took of their goods, but then the thief got so small a share that the encouragement was very small, and had it continued so, the thieving trade might, for aught I know, have been in danger of being lost; for the receivers running so extreme a hazard, they got all the profit, and the poor lifter or housebreaker was glad to part with things of the greatest value for a trifle.

DEFOE 2004, 83–84; see CLEGG 2003

The receiving trade was not, in fact, 'spoiled all at once' and neither was the thieving trade 'lost', but the equilibrium between the two may have altered. In *Moll Flanders* Defoe puts into the mouth of his first fictional thief sentiments very much like those he was soon to attribute to the actual 'poor adventurer' who twice risks his life, and is forced to sell his purchase 'for a trifle'.

3   Moll Flanders' Super-fence

Having accumulated, in addition to the contents of the little white bundle, gold beads slipped from the neck of a trusting child, lengths of lustrous silks and velvet dumped by a fleeing thief and the two rings filched from the window of a Stepney house, Moll Flanders faces up to the problem of how to sell her booty profitably:

I WAS now at loss for a Market for my Goods, and especially for my two Peices of Silk, I was very loth to dispose of them for a Trifle; as the poor unhappy Thieves in general do, who after they have ventured their Lives for, perhaps a thing of Value, are fain to sell it for a Song when they have done; but I was resolv'd I would not do thus whatever shift I made, unless I was driven to the last Extremity.

MF, 155

The 'shift' that saves Moll from having to sell 'for a Song' to miserly cheats like the Glanisters involves the woman who had managed the last of her pregnancies, and whom she now finds – by one of those marvellous coincidences that J. Paul Hunter (1990, 208–217) notes as punctuating early novels – has 'turn'd *Pawn Broker, and liv'd pretty well*'. She passes the things off as her own, and the Governess sells them on to the 'proper Agents that bought them, being in her Hands, without any scruple, and gave good Prizes too' (*MF*, 156). Since this 'necessary Woman' also provides Moll with a cheap lodging and negotiates a better deal with the family fostering her son, this enables her to get by for a while by doing 'Quilting-Work for Ladies Beds' (*MF*, 157)

This makeshift period, in which occasional, opportunity thefts supplement income from legitimate employment (Shore 2003), does not last long. The Devil, who had 'resolv'd I should continue in his Service',[1] leads his acolyte to an alehouse door through which she sees an unguarded silver tankard. Moll brings off the theft of it smoothly, listening carefully to exchanges between the serving boy and the woman at the bar to make sure that the tankard will not be quickly missed; cheekily simulating the part of an officious customer, she leaves with a parting reminder to the boy to 'take care of your plate child'. But, having got her tankard, how will she make money from it without risking the fates of Elizabeth Eves, Hannah Graham, Hannah Connor and Sarah Herbert? The prospect of being pursued to gaol and on to the gallows by vindictive tavern keepers is the bogey the Governess uses to terrify Moll when she reveals 'the whole Story of Tankard' and asks whether she should not 'carry it again':

> CARRY it again! *says she.* Ay, if you are minded to be sent to *Newgate* for stealing it; why, *says I*, they can't be so base to stop me, when I carry it to them again? You don't know those Sort of People Child, *says she*; they'll

---

[1] This, like Moll's other references to the Devil as instigator of crimes, reads like a lame excuse to modern readers, but might have been taken seriously in an eighteenth-century courtroom. Like poverty, drink and insanity, 'Satanic inspiration' was often evoked as exonerating the accused of responsibility for his or her actions and for mitigating punishments; see Davies 2007. Rabin discusses the language of mental states as used in the courtroom and the close relationship between poverty and insanity which haunts Moll Flanders (2003, 98 and 2004, 64–65).

not only carry you to *Newgate*, but hang you too, without any regard to the honesty of returning it; or bring in an Account of all the other Tankards they have lost for you to pay for: What must I do then? *says I*; Nay, *says she*, as you have plaid the cunning part and stole it, you must e'en keep it, there's no going back now; besides Child, *says she,* Don't you want it more than they do? I wish you cou'd light of such a Bargain once a Week.

THIS gave me a new Notion of my Governess ...

MF, 158

This conversation marks a watershed in the relationship between the two women, from now on bound to each other by dangerous, reciprocal knowledge. On the one hand, the Governess has heard her protégé confess to a capital felony and can pressure her into supplying her regularly with such 'bargains'. On the other, Moll's eyes have been opened to the true nature of the Governess's business. The 'Sort of People about her', she now notices, are 'none of the honest ones that I had met with there before':

I HAD not been long there, but I discover'd it more plainly than before, for every now and then I saw Hilts of Swords, Spoons, Forks, Tankards, and all such kind of Ware brought in, not to be Pawn'd, but to be sold down right; and she bought every thing that came without asking any Questions, but had very good Bargains, as I found by her Discourse.

I FOUND also that in following this Trade, she always melted down the Plate she bought, that it might not be challeng'd; and she came to me and told me one Morning that she was going to Melt, and if I would, she would put my Tankard in, that it might not be seen by any Body; I told her, with all my Heart; so she weigh'd it, and allow'd me the full value in Silver again; but I found she did not do the same to the rest of her Customers.

MF, 158

Able to summon distribution agents at the drop of a hat and equipped with a forge for smelting down engraved silver, the Governess is an exceptionally well-organised receiver, and not only that. The manager of a network of thieves, she co-opts Moll, has her train under an expert and become 'as impudent a Thief, and as dextrous as ever Moll Cut-Purse was'. With this analogy Defoe promotes his protagonist from part-time pilferer to top slot in the professional thieves' hall of fame,[2] so it is appropriate that her receiver be represented as a super-fence. Far superior in entrepreneurial, organisational and technical expertise to all of those actually tried for receiving in 1720–1722 (except perhaps the Glanisters), the Governess anticipates the myth-in-the-making of organised crime that was soon to be perfected with the literary and graphic packaging of Jonathan Wild (Clegg 2003). In the episode to which we now turn, she also acquires the skill of selling stolen goods back to their owners by which, Defoe was to explain in his *True and Genuine Account*, Wild defeated the purposes of William's, Anne's and George I's anti-receiving legislation and made the 'thieving trade' worth pursuing again.

4   Brokers 1720–1722

The practice of 'payback', the selling stolen items back to their legitimate owners was a long established one. In 1663 the Recorder for the City of London complained that shopkeepers were especially prone to negotiate with thieves for the return of their goods (Wales 2000, 69), and in 1699 *The Great Grievance of Shopkeepers* ([1699]) listed as the fourth cause of the increase in shoplifting 'the chief Receivers and Heads of this Body, and those who know their Walks and Gangs, restoring the Goods stolen, but at the Expense of more than half the Value, and Promises of not prosecuting'. Two years later, the author of *Hanging, Not Punishment Enough* (1701) attributed the frequency of 'Private compositions' to victims' reluctance to undertake expensive prosecutions which did not necessarily result in the return of their property (cited in Beattie 2001, 249). Paradoxically, the removal of benefit of clergy from shoplifting in 1691 and in 1713 from servant theft may have reinforced retailers' and employers' reluctance to prosecute, making compounding the preferred option. Pickpocketing had long been a capital offence and for that, as well as other reasons, under-prosecuted: both victims who lost valuables to prostitutes and merchants and financiers robbed of credit notes would have been more eager to get their property back than to take their predators to court and perhaps to the gallows. As John Beattie (2001, 249) explains, there were benefits for all involved:

> Many victims were clearly willing to pay for the return of their goods – an outcome the criminal law could not guarantee. Such transactions

---

[2]   On Moll Cutpurse, celebrity criminal, see Liebe 2021.

were also presumably attractive to thieves who might find returning the goods for a portion of their value (and a promise not to prosecute) safer and more profitable than dealing with a receiver.

The recent stiffening of the laws against receiving, moreover,

> made receiving apparently riskier than it had been – and that in turn made it riskier for thieves to deal with receivers they could not entirely rely on. Returning the stolen goods to their owner for a portion of their value may have come to seem a safer option. In the case of objects with little inherent value, or at least with value that could not easily be realized – shopbooks, or bills of exchange, or other commercial papers for example – the usefulness of negotiating with the victim for their return was even more obvious.
> BEATTIE 2001, 251

But how were such exchanges arranged? Some would have been agreed directly between victim and thief, as Elizabeth Lockwood, alias Logwood, and Christian Hurst attempted to do when apprehended by the man whose watch they had stolen: 'both confest (when in Custody) that they had pawn'd it for a Guinea, which if he would advance he should have it again' (*OBO*, t17210301-50). In trying to make such bargains, however, thieves admitted their guilt, thus providing evidence that could be used against them in court. For pickpocket Martha Purdew, the consequences were fatal: taken 'in a poor Garret wherein there were a few Flocks and Rags' she 'owned she took the Prosecutor's Money' and made matters worse for herself by claiming that 'she had Gold, if the Prosecutor would make it up' (*OBO*, t17201012-11; *OA*, 17201026).

Thieves could hope to minimise such risks, and victims had a better chance of getting their things back again, by going through intermediaries. Richard Hilliard told the Old Bailey how, soon after missing his snuffbox in the Guildhall, he was

> accidentally in Company with a Gentleman afterwards, he was speaking of his Loss, describing his Box, and the Prisoner, whom he suspected, the Gentleman told him he believed he could help him to it again; for that his Description answered what a Gentleman brought to Mrs. Champman to pawn for him; that he went to Mrs. Chapman, redeemed the Box for 5 s. 1 1\2
> *OBO*, t17210712-17

One suspects that the meeting with the helpful 'Gentleman' was not accidental, and that the intermediary got a tip and perhaps a cut out of Mrs. Champman's (or Chapman's) five shillings and a penny halfpenny. Certainly, many thief-takers (of whom more later) supplemented the income they derived from apprehending and prosecuting criminals by brokering such deals:

> there was a potentially lucrative service to be offered by those who could put victims of such offences in touch with those who had stolen from them and negotiate the return of the goods for a fee. This required the same kind of information about thieves, receivers, and suspicious alehouses that thief-takers needed if they were to engage in the more dangerous business of prosecution .... Acting as an intermediary must surely have been an attractive option in cases in which rewards were not available even though compounding a felony in this way was illegal.
> BEATTIE 2001, 248–249

By the turn of the century the role of thief-takers in compounding was familiar enough for the meaning of the word to have undergone drastic slippage, as is illustrated by the first definition given by B.E. in his *New Dictionary of the Terms Ancient and Modern of the Canting Crew in its Several Tribes of Gypsies, Beggars, Thieves, Cheats etc* (1699; cited in Beattie 2001, 232): 'a Thief Taker: one who makes a Trade of helping people (for a gratuity) to their lost Goods and sometimes for Interest or Envy snapping the Rogues themselves, being usually in fee with them and acquainted With their Haunts.' Burglar John Read explained how brokering combined with receiving: 'the practice of pretended Thief-takers was to compound Felonies for the Thieves, to prevent their Prosecutions, and to harbour them, and receive their stoll'n Goods' (*A Short State of the Case of Joseph Billiers*, 1709, cited in Beattie 2001, 249). Charles Hitchen, under Marshall to the City of London, was adept at this: he was said to have demanded huge sums for arranging the return of exchequer bills stolen by the young pickpockets he himself managed (Beattie 2001, 253–254). In my early 1720s sample, William Kirby told the Old Bailey court that he had not wanted to prosecute the two women with whom he had been drunk in bed when his silver watch was stolen but had been forced to so do to get rid of 'the Thief-Taker following him to extort money' (*OBO*, t17211083o-47). Jonathan Wild, pupil and then rival to Hitchen, drummed up custom by placing advertisements in newspapers conveying veiled blackmail demands to gentlemen who had 'lost possessions in the vicinity of brothels (Beattie 1986, 53 and 2001, 252; Wales 69–70; Lamb 2004). He was not the first broker to take advantage of the growth of the press to contact potential clients. Already during the reign of Anne, John Bonner was singling out a type of victim and the 'environment of pickpocketing' favoured by Moll Flanders by advertising that 'Ladies and others who lose their watches at Churches, and other Assemblies, may be served by him ... to his utmost power, if desired by the rightful Owner, he being paid for his Labour and Expenses' (Ashton 1919, 422, cited in Wales 2000, 70).

By the end of the second decade of the century the government had begun trying to disentangle the taking of thieves from brokering. Until 1718 it had been only a misdemeanour to return stolen goods for a fee without prosecuting the thief, but the 'Felons' or 'First Transportation Act', which was also known as 'the Jonathan Wild Act',[3] contained a clause which made it a felony, and a capital felony if the offence in which the goods had been taken had been excluded from clergy (Beattie 2001, 256). In 1720 the second Transportation Act added a reward of £40 to 'encourage some of the parties to these arrangements to turn informer' (Beattie 2001, 379).

Not many seem to have taken the bait, so we do not find many trials for compounding in the *Proceedings*. One, paradoxically, shows how readily victims of thefts submitted to blackmail by brokers, only turning them in when exasperated by their demands. In April 1721 an unnamed prosecutor told the Old Bailey how John Thompson, alias Williams, who claimed that it 'was his Business to take up Pick-pockets and Idle People', had settled for twenty guineas for 'helping' him to valuables stolen while he was 'in Liquor' and 'ill Company'. This might have been the end of the story had Thompson not returned to squeeze more money out of the victim and threatened to charge him with fathering a bastard, 'Whereupon he caused the Prisoner to be apprehended' (*OBO*, t17210419-10). Thompson claimed to know nothing of the statute under which he was indicted, unlike brokers Edward Wooton, George Beal, Charles Motherby and John Hornby, who were evidently well aware of the danger they ran. When they met Elizabeth Carter and Elizabeth Hatchet to receive the six guineas agreed on for helping them to their stolen jewellery, Motherby, wearing a large black coat and a very large hat, impersonated

---

3   In *The True and Genuine Account* (2004, 107) Defoe himself described the Act as 'directly aimed at Jonathan's general practice'. Beattie (2001, 379) explains that 'it is better regarded as part of a broader policing policy strategy than that – as a way of encouraging thief-takers to engage more actively in prosecution while discouraging the kind of mediation between victims and offenders that could only make street and other crime more attractive'.

the thief, and a scrivener was brought in to draw up 'Releases' exculpating them (*OBO*, t17221205-43).

Unusually, in both this and the Thompson case, the *Proceedings* spelled out the provisions of the relevant statute, presumably in a bid to publicise the measure and boost the prosecution rate. In dedicating to compounding one long episode in *Moll Flanders* and two even longer ones in *Colonel Jack*, Defoe was not only being topical but also exposing a widely tolerated practice that allowed thieves to escape justice and frustrated government efforts to make property crime less profitable.

5   Private Compositions

5.1   *Moll's Governess Makes a Booty*

In a sequel to her despoiling the drunken gentleman of his valuables, Moll describes him to her Governess and is alarmed to hear that she thinks she knows who he is:

> I AM sorry you do, *says I*, for I would not have him expos'd on any account in the World; he has had Injury enough already by me, and I would not be instrumental to do him any more: No, no *says she*, I will do him no Injury, I assure you, but you may let me satisfie my Curiosity a little, for if it is he, I warrant you I find it out: I was a little startled at that, and told her, with an apparent concern in my Face, that by the same Rule he might find me out, and then I was undone: *she return'd warmly*, why, do you think I will betray you, Child? No, no, *says she*, not for all he is worth in the World; I have kept your Counsel in worse things than these, sure you may trust me in this: So I said no more at that time.
>
> MF, 180

Two possibilities are hinted at here. The Governess may extort money from a rich man with a reputation to lose; alternatively, she may betray Moll to a potential prosecutor. She does neither but, as with other unrealised outcomes, the fact that in satisfying her curiosity she may bring disaster on Moll keeps the tension high during the delicate negotiations that follow. Through a friend of the family, the Governess gets to speak with the baronet and introduces herself as having come 'with a single design of doing him a Service', one which, she promises, will 'remain a Secret to all the World, unless he expos'd it himself' (*MF*, 182). Many circumlocutions and *litotes* are employed by this 'Mistress of her Tongue' to intimate that she is familiar with the details of his night of sin and could, if she wanted, demand compensation for keeping quiet:

> Sir I do not come to make a Booty of you, I ask nothing of you ... and yet perhaps I may serve you farther still, for I did not come barely to let you know, that I was inform'd of these things, as if I wanted a Bribe to conceal them; assure your self, Sir, *said she,* that whatever you think fit to do or say to me, it shall be all a secret as it is, as much as if I were in my Grave.
>
> MF, 183

Moll's Governess has indeed not come *barely* to let the gentleman know that she is 'inform'd', but she certainly *does* want to 'make a Booty' of him. After much beating about the bush, the main object of the exercise is revealed and a deal is quickly wound up:

> THEY had some Discourse upon the Subject of the things he had lost, and he seem'd to be very desirous of his Gold Watch, and told her if she cou'd procure that for him, he would willingly give as much for it, as it was worth, she told him she would endeavour to procure it for him, and leave the valuing it to himself.
>
> ACCORDINGLY the next Day she carried the Watch, and he gave her 30 Guineas for it, which was more than I should have been able to make of it, tho' it seems it cost much more. He spoke something of his Perriwig, which it seems cost him threescore Guineas, and his Snuff-box, and in a few Days more, she carried them too; which oblig'd him very much, and he gave her Thirty more, the next Day I sent him his fine Sword and Cane *Gratis,* and demanded nothing of him ...
>
> MF, 184–185

Careful readers might notice that the gentleman does not quite honour his promise to give for his watch 'as much for it as it, was worth', for it had 'cost much more' than the thirty guineas he hands over, and that the second thirty has to cover not only a perriwig that had cost him sixty guineas but also his snuffbox, while his fine sword and cane are thrown in at no extra charge. We assume, however, that Moll's overall gain of sixty guineas represents more than she would have made through her Governess's agents, and do not much blame the two of them for exploiting the baronet's fear of being exposed. We are surely, however, meant to take a dim view, not only of

AFTER THE FACT I: A MARKET FOR MY GOODS

his lechery and boozing, but of his collusion in a practice that encouraged property crime no less than the universally decried receiving trade. That Defoe intended this is made more likely by his devoting two long episodes in *Colonel Jack* to the practice of compounding.

5.2   *Colonel Jack's Errand of Consequence*

Jack and Will must undertake longer and trickier negotiations than those conducted by the Governess if they are to profit safely from their Customs' House booty, pickings far more dangerous to handle than watches and snuff boxes. This they quickly realise when they sit down in Leadenhall market to inspect their first day's prize:

> IT was not a Meat-Market Day so we had room to sit down upon one of the Butcher's Stalls, and he bad me Lug out; what he had given me, was a little Leather Letter Case, with a *French* Almanack stuck in the inside of it, and a great many Papers in it of several kinds.
>
> WE look'd them over, and found there was several valuable Bills in it, such as Bills of *Exchange,* and other Notes, things I did not understand; but among the rest was a Goldsmith's Note, *as he call'd it,* of one Sir *Stephen Evans* for 300*l.* payable to the Bearer, and at Demand, besides this there was another Note, for 12*l.* 10*s.* being a Goldsmith's Bill too, but I forget the Name; there was a Bill or two also written in *French,* which neither of us understood, but which it seems were things of value, being call'd foreign Bills accepted.
>
> CJ, 77–78

Like Moll's little white bundle, the 'little Leather Letter case', so diminutive and apparently ordinary, is endowed with mystery, and so are the things it contains. The papers with which it is stuffed have meaning in the world of international high finance, a world geographically near to, but in all other senses far from the boys' East London habitat. Jack the novice is mystified by all the papers, and even his teacher is stumped by those 'in *French*'. Will is fast enough on his feet to get to Lombard Street and, miming the mien and gestures of a merchant's boy, have the smaller bill exchanged for gold 'without any Stop or Question ask'd' (*CJ,* 78). The £300 credit note issued by Sir Stephen Evans, whom many of Defoe's early readers would have recognised as one of the most powerful London goldsmith-bankers of the time, he knows to be 'too big … to meddle with'. As Will explains to Jack, and indirectly to the reader,

> if I, *says he,* that am but a poor Lad should venture to go for the Money, they will presently say, how should I come by such a Bill, and that I certainly found it or stole it, so they will stop me *says he,* and take it away from me, and it may be bring me into Trouble for it too; so, *says he,* I did say it was too big for me to meddle with, and that I would let the Man have it again if I could tell how; but for the Money *Jack,* the Money that we have got, I warrant you he should have none of that; besides *says he,* who ever he be that has lost this Letter Case, to be sure, as soon as he miss'd it, he would run to a *Goldsmith* and give notice, that if any body came for the Money, they should be stopp'd, but I am too Old for him there, *says he.*
>
> CJ, 79

The solution to the boys' seemingly intractable problem is suggested next day by the victim's fellow financiers. The Customs House commissioners who, as we saw earlier, have failed to get Will to confess,

> carry'd him into an Ale-house, and there they told him that the Letter Case had Bills in it of a great Value, that they would be of no use to the Rogue that had them, but they would be of infinite Damage to the Gentleman, that had lost them, and that he had left word with the Clerk, and who was there with him, that he would give 30l. to any one that would bring them again, and give all Security that could be desir'd that he would give them no Trouble, whoever it was.
>
> CJ, 86

Jack urges his tutor to accept the deal, but as Defoe signals through Will's anxious reaction, the execution of it is riddled with risks:

> *Why,* says he, *how shall I get them to him? who dare carry them? I dare not to be sure, for they will stop me, and bring me the* Goldsmith *to see if he does not know me, and that I received the Money, and so they will prove the Robbery, and I shall be hang'd, would you have me be hang'd* Jack?
>
> CJ, 86

What Will needs, of course, is an intermediary to shield him from direct contact with his victim and potential prosecutor. Lacking a governess figure, he assigns the task to Jack, who solemnly swears that he will never betray his comrade and sets off on 'an Errand of too much Consequence indeed to be entrusted to a Boy ... with a manly Heart, tho' a Boy's Head'.

The dangerous and delicate nature of Jack's task is reflected in the long drawn-out narrating of the multiple interactions that follow, which are rendered mainly in dramatic mode. First Jack listens in on a conversation between a customs clerk and a gentleman in which the latter tells the former how the merchant may recover his bills. He must publicly advertise a reward for the return of his papers, and must add

> that he will promise, not to stop, or give any Trouble to the Person that brings them.
> He has done that too, *says he* [the clerk], but I fear they won't trust themselves to be Honest, for fear he should break his Word.
> Why? it is true he may break his Word in that Case, but no Man should do so; for then, no Rogue will venture to bring home any thing that is stolen, and so he would do an Injury to others after him.
>
> cj, 88–89

It was not unknown for advertisers to break promises not to prosecute, and the possibility that this victim may do so keeps the tension high throughout the episode.[4] Fearfully, Jack approaches the clerk and, in a whispered exchange, receives a promise that he will neither be harmed himself nor made to name names. Yet when he brings the letter case to the clerk's house that evening, the victim demands to know the whereabouts of the thief, proposes giving less than the promised £30 reward, and asks Jack his name. It is only thanks to the clerk, who acts as umpire and shields the boy from being interrogated further, that the negotiations are successfully concluded (*cj*, 91).

In the second compounding episode, the stakes are even higher. Having observed 'two Gentleman mighty Eager in Talk' (*cj*, 99), Jack relieves one of a carelessly put away pocket-book and finds it to contain, in addition to bills to the astronomical value of £2,304, 'a Paper full of loose Diamonds' valued at £435. Such a loss could well make a businessman's nightmare of bankruptcy come true, so it is no wonder that Jack's victim takes to 'Raving and [is] half Distracted; He Stamps and Crys, and Tears his very Cloths, *he says*, he is utterly undone, and ruin'd' (*cj*, 100). With so much at stake, there is no question that

---

[4] In October 1719 John Metcalf told the Old Bailey court how, after missing a silver tankard, he had 'advertised it in the News, with a Reward for any who should bring it, and it was brought home', but had nevertheless prosecuted a hawker of broken glass and old clothes who had been noticed in Newgate market with a tankard under her apron (*obo*, t17191014-8).

the only way for Jack to profit safely from his coup is by selling the things back to the merchant himself:

> as for the Bills, there was no room to doubt, but unless they had been carried that Minute to the Goldsmiths for the Money, he would have come with Notice to stop the Payment, and perhaps come while the Money was Receiving, and have taken hold of the Person; and then as to the Diamonds there had been no offering them to Sale, by us poor Boys to any Body, but those who were our known Receivers, and they would have given us nothing for them, compar'd to what they were worth; for as I understood afterwards, those who made a Trade thus of buying stolen Goods, took care to have false Weights and Cheat the poor Devil that stole them, at least an Ounce in Three.
>
> CJ, 108

As Faller notices (1993, 193), Jack is an excellent negotiator, but Will, who now takes over the role of intermediary, proves just as skilful (*CJ*, 102–107). Having circumspectly approached the distraught victim and his associates, he intimates that he is 'concerned in a Business where a great many of the Gangs of little Pick-pockets haunted' and might 'get the things again (*CJ*, 102)'. He then delays contacting them for three days in order to 'make it appear as Difficult as possible' and, on returning to find the merchants 'uneasie', chastens them into submission by threatening to abandon the enterprise (*CJ*, 103).

In the exchanges that follow Will maintains the upper hand by rejecting one conciliatory offer after another. When the merchants assure him that the thieves 'shall not be Stop'd, Question'd, or call'd to Account before a Magistrate', he answers that this assurance has no value:

> for when a poor Fellow is in your Clutches, and has shown you your Goods, you may Seize upon him for a Thief, and it is plain he must be so; then you go take away your Goods, send him to Prison, and what amends can he have of you afterward?
>
> CJ, 104

In their offer to pay him in advance and give him a half-hour start, he scents treacherous intentions: 'NO Gentlemen, *says he,* that won't do now; if you had talk'd so before ... I should have taken your Words; but now it is plain you have had such a thought in your Heads, and how can I, or anyone else be assur'd of Safety'. When others propose that Will be given a bond of £1,000 as security, he objects that such a bond would be unenforceable. At the suggestion that 'he should take the things of the Boy, if it was a Boy', he laughs: 'No Gentlemen, as I am not the Thief, so I shall be very loth to put my self in the Thiefs stead, and lye at your Mercy'. Finally, 'confounded with the difficulty', the merchants propose signing a release of the kind the scrivener drew up for wootton Beal, Motherby and Hornby:

> THEY then offer'd to give it him under their Hands, that they did not in the least Suspect him; that they would never Charge him with any thing about it; that they Acknowledg'd he went about to Enquire after the Goods at their Request; and that if he produced them, they would Pay him so much Money, at, and before the Delivery of them, without Obliging him to Name or produce that Person he had them from.
>
> CJ, 104–105

Taking the further precaution of having the contents of the pocket-book listed, Will finally hands it over, opportunely 'wrapt up in a Dirty piece of colour'd Handkerchief, as Black as the Street could make it, and Seal'd with a piece of sorry Wax, and the impression of a Farthing for a Seal'. He receives the agreed £50 for his services, but of the fifty intended for the thief returns twenty, to the surprise of the gentlemen, 'for till that time they were not quite without a secret Suspicion that he was the Thief'.

They would have done well to follow their instincts, Defoe surely meant his readers to conclude, instead of assuming that willingness to part with £20 proves that Will is no thief. These wealthy merchants have been beaten at their own game of negotiating deals, and by a street urchin at that.[5] They have also been exposed as having allowed two criminals to evade justice and supplied them with a lucrative way of converting their pickings into ready money.

6 Conclusion

In this chapter we have seen actual shopkeepers and their employees tracing and catching thieves 'after the fact', thus playing key detective roles in citizen

---

5 Sill and Cervantes note that the actual goldsmiths who appear in this list of bills include a Tory M.P. satirised by Defoe in the *True-Born Englishman,* a former Lord Mayor of London who, though initially a Whig, broke with his party, and 'one *Stewart* that kept an Wager Office' (*CJ,* 105).

law enforcement. When approached by someone with something to sell, many must have suspected nothing, or turned a blind eye, and got themselves bargains; of these we have little or no record. The dealers mentioned in trial reports, on the other hand, made enquiries, stopped those offering for sale, sent word to whoever they thought was the legitimate owner, and came to court to testify. In most cases one has the impression of individuals motivated by solidarity with fellow traders, but some may have acted out of fear of being prosecuted for receiving at a time when governments were trying to crack down on the trade in stolen goods.

On the other hand, the compounders and brokers of 'private compositions' complained about in some pamphlets very rarely ended up in court, at least in the early 1720s, so we know even less about them than we do about receivers. One suspects that, in spite of government efforts to suppress the practice, compounding was too advantageous to all those involved for the practice to be abandoned, especially by wealthy victims who risked losing huge amounts and even ruin if they failed to recover their property. In narrating the marketing of stolen goods, Defoe highlights practices which trial reports inevitably leave in the shadows. Bringing both poor thieves and rich victim/clients above Gladfelder's 'threshold of social visibility' (2001, 68), his crime fictions imagine for us the difficulties faced by Moll Flanders, Colonel Jack and his partner, Will, in trying to turn their loot into cash, but also vividly illustrate the 'singular and secretive procedure' that was illegal but commonly practised in the grey economy of his time.[6] Moll is supplied with a super-fence who sells her booty on, but who also doubles as a broker. Will and Jack are attributed superb negotiating skills that enable them to make deals more lucrative than they could have obtained from professional receivers.

How did Defoe expect his early readers to respond to his dramatisations of such dealings? In her role as a fence, Moll's Governess is clearly portrayed as criminal, but as go-between she shares criminal responsibility with the fine gentleman who agrees so readily to buy back his valuables. His case is complicated, however, by the heavy censure heaped on him for whoring and drinking, and by his class. The merchants and bankers to whom Will and Jack sell back credit notes and diamonds are blameless in these respects, although not

---

6 Lamb (2004,953). As Lamb underlines (955–956), in newspaper advertisements for 'lost things' the things are often lovingly *described*, but the *narrative* of 'how the thing went missing and how it will return, is sedulously avoided', merely suggesting the outline of a story 'not at all flattering to the former owner'.

in others. They are robbed while engaged in commercial dealings that many of Defoe's readers would have held in high regard, yet, preoccupied with business worries, they are careless with their property, prove less observant, acute and articulate than the plebeian youths who prey on them, and supply the latter with a safe and profitable market for stolen goods. Defoe thus indirectly accuses not only members of England's upper classes but also the 'big bourgeoisie' of complicity with the criminal economy and of putting private interest before public good. At a practical level, he also offers cultural support for new judicial measures, such as the anti-receiving and anti-compounding clauses in the 1718 and 1720 Transportation Acts, that were proving difficult to enforce.

CHAPTER 5

After the Fact II: Thieves Discovering Thieves

1   Introduction

The second of my chapters on catching thieves 'after the fact' examines the parts played by thieves themselves, and by thief-takers. Crucial here are the pardons guaranteed to those who 'discovered' felons and gave evidence leading to conviction, and the rewards offered for apprehending and convicting. Both pardons and rewards had been frequently used on an *ad hoc* basis as incentives to inform against a wide range of offenders, dissidents and transgressors of trading regulations (Clegg 2004), but it was only after the Revolution of 1688–1689 that they were formally countenanced and enshrined in statutes directed against certain types of property crime. First and foremost among these was robbery (namely theft involving violent assault or 'putting in fear') committed on the king's highway, a crime perceived as a threat to inland trade. The 'Act for encourageing the apprehending of Highwaymen' of 1692 established

> That if any person or persons being out of Prison shall from and after the Five and twentieth day of March committ any Robbery and afterwards discover Two or more person or persons [who] already hath or hereafter shall commit any Robbery so as two or more of the person or persons discovered shall be convicted of such Robbery any such discoverer shall himselfe have and is hereby entituled to the gracious pardon of Their Majesties Their Heires and Successors for all Robberies which he or they shall [have] committed att any time or times before such discovery made Which pardon shall be likewise a good bar to any Appeal brought for any such Robbery.

As John Langbein explains (2005, 158 n.), the royal pardon was in fact 'virtually never needed, because in routine circumstances the crown witness was not prosecuted and thus suffered no conviction needing pardon'. The guarantee must nevertheless have been thought useful, for during the reigns of William and of Anne it was extended to discoverers and prosecutors of felons of various types, including coiners and counterfeiters and, in 1699, to those of 'Felons that commit Burglary, Housebreaking, or Robbery in Shops, Warehouses, Coach-houses or Stable, or that steal Horses'.

In another sense too, the 1692 statute set a pattern. The Act established that 'persons who shall apprehend and take One or more such Thieves or Robbers and prosecute him or them ... until he or they be convicted of any Robbery ... shall have and receive ... for every such Offender so convicted the sum of Forty pounds' and in addition 'have and enjoy' any horse, equipment, money or other goods taken with the robber. The 1699 Act added the offer of a 'Tyburn ticket', 'a Certificate ... by which apprehenders of burglars, shoplifters and horse-thieves, shall and may be discharged of and from all and all manner of Parish and Ward Offices within the Parish or Ward wherein such Felony or Felonies shall be committed' and from 1706 £40 rewards were available for convicting burglars and housebreakers.[1] Even greater rewards were instituted as, after the coming of peace in 1713 and subsequent demobilisation of thousands of soldiers and sailors, violent crime seems to have been on the increase, especially in and around the capital (Beattie 2001, 372–373). The Transportation Act of 1718 included a clause stipulating that all the streets of London – including lanes and courts – were to be considered highways under the 1692 Act, while in January 1720 a royal proclamation added a massive £100 over and above the statutory £40 for convicting a robber committing an offence within a five-mile radius of Charing Cross. 'The policy established by the 1720 proclamation was something entirely new', Beattie comments:

> It offered rewards on an entirely different scale than anything seen in the past. The combined rewards for the conviction of one robber in London would now be one hundred and forty pounds – the equivalent of three years' income of a London journeyman, much more than that of a labourer. Indeed, it was so large a sum that it is likely to be explained not as a means of getting ordinary victims of robberies to prosecute – forty pounds would do that – but to encourage members of gangs to take on the risk of impeaching their colleagues and to persuade private thief-takers like Jonathan Wild to take up the prosecution

---

1   As Beattie remarks (2001, 330), in shoplifting cases, where it would have been up to the shopkeeper to prosecute, the promise of exemption from office was well-judged to induce 'men who, precisely at this time, were becoming increasingly reluctant to serve as constables and perhaps in other parish and ward offices ... the device of the Tyburn Ticket was well judged to induce shopkeepers to overcome their reluctance to undertake prosecutions'.

of offenders rather than mediating between them and their victims for the return of stolen goods for a fee.

BEATTIE 2011, 379; see also CLAYTON AND SHOEMAKER 2022

Defoe's early readers, and especially the many Londoners among them, would have been aware of these measures, if only because impeachers and thief-takers appear so frequently in reports of trials celebrated at the Old Bailey in the years just before and after the publication of his criminal fictions.[2]

2 Thieves Discovering Thieves 1720–1722

2.1 *Shoplifters Discovered*

Nineteen of the seventy-five prosecutions brought for shoplifting between 1720 and 1722, just under a quarter, relied on the testimony of men and women who claimed to have partnered the accused in the theft. Typical is James Gush, who testified that he, John Vaughan and Walter Shelton, had 'carry'd off' twenty yards of linen from a shop, and that Vaughan and Shelton had broken into a house and taken a trunk containing smocks and napkins (*OBO*, t17220112-28). Similarly, Thomas Yeomans testified that Reynolds Winter had taken bath metal rings and sword belt locks from John Siddal's shop, and that he had stood to watch while Reynolds took a chintz gown and other things from a silk dyer's shop (*OBO*, t17220228-8). In another case, Richard Arnold told how, three weeks after losing three wigs from his shop, he found one of the thieves 'by Robert Halfpenny's Direction', and at the trial of Thomas Williams and Joseph Bury,

> Halfpenny deposed that himself and the prisoners coming by the Prosecutor's Shop, Williams lookt in, and told em it was a Rum Ken, i.e. a Shop easy to be rob'd. Williams went in and took one Wig, Bury followed him and took the other two, and gave them to this Evidence.
>
> *OBO*, t17220907-67

---

[2] This chapter was written before Clayton and Shoemaker's systematic study of the impact of the rewards on criminal justice was published, but my suggestions are supported by their findings. I have, however, placed more emphasis than they do on the role of rewards in encouraging accomplices and thief-takers to discover and give evidence; as they show, the rewards policy probably had more influence on the behaviour of victims, making them more likely to indict, to bring more serious charges and to press for full convictions and the latter to help arrest, search and obtain convictions.

Halfpenny, Williams and Bury probably made up or formed part of one of those networks perceived at this time as 'gangs'.[3] John Courland was another; in two separate, consecutive trials he testified to stealing from three shops, first with Thomas Beaul, alias Handy (*OBO*, t17210301-43), and then with Edward Cotterel (*OBO*, t17210301-44).

It was probably easy to frighten child thieves into spilling the beans. 'James Lanman, (aged 11)' was caught by a porter immediately after taking a silver snuff box from the window of Simon Hansel's shop; 'Samuel Armstrong, alias Welshman, (aged 13)', got away, but was later taken on information from Katherine Rider, who had 'stood to watch' (*OBO*, t17220228-19). In the next trial to come on, Rider testified against Lanman, this time for stealing patch and snuff boxes together with Robert (or Robin) Drumman, whose mother 'knew where to dispose of them' (*OBO*, t17220228-20). In the next the girl again took the stand against Drumman and implicated two others 'not yet taken' (*OBO*, t17220228-21). George Bow quickly missed two snuff boxes from his show glass, pursued and caught 'James Hopkins, (a little Boy)' together with the 13-year-old Luke Anderson, who had shielded James while he lifted up the glass, and Henry Thorp, the boy who actually took the box. Anderson gave evidence in court against Hopkins and must have informed on Henry Thorp and James Bird, of whom the prosecutor 'had no suspicion [and] ... whom he had not seen at his Window' (*OBO*, t17220907-41).

None of these evidences appear as defendants in the *Proceedings* for these years, so they all presumably negotiated immunity from prosecution according to the procedure described by Beattie (1986, 367):

> The process by which one of a group of offenders was persuaded to become a witness for the Crown, or by which he persuaded the authorities to allow him to assume that role, frequently began as soon as one or two members of a gang of suspected offenders were apprehended. The negotiations commonly involved the victim of the offense and constables and others with an interest in seeing a successful prosecution, and must have been conducted by means of a combination of threats and

---

3 See Sill 1983 and Wales 2000. In fact, thieves did not usually form large, cohesive groups specialising in any one type of crime, method or territory, but operated in loosely linked networks of whom only a few men would participate in any given robbery (Beattie 2001, 373; Shoemaker 2006, 386). In this respect Defoe's representation of Will's gang in *Colonel Jack* is true to life.

inducements. But the arrangement depended mainly on the examining magistrate, for it was his willingness to admit a suspect as 'an evidence' that induced such men to confess and act as witnesses for the Crown.

All of the accused mentioned so far in this chapter were found guilty, and most were given transportation, but four were sentenced to death.[4] Whether those who gave evidence benefited financially from the parts they played in getting convictions, either in the form of a private reward or of a share in proceeds of a sale of a 'Tyburn ticket', does not emerge from the *Proceedings*. Given the huge sums on offer for convicting robbers it is more likely that rewards were a bigger factor in getting our next group of offenders convicted.

2.2 *Street Robbers Discovered*

Late at night on 1 July 1722 James Carrick, John Molony and Daniel Carrol held up at pistol point two chairmen, William Grindal and John Brooks, who were carrying William Young Esq. from a Covent Garden tavern, and relieved their fare of his gold watch, crystal snuff box, silver-hilted sword and £42 in money. The chairmen carried Young a little further but then pursued the robbers, and saw Moloney stopped by watchman John Felton, get loose and be seized again by Felton's dog. Taken to the roundhouse, Moloney at first denied his guilt but later sent for Young and told him that Carrick and Carrol had been with him. Carrol seems to have got away, but Carrick was later recognised by a salesman while buying a suit of clothes in Monmouth Street; he was followed and, with assistance from others, taken coming out of another shop (*OBO*, t17220704-51).

The taking of James Carrick involved action by a watchman, two chairmen, a salesman, a shopkeeper and an unspecified number of others. It is important to remember that many ordinary men and women who were assaulted and robbed on the streets of London managed to apprehend their attackers at the scene, frequently with help from casual passers-by, and even in the face of threatened or actual physical violence. Reports of one hundred and eleven trials for highway robbery robbery between 1720 and December 1722 suggest that about a third of the accused were taken in

---

4 Reynolds Winter, James Lanman, Samuel Armstrong and Robert Drumman. The last two little boys certainly received conditional pardons, and Lanman probably also, for he is not mentioned in the Ordinary's *Account*. Winter, on the other hand, went to his death and in a wretched condition, 'loaded with distempers ... his Pains and Cries not only molesting himself, but disturbing likewise all those near him' (*OA*, 17220314).

this way.[5] But crucial to the capture of Carrick and another twenty-three indicted for robbery in the early 1720s was information supplied by partners who must have obtained immunity from prosecution and may have had a share in the £140 reward on offer for convicting.

Some of the 'highwaymen' impeached were probably small-time opportunity thieves,[6] barely distinguishable from pickpockets. William Falkner, for instance, deposed that with Jeremy Rand he had attacked a porter and taken the clock he had been delivering (*OBO*, t17220510-24), while John Boon accused Thomas Bishop and David Pritchet of having with him snatched the pockets of Sarah Reed and of 'several others' (*OBO*, 17200303-23). James Carrick, on the other hand, was a member of a gang which went for large pickings and was prepared to use violence, as was William Hawkins (see Howson 1970, Chapter 17 and Appendix 3). In December 1721 Hawkins testified that he, his brother John and James Wright had together held up a hackney coach at pistol point, Wright countering that 'Hawkins would swear any thing to save his own Life' (*OBO*, t17211206-66). John Hawkins together with George Simpson was later arrested for robbing the mails on the directions of confederate Ralph Wilson (*OBO*, t17220510-3). John Winship was one of several highwaymen who regularly took the stand against partners. In two separate trials held in March 1720, he got first Richard England (*OBO*, t17200303-26), and then James Shepherd (*OBO*, t17200303-28) condemned to death; three months later he deposed – unsuccessfully this time – against John Morgan (*OBO*, t172006-14). James Reading was another repeater. In March 1721 he impeached his partner, William Giles, for burglary (*OBO*, t17210301-41) and for highway robbery, John Cobidge together with two named Shaw and Dickinson (*OBO*, t17210301-57); shortly afterwards he testified again against Dickinson as well as William Barton (*OBO*, t17210419-37), and in May against William Wade (*OBO*, t17210525-5). Other names to be added to the list of robbers who turned king's evidence against their wretched partners are those of John James (*OBO*, t17220510-29), and Oliver Fen (*OBO*, t17221010-25). Reading made

---

5 See, for example, *OBO*, t17210712-42; t17201012-4; t17200427-33; t17200303-23; t17220510-32; t17220228-61; t17200712-17; t17200303-15; t17220907-40; t17220704-24; t17211206-45. Constables and watchmen also participated in a number of arrests of street robbers.
6 'Highwayman' is often used to mean a horseman working heaths and roads leading into and out of London, as opposed to a robber working city streets on foot. In law, however, there was no distinction between the mounted and unmounted, and from 1719 even the narrowest of London alleys counted as a highway. Confusions like these are exacerbated by supposed social distinctions of rank which may have held good for an earlier period but by our period had become slippery or changed meaning altogether; Spraggs 2001, Chapter 14.

no bones about sending his accomplices to the gallows, bragging that 'rather than be Hang'd himself, he'd hang half the Nation, nay he'd Hang the Devil' (*OBO*, t17210525-57), while Isaac Drew likewise declared that 'he would Hang a hundred before he would be hang'd himself' (*OBO*, t17211011-28).

Reading and Drew were among those who probably made money by giving evidence, false or true. On trial for highway robbery and murder in January 1722, footpad James Shaw alleged that Drew 'swore his Life away, for the sake of 140 l. Reward' (*OBO*, t17220112-14). When Roger Barry (or Berry) deposed that he had seen Hugh Kelley assault Mercia Porter on the highway, Kelley countered that his accuser 'did not appear against him till the Proclamation was out, and then appear'd for the Lucre of the Reward' (*OBO*, t17200303-24). Reading seems also to have made money by *not* giving evidence: the James Shaw convicted in 1722 may have been the 'one Shaw' from whom, according to William Barton, he had earlier extorted ten guineas under threat of impeachment (*OBO*, t17210419-37).[7]

The ones to profit most systematically from the rewards, however, would have been the professional thief-takers (Shoemaker 2004, 38, 237). Among those who feature in early 1720s trials are the Mr. and Mrs. Murrel whom Elizabeth Cole contacted – with help from a boatman – in order to track down pickpockets Thomas and Ann Tompion (*OBO*, t17201012-5). Jonathan Wild, self-styled 'Thief Catcher General', was so well known that he would be approached directly by victims and by robbers eager to turn evidence. When Elizabeth Knowles was kicked in the leg and robbed of her silk pocket by four footpads she went straight to Wild, who took first Thomas Eades alias Eaves, and with his help three others, all of whom 'confest that they design'd to become Evidences, if they were not already impeach'd' (*OBO*, t17220228-59). At the trial of John James of Ealing for assaulting Collet Mawhood and taking a gold ring of sentimental value, Wild deposed that Nathaniel Hawes 'sent to him and told him he would come in, and make himself an Evidence, told him of this Robbery and discover'd the Prisoner; that when he (this Evidence) took

---

7 A similar accusation was laid by the witness called in his defence by William Wade, who deposed 'that Reading told Strut that he was the King's Evidence; and if he would not give him 5 pieces he would hang him. That Strut gave him 3 Guineas, and a Note for 2 more; which not being paid, he swore a Felony against him' (*OBO*, t17210525-57). At the same trial William Wagland confirmed 'that Reading got 2 Guineas out of Strut, and said he should give him more' while Charles Newman deposed 'that he bailed a Friend of his out of New Prison, who told him, if he did not, Reading would swear away his Life; that Strut was taken up again, and the Constable had 2 Guineas of him, and he (this Evidence) gave Reading Half a Crown, who swore that he was not the Person'.

the prisoner he found the Ring produced in Court in his Pocket' (*OBO*, t17211011-16). John Dikes and Isaac Drew competed to be made evidences in prosecutions organised by Wild (*OBO*, t17211011-28), as did James Wilson, John Homer and William Field (*OBO*, t17200907-33). Wild was also behind the prosecutions for highway robbery of James Wright (*OBO*, t17211206-66), of Butler Fox (*OBO*, t17211206-41), of William Colthouse (*OBO*, t17220112-10), of our old acquaintance James Reading, to whom it availed nothing that he reminded the court that he had 'been an Evidence against others' (*OBO*, t17210830-50), and of John Wigley (*OBO*, t17210830-51). Wigley, who was accused by William Burridge, his partner in crime and rival in love, must have regretted not following his usual practice of operating alone; while awaiting execution in Newgate he told the Ordinary that

> it was not his Method to robb in Gangs, or with Comrades; for that tho' they even gave their Oaths to be true to each other, and there was sometimes found some Faith among them, yet when their Lives were touch'd, they were regardless of their former Promises, and would betray and impeach the nearest Friends.
>
> *OA*, 17210911

The ethics of hanging others to save oneself seems to have been a common topic of conversation in Newgate, where the condemned were urged both to discover confederates and to forgive those who testified against them. Chaplain Thomas Purney wrote that Thomas Wilson was

> told by a Gentleman, that he ought to make all the Discoveries of Robberies committed, he could, because 'twas doing Justice to the World, as innocent Men might be suspected, of what he had perform'd and also that Injur'd Persons might receive Satisfaction as to the Persons who robb'd them, at least, if not as their Goods.
>
> And being told farther, that 'twas in vain for him to fancy his Repentance was sincere, unless he was Candid and Ingenious, and took the shame due to his Offences upon himself; (whatever Ill-designing People might tell Malefactors to the contrary;) he, upon this, said, he was ready to give any Account of his Robberies that should be required of him.
>
> *OA*, 17220924

Others resisted these arguments. Against Ralph (or Richard?) Wilson, who had snitched on him and John Hawkins, George Simpson 'had nothing to say'; Wilson, he admitted, had been

> Compel'd to end his own Days, or to shorten theirs … yet [he] did believe, that there was such Tye and Obligation in Oaths, especially taken at a sacred Time, that he might question, whether even the Good of the publick could excuse the breaking thro' them.
>
> OA, 17220521.

Similarly, Hawkins forgave but could not justify his accuser:

> told by a Gentleman, that he ought to bear no Malice towards Richard Wilson, his Friend and Accuser, because he Acted not out of Ill-will to him, but to preserve his Life; he answered, That Life was sweet, especially to those in their Course of Life; yet, he himself would have died more Deaths than one, rather than have betray'd his Friend, and embru'd his Hands in the Blood of his Companion; however, he freely forgave him from the very Bottom of his Heart, and wish'd that the Creator would so forgive him.
>
> OA, 17220521

James Wright found it hard to pardon William Hawkins, the 'Friend and Companion' who had testified against him; he told the Ordinary

> that as his Companions in Sin might Repent, and be reclaim'd from their vicious Courses, he had resolv'd never to discover them; and that he believed they were all of his Nature and Disposition, desirous to benefit themselves as little to the Loss and Detriment of others, as that sad Way of Life would possibly admit of.
>
> OA, 17211222

Such talk would have interested Defoe, who was probably frequenting Newgate at this time (Novak, 2001, 600). In accordance with the line of reasoning expounded by Wright, he gives both Moll and Jack many a second chance and succeeds in reclaiming them from their 'vicious Courses'. To do that, however, he must first save them from their respective partners in crime.

3   Fear of Witnesses

3.1   *Moll's Joyful News*

To read Defoe's crime fictions in the light of reports on 1720s trials that relied on accomplice evidence is a grim but illuminating experience. The possibility that she may be betrayed and end up on the gallows hangs over Moll Flanders like a black cloud throughout her thieving career. In Chapter 3 we came across her 'Teacher, with another of her Scholars' being 'snap'd' during an attempt on a Cheapside linen draper, but what earns them death sentences is their being recognised in Newgate, 'where they had the Misfortune to have some of their former Sins brought to Remembrance; two other indictments being brought against them, and the Facts being prov'd upon them, they were both condemned to Die' (*MF*, 161).

Defoe does not spell out for us who 'brought to Remembrance' of the two women's 'former Sins', but early readers would have supposed that some prisoner had seized her or his chance to get an indictment deferred. This is what Moll's Governess fears the 'Teacher' will do:

> [she] was for a while really concern'd for the Misfortune of my Comerade that had been hang'd, and who it seems knew enough of my Governess to have sent her the same way, and which made her very uneasy; indeed she was in a great fright.
>
> IT is true, that when she was gone, and had not open'd her Mouth to tell what she knew; My Governess was easy as to that Point, and perhaps glad that she was hang'd; for it was in her power to have obtain'd a Pardon at the Expence of her Friends: But on the other Hand, the loss of her, and Sense of her Kindness in not making her Market of what she knew, mov'd my Governess to Mourn very sincerely for her; I comforted her as well as I cou'd, and she in return harden'd me to Merit more compleatly the same Fate.
>
> *MF*, 164

As Maximilian Novak pointed out in his classic essay on the complexity of the novel (1970, 358), Moll 'does not render this [the Governess's] mixture of regret ... and apprehension ... in anything resembling straight description ... the language is sometimes pointed, sometimes neutral in a situation that is inherently ambiguous'. The passage abounds with adversatives and oppositions, reflecting sickening swings between being 'uneasy ... in a great fright', then 'easy ... perhaps glad that she was hang'd', yet grateful for the woman's 'Kindness in not making her Market of what she knew' and 'mov'd to mourn very sincerely'.

Moll herself will experience similar psychic conflicts. Over five years she comes to be 'the greatest Artist of my time ... and the People at *Newgate* ... had heard much of me indeed, and often expected me there, but I always got off' (*MF*, 168–169). Moll's very success in evading capture puts her at risk:

> ONE of the greatest Dangers I was now in, was that I was too well known among the Trade, and some of them whose hatred was owing rather to Envy, than any Injury I had done them began to be Angry, that I should always Escape when they were always catch'd ...
>
> I WAS soon inform'd that some of these who were gotten fast into *Newgate*, had vowed to Impeach me; and as I knew that two or three of them were but too able to do it, I was under a great concern about it, and kept within Doors for a good while ...
>
> MF 169

Her Governess, however, grows 'something impatient of ... [her] leading such a useless unprofitable Life', dresses her in man's clothing and teams her up with a young man who is 'Nimble enough at his Business' but perilously rash (*MF*, 169). He insists on breaking into a warehouse, they are detected and pursued, and although Moll gets away, he is seized with two pieces of silk upon him:

> MY poor Partner in this Mischief was now in a bad Case, for he was carried away before my Lord Mayor, and by his Worship committed to *Newgate*, and the People that took him were so willing, as well as able, to Prosecute him, that they offer'd themselves to enter into Recognisances to appear at the Sessions, and persue the Charges against him.
>
> HOWEVER, he got the Indictment deferr'd, upon promise to discover his Accomplices, and particularly, the Man that was concern'd with him in this Robbery, and he fail'd not to do his endeavour, for he gave in my Name who he call'd *Gabriel Spencer*, which was the Name I went by to him ...
>
> MF, 172

Defoe here follows the procedure described by Beattie: the examining magistrate – in this case the Lord Mayor of the City of London – delays drawing up a formal charge to give the young man a chance to find out his partner, but to no end:

> HE did all he cou'd to discover this *Gabriel Spencer*; he describ'd me, he discover'd the place where he said I Lodg'd, and in a word, all the Particulars that he cou'd of my Dwelling, but having conceal'd the main circumstances of my Sex from him, I had a vast Advantage, and he never cou'd hear of me ...

> THIS turn'd to his Disadvantage, for having promised Discoveries, but not being able to make it good, it was look'd upon as a trifling with the Justice of the City, and he was the more fiercely persued by the Shopkeepers who took him.
>
> MF, 172

In the meantime, Moll has prudently fled London for Dunstable, where she continues very 'uneasie ... least this Fellow should some how or other find me out ... he might ... have bought his own Life at the Expence of mine':

> THIS fill'd me with horrible Apprehensions: I had no Recourse, no Friend, no Confident but my old Governess, and I knew no Remedy but to put my Life in her Hands, and so I did, for I let her know where to send to me, and had several Letters from her while I stayed here, some of them almost scar'd me out my Wits; but at last she sent me the joyful News that he was hang'd, which was the best News to me that I had heard a great while.
>
> MF, 173

It is not simply relief, but *joy* that Moll feels at hearing that her 'poor Partner' has gone to the gallows. Defoe surely expected his readers to be shocked by this chilling exemplification of emotional hardening, but some might have reflected on the morally degrading effects of official inducements to buy one's life at the expense of another's.

The lesson Moll and her manager learn from the episode of the rash young man is the more practical one that the lone wolf method preferred by John Wigley is safest. Coming merrily back to London, Moll finds her

> Governess as well pleas'd as I was; and now she told me she would never recommend any Partner to me again, for she always found, *she said*, that I had the best luck when I ventur'd by my self; and so indeed I had, for I was seldom in any Danger when I was by my self, or if I was, I got out of it with more Dexterity than when I was entangled with the dull Measures of other People, who had perhaps less forecast, and were more rash and impatient than I; for tho' I had as much Courage to venture as any of them, yet I used more caution before I undertook a thing, and had more Presence of mind when I was to bring myself off.
>
> MF, 174

Defoe has allowed his narrative to get out of chronological sequence here, and to give further illustration of the perils of partnership has to flash back to the episode in which a comrade is seized by a mercer's messengers while Moll, watching from an upstairs lace chamber, has 'the Satisfaction, or the Terror' of seeing her dragged off to face a justice (*MF*, 174). Once again, that coupling of opposite emotions: satisfaction with terror, sadness and regret 'for the poor Woman, who was in Tribulation for what I only had stolen', with self-congratulation for having concealed her true name and lodging (*MF*, 175). Moll conveys money to her comrade in Newgate, but keeps 'close a great while ... I knew that if I should do any thing that should Miscarry, and should be carried to Prison she would be there, and ready to Witness against me, and perhaps save her Life at my Expence' (*MF*, 175). Her ability to predict the chain of consequences that would follow any imprudence proves a life saver. When her partner comes to trial,

> she pleaded she did not steal the Things; but that one Mrs. *Flanders*, as she heard her call'd, (for she did not know her) gave the Bundle to her after they came out of the Shop, and bade her carry it Home to her Lodging. They ask'd her where this Mrs. *Flanders* was? but she could not produce her, neither could she give the least Account of me; and the *Mercers* Men swearing positively that she was in the Shop when the Goods were stolen; that they immediately miss'd them, and purs'd her, and found them upon her; Thereupon the Jury brought her in Guilty; but the Court considering that she really was not the Person that stole the Goods, an inferiour Assistant, and that it was very possible she could not find out this Mrs. *Flanders, meaning me,* tho' it would save her Life ... they allow'd her to be Transported, which was the utmost Favour she could obtain, only that the Court told her, that if she could in the mean time produce the said Mrs. *Flanders*, they would intercede for her Pardon, that is to say, if she could find me out, and hang me, she should not be Transported: This I took care to make impossible to her, and so she was Shipp'd off in Pursuance of her Sentence a little while after.
>
> *MF*, 175

The reader is left in no doubt about what is required from the 'poor Woman' if she is to avoid several years' hard labour in the colonies. Would she have hanged Moll, had it not been made 'impossible to her'? Would we have blamed her if she had? Or questioned the ethics of the bargain offered by the court in its pursuit of the untaken thief? The moral issues that complicate the behaviour of the judiciary, of the accused and of Moll herself are evident in the laboured reflections that close the episode:

> I MUST repeat it again, that the Fate of this poor Woman troubl'd me exceedingly; and I began to be very pensive, knowing that I was really the Instrument of her disaster, but the Preservation of my own Life, which was so evidently in Danger, took off all my tenderness; and seeing she was not put to Death, I was very easie at her Transportation, because she was then out of the way of doing me any Mischief whatever should happen.
> MF, 175–176.

'Very pensive' at having been the cause of 'her Disaster', but 'very easie ... because she was then out of way', Moll evaluates the question first through an empathetic lens, then through a purely egotistical one. It is the latter that colours her brutal summary of the fates of *all* her partners in crime: 'I WAS now easie as to all Fear of Witnesses against me, for all those, that had either been concern'd with me, or that knew me by the name of *Moll Flanders*, were either hang'd or Transported' (*MF*, 176).

Defoe surely expected his readers to learn with dismay of Moll's complacency at the fates of anyone who knows her adopted name, but spares them from having to read in the novel of its protagonist betraying or being betrayed for a reward. Only indirectly and briefly are we given glimpses of the temptation these inducements constituted. As receiver, compounder, organiser and maker of thieves, Moll's Governess plays all the roles played by Jonathan Wild *except* that of turning in the thieves who supply her. In the fine gentleman episode, however, she feels the need to *deny* that she means to betray Moll, thus reminding us that she might have done so. More lucrative is the information about smuggled lace which Moll passes on to a customs officer, after which she makes it her business to 'enquire out prohibited Goods; and after buying some, usually betray'd them' (*MF*, 166). If these references to the use of rewards in law enforcement seem cursory, even more noticeable is the omission of any reference to them in Defoe's narrating of Colonel Jack's experience of assaulting and robbing Londoners of all and every sort as they go about their business on the streets of the city.

3.2   *Will's Brave Gang*
In accordance with the traditional pattern of criminal biography, Will's and Jack's thieving careers follow a rising curve of violence which corresponds to a downward slide in moral and spiritual terms. From picking pockets, Defoe has

them move on to work through 'a catalogue of the varieties of street robbery' (Gladfelder 2001, 105). First comes a mugging in Smithfield meat market, where the young men notice 'an antient Country Gentleman' who has just been paid for a sale of bullocks. When their target is overtaken by a fit of coughing that leaves him breathless, Will makes an 'artificial stumble' against him; the 'violence of the blow' beats the old Gentleman quite down, Jack runs to get hold of his Bag of Money, gives it 'a quick snatch … [pulls] it clean away, and run[s] like the Wind (*CJ*, 109). Thick with verbs of beating and pulling, snatching and running, Defoe's description of two healthy youths mugging a frail old man strains our sympathy for Jack and his tutor (see Gladfelder 2001, 106). Half-strangled by his cough and 'frighted with the fall', their victim 'could not recover himself to speak till some time … nor could he call out stop Thief, or tell any Body he had lost any thing for a good while'. It is implicit here that if he had managed to give the proper alert in time, the 'People' nearby would have come to his aid and perhaps caught his attackers.

There is no one to come to the aid of Will and Jack's next target, a 'young Fellow' who might have given them more trouble if he had been attacked in daylight and on a busy street. Instead, in a half-enclosed court off Lombard Street, Jack and Will notice at dusk one evening a woollen-draper's apprentice paying in money at a goldsmith's shop. They wait until he comes out with 'still a pretty large Bag under his arm', by which time it is 'Very Dark'; Will

> flyes at the young Man, and Gives him such a violent Thrust, that push'd him forward with too great a force for him to stand, and as he strove to recover, the Threshold took his feet, and he fell forward into the other part of the Court, as if he had flown in the Air … I stood ready, and presently felt out the Bag of Money, which I heard fall, for it flew out of his Hand, he having his Life to save, not his Money: I went forward with the Money, and *Will* that threw him down, finding I had it, ran backward …
>
> *CJ*, 110

The force used during this attack might have been fatal to the apprentice, Defoe reminds us, for he had 'his Life to save'. Worse is to come: 'My Companion Will, who was now grown a Man, and encourag'd by these Advantages fell into quite another Vein of Wickedness, getting acquainted with a wretched Gang of Fellows that turn'd their Hands to every Thing that was vile' (*CJ*, 111). Pressing Jack to leave off what he now sees as the childish game of pickpocketing, he boasts: 'I am got into better Business I assure you, and you shall come into it too, I'll bring you into a brave Gang *Jack, says he*, where you shall see we shall be all Gentlemen' (*CJ*, 112). Will here glosses his new 'Business' in terms of a long-standing tradition that celebrated highwaymen as paradigms of daring, courage and politeness (see Spraggs 2001; Parrinder 2001; Shoemaker 2006, 381-2; McKenzie 2007, 105; Clegg 2016, 227). The invitation is irresistible to a young man obsessed with notions of his own gentility,[8] resentful of having been excluded from the 'Society' of young pickpockets led by his 'happy' brother, the Major (*CJ*, 74), and suffering from a deficit of 'manliness' and a 'subaltern psyche' (Gregg 2009, 106).

Seen in operation, the 'brave Gang' turns out to be anything but courageous or gentlemanly. Jack's account of a long night of miscellaneous mayhem in which he joins Will and two others realises the distinctly unglamorous stereotype of the other tradition discussed by Shoemaker: that of the robber as a brutal and cowardly predator. On the road from Kentish Town a lone foot traveller strikes with his cane at Will, but is wrestled to the ground, forced to beg for his life and left tied up by the side of the road. A doctor and apothecary in a coach who yield their fees, watches and silver surgical instruments without resisting perhaps excite more humour in the reader than sympathy, but the 'easie ... Bargain' assigned to the novice Jack arouses only contempt. In confronting his targets, a 'Couple of Poor Women, one a kind of a Nurse, and the other a Maid-Servant', he begins with the kind of polite banter ascribed to gallant highwaymen (Spraggs, 185), but when the women scream adopts an ugly, threatening tone: 'hold, *says I*, make no Noise, unless you have a mind to force us to murther you whether we will or no, give me your Money presently, and make no Words, and we shan't hurt you' (*CJ*, 115–116). The maid hands over 5s. 6d., the nurse a 'Guinea, and a Shilling, crying heartily for her Money, and said, it was all she had left in the World; well we took it for all that, tho' it made my very heart bleed to see what agony the poor Woman was in at parting with it'.

As Geoffrey Sill (2014) has noted, Defoe here disqualifies his robbers from being 'gentlemen' by showing them to be unfeeling. In the next few segments, he also casts doubt on their courage and determination. When they hold up a gentleman and a punk in a coach in Hyde Park the client hands over his money, but from 'the Slut' they get an earful of abuse – and 'not one Six-penny Piece'. Three gentlemen crossing Chelsea Fields prove 'too strong for us to meddle with', for they have 'hired three Men at Chelsea, two with Pitch-Forks, and the third, a Waterman, with a Boat-Hook-Staff to Guard

---

8 McBurney (1962, 325) long ago identified gentility as the 'dominant motif' of the novel, and David Blewett (1979) has explored its relevance to Defoe's representation of Jacobites.

them'; challenged by this rudimentarily armed bodyguard, the four robbers scuttle off. They cut no better figure in a bungled attempt at burglary: they have bribed a footman to let them in to a house, but the 'Rogue' has got drunk and been shut out. What turns out to be a farce, Jack reminds us, could have resulted in a massacre: 'it was a happy Drunkenness to the Family, for it sav'd them from being robb'd, and perhaps murther'd, for they were a cursed bloody Crew'. The night concludes, prosaically, with the gang breaking into a brew-house and wash-house to steal 'a small Copper and about a Hundred weight of Pewter', goods which next day they sell for half their value.

Jack's experience, and especially the callous taking of the poor nurse's last guinea, sparks off a revulsion from violent crime: 'it came into my Head with a double force, that this was the High Road to the Devil. And that certainly this was not the Life of a Gentleman!' (*CJ*, 118). Will, on the other hand, is 'Mighty full' of the gang's success, and eager for even greater things: 'we will buy a Couple of good Horses, and go further a Field … we will take the Highway like Gentlemen, and then we shall get a great deal of Money indeed … then, *says he*, we shall live like Gentlemen'. The plan deploys current assumptions about the mounted highwayman's social superiority to the lowly footpad (Shoemaker 2008, 387; Beattie 1996, 151), assumptions Jack rejects in a tart reply which leads to a heated exchange:

> Why *Will*, do you call this way of Living the Life of a Gentleman?
> WHY, *says Will*, why not?
> WHY, *says I*, was it like a Gentleman for me to take that Two and Twenty Shillings from a poor antient Woman, when she beg'd of me upon her Knees not to take it, and told me it was all she had in the World to buy her Bread for her self and a sick Child which she had at home, do you think I could be so Cruel if you had not stood by, and made me do it? why, I cry'd at doing it, as much as the poor Woman did, tho' I did not let you see me.
> YOU Fool you, *says Will*, you will never be fit for our Business indeed, if you mind such things as those, I shall bring you off of those things quickly; why, if you will be fit for Business, you must learn to fight when they resist, and cut their Throats when they submit; you must learn to stop their Breath, that they may beg and pray no more; what signifies pity? prethee, who will pity us when we come to the *Old-Baily*? I warrant you that whining old Woman that beg'd so heartily for her Two and Twenty Shillings would let you, or I beg upon our Knees, and would not save our Lives by not coming in for an Evidence against us; did

you ever see any of them cry when they see Gentlemen go to the Gallows?

CJ, 119

Will's sketch of what his kind of 'gentleman' must do in order to save his neck is chilling. Built into it is the notion that his gang will inevitably 'come to the *Old-Baily*' sooner or later, but that by killing all potential witnesses against them they may avoid the gallows. The speech prepares the reader to feel less pity for Will when he is finally taken and hanged – not on the evidence of a whining old woman – but, ironically, on that of a not-so-brave gentleman like himself.

The catastrophe comes in a thirteen-man attack on a Hownslow house in which Jack fortunately does not take part. The gang come up against armed resistance from a posse of neighbours and a gardener loses his life: 'the Gentlemen Rogues were pursued, and being at *London* with the Booty, one of them was taken' (*CJ*, 120). One is enough. George, as the captured robber turns out to be called, 'upon promise of Favour, and of saving him from the Gallows, discover'd his Companions, and *Will* among the rest, as the principal Party in the whole Undertaking' (*CJ*, 121). Four days later Jack hears that Will is in Newgate and destined for the gallows. 'I would advise you to shift for yourself', Jack's poor shoemaker friend warns him: 'if he can lay any thing to you he will do it you may be sure; he will certainly hang you to save himself' (*CJ*, 122). This Will does not, but Jack knows that if he should confess to the whereabouts of the silver plate he has hidden under his (Jack's) bed, 'I should be undone, and should be taken up for a Confederate'. Jack manages to get rid of the incriminating goods, but is apprehended on an erroneous tip-off, and, as we shall see in Chapter 7, it takes all his genius for negotiating to get himself off the hook. As for Will, he assures Jack that 'it would do him no good to accuse me, who was never out with any of them, but that once' (*CJ*, 131).

As readers of the *Proceedings* would have known, just one robbery would have been enough to attract a death sentence, and in any case, the 'once' Will refers to had consisted of a whole series of violent assaults on travellers. Wisely, Jack decides to flee to Scotland with his brother, the Captain, where they will be beyond the reach of English law and of information laid by erstwhile comrades. Before leaving London, however, Jack seeks out the poor nurse and returns her guinea with 'a Crown more' (*CJ*, 136). In so doing he puts himself at risk of being recognised, but is saved by the compassion of his victim, who disclaims all memory of her attacker and, in a tearful scene, heartily forgives 'him and all that were with him'. In this act of gratuitous, Christian forgiveness, did Defoe wish his readers to recognise one that differs radically from the 'gracious Pardons' offered, in the king's name, in exchange for sending a partner or two to the gallows?

In the meantime, the other main provision of the Highwaymen Act, the £40 reward – raised to £140 by the proclamation of 1720 – has become something of an elephant in the room. The only motive given for George's impeachment of his confederates is 'to save his Life', yet from the twelve other gang members who had been 'out' on the night of the Hounslow burglary, and had perhaps murdered a gardener as they escaped, he would have stood to earn not only immunity from prosecution but a share of £1,680 as well. Even if *he* had not been after the reward, the loosely organised, incompetent and cowardly band of thugs described by Jack would have been perfect targets for any averagely intelligent thief-taker.

As in *Moll Flanders*, in *Colonel Jack* Defoe gives little prominence to financial inducements to catch thieves, allowing them to surface briefly on only one occasion. In the second compounding episode, Will offers to infiltrate the gangs of young pickpockets who may have stolen the merchant's pocketbook: 'by some Inquiries, offering them Money and the like,' he suggests, 'he believ'd they would be brought to betray one another, and that so he might pick it out for them'. Nothing comes of the suggestion, but it is a disquieting one nevertheless. Given the topicality of the rewards and the visibility in trial reports of those who made fortunes out of them, we may conclude that if in his criminal fictions Defoe is practically silent on the topic, he must have been so deliberately.

4   Conclusion

In this chapter we have seen how, in the thirty years between the Glorious Revolution and the publication of *Moll Flanders* and *Colonel Jack*, English governments enacted provisions aimed at encouraging prosecutions of a range of property offenders by guaranteeing royal pardons to thieves who convicted associates, and by offering ever larger financial rewards to those prepared to aid with law enforcement. Accomplices trying to save their lives by acting as crown witnesses appear regularly in 1720s trial reports, which sometimes record defendants' counter accusations. Defoe's narratives of thieves discovering thieves are fraught with dreadful psychological conflicts and suggest the morally degrading effects both on those who turn evidence and on those who stand to lose their lives as a consequence of their doing so. His near silence on 'blood money', and the total absence of thief-takers from his cast of characters at a time when they were playing an increasingly important and very public part in catching and prosecuting criminals, is deafening. We may not conclude from Defoe's mode of representing betrayals of partners, or from the absence of reference to rewards, that in *Moll Flanders* and *Colonel Jack* he is attacking this important component of the 'Bloody Code', but he was surely asking his early readers to think critically about some of its unintended human and moral consequences.[9]

---

9 If I am right about this, Defoe is ahead of his time. Clayton and Shoemaker (2022, 97) argue that over the course of the eighteenth century 'the rewards system undermined the twin pillars of early modern criminal justice. The rewards which stimulated so many capital convictions came to be labelled as 'blood money', and they added to growing doubts about the use of the 'bloody code' ... Moreover, the practice of the state paying for the cost of apprehending and prosecuting criminals contributed to the development of modern forms of policing and, paradoxically given that victims were principal initial beneficiaries of rewards, their long-term marginalisation in criminal justice.'

PART 2

The Intricacies of Office

∴

CHAPTER 6

What It Is to Be a Constable

> ... the Mistress of the House was mov'd with Compassion, and enclin'd to have let me go, and had almost perswaded her Husband to it also, but the sawcy Wenches were run even before they were sent, and had fetch'd a Constable, and then the Master said, he could not go back, I must go before a Justice, and answer'd his Wife that he might come into Trouble himself if he should let me go.
>
> THE sight of the Constable indeed struck me with terror, and I thought I should have sunk to the Ground; I fell into faintings, and indeed the People themselves thought I would have died ...
>
> MF, 214

∴

> I went to Sleep at first, but notwithstanding, I was so weary I Slept little or none, for several Hours; at last being overcome with Sleep, I Dropt, but was immediately Rouz'd with Noise of People knocking at the Door, as if they would beat it down, and Crying and Calling out to the People of the House, Rise, and let in the Constable here, we come for your Lodger in the Garret.
>
> I WAS frighted to the last degree, and started up in my Bed; but when I was awake, I heard no Noise at all, but of two *Watch-men* thumping at the Doors with their Staves, and giving the Hour past Three a Clock, and a Rainy wet Morning *for such it was*: I was very glad when I found it was but a Dream, and went to Bed again, but was soon Rouz'd a Second time, with the same, very same Noise, and Words: Then being sooner awak'd than I was before, I Jumped out of Bed and run to the Window, and found it was just an Hour more, and the *Watch-men* were come about past four a Clock, and they went away again very quietly, so I lay me down again, and slept the rest of the Night quietly enough.

I LAY'D no stress upon the thing call'd a Dream, neither till now did I understand that Dreams were of any Importance
CJ, 124–125

∴

1 Introduction

The two passages quoted above mark crucial transitions in the progress of Defoe's criminal protagonists along the 'corridor' of cultural spaces that made up early modern England's system of justice. As we have seen in Part 1 of this book, detecting and apprehending was a task left largely up to ordinary citizens, many of whom let their captives off with some informal punishment rather than instituting a prosecution which would cost time and money, might bring disrepute upon the prosecutor, result in a harsher sentence than desired, or an acquittal, and probably not restore the stolen goods. Of those who did opt for formal process, many would call upon the assistance of a constable to 'carry' their suspect before a justice of the peace and, if so directed, to prison to await trial. Hence the terror the appearance of constables induces in Moll and Jack. The officer before whom the former falls 'into faintings' will indeed march her off to a magistrate, who then commits her to Newgate. The latter will learn 'the importance of dreams' when he sees a flesh-and-blood officer and three men running towards him, finds that they bear an arrest warrant and is marched off to face interrogation by a justice of the peace. Yet Jack manages to show the officer to have mistaken his man, and on a series of earlier occasions Moll has fallen into but wriggled out of an arrest. They succeed in this, I suggest, through a combination of the accumulated legal knowledge on which Beth Swan has remarked (1998, 41), and a talent for 'Watch[ing] the Advantages of other People's Mistakes' (*MF*, 211).

Michel de Certeau's distinction between 'strategies' and 'tactics' is useful here. Whereas the former 'postulates a *place* that can be delimited as its own and serve as a base from which relations with an exteriority composed of targets or threats … can be managed', the latter are of necessity constantly mobile, and

> must accept the chance offerings of the moment, and seize on the wing the possibilities that offer themselves at any given moment. It must vig-

ilantly make use of the cracks that particular conjunctions open in the surveillance of the proprietary powers. It poaches in them. It creates surprises in them. It can be where it is least expected. It is a guileful ruse.
> 1988, 37

Tim Hitchcock and Robert Shoemaker have used this idea to explain the limited but 'real and effective agency' of eighteenth-century plebeian Londoners:

> the very poverty and apparent powerlessness of the poor and the criminal – their identification as 'problems' – both ensure that they become the object of 'strategies' and in turn give greater significance to their 'tactics'. Additionally, the highly pressured circumstances they confront – hunger and possible execution – make them doubly motivated to develop a profound knowledge of the narrow social system with which they were forced to engage.
> 2015, 20

This chapter will illustrate the knowledge and the tactics used to open up 'cracks ... in ... surveillance' in three episodes involving constables in *Moll Flanders* and one in *Colonel Jack*. In narrating these incidents Defoe could take for granted his readers' familiarity with customs, laws and apparatus of norms, regulations and provisos that no longer apply, and which we shall need to recover with the help of conduct books and trial reports of his time. But it will be useful to begin by briefly surveying what historians of crime and justice can tell us about the functions and powers of early modern constables and how these were being *de facto* bureaucratised and in part professionalised over the long eighteenth century.

2 An Insupportable Hardship

Of all the 'punishments' that could be inflicted on a householder by a parish vestry, thundered Defoe in his guise as Andrew Moreton,

> the most terrible is that of the Constable, or Parish-Drudge, for he is in Effect a greater Slave than the Beadle ... The Imposition of this Office is an insupportable Hardship; it takes up so much of a Man's time that his own Affairs are frequently totally neglected, too often to his Ruin; yet there is neither Profit nor Pleasure therein, but an inconceivable Fa-

tigue. Besides the Office is so intricate, that a Man is generally out of his Constableship before he has learn'd half his Duty.

[1727], 16–17

The constableship had certainly become 'intricate' by the eighteenth century, although it had never been a simple institution. Originally heads of local self-governing communities, by the late fourteenth century constables had been subordinated to the central government judiciary, a change which forced them into what Joan Kent calls a 'dual allegiance': 'On the one hand, the constable was the lowest officer in a hierarchy of authority that stretched from the monarchy to the village … On the other hand, the constable also had to represent the village's interests to his superiors' (1981, 30–31). In another classic essay, Keith Wrightson described early modern constables as torn between 'two concepts of order': on the one hand, they were responsible for 'the maintenance of harmony between neighbours in the face-to-face and day-to-day relationships', on the other, they had to uphold 'a pattern of authority and an ultimate scheme of values' (1980, 24 and 32). Their ability to do either would have been limited by the temporary nature of their mandate and consequent reliance on local goodwill, aspects of the constableship underlined by Cynthia Herrup:

> Both the staff [of office] and its aura of expertise would, within a few months, be transferred into new hands … at best the headboro or the constable was an equal among equals; that meant that he was likely to be resisted at times by other people, and that he could not counter that resistance easily without popular support.
>
> 1989, 70

Over the sixteenth and seventeenth centuries the duties of constables became increasingly burdensome as the scope of criminal, social and economic legislation expanded. Traditionally, they had been responsible for apprehending or reporting breakers of the peace, nightwalkers and 'lewd men and women'; to these were by stages added other perpetrators of victimless offenses: vagrants, disorderly persons and gamblers, tipplers, certain kinds of religious offenders, violators of social and economic regulations, and

> such diverse offenders as conventiclers, profaners of the Sabbath, keepers of unlicensed or disorderly alehouses, prostitutes, players of 'drolls and interludes', singers of seditious ballads, people who sold oranges

from wheelbarrows, and landlords who divided tenements or kept inmates.
SHOEMAKER 2008b, 217

In the rapidly growing capital, they had also to direct increasingly chaotic traffic and keep the peace among 'more and bigger crowds of people, more frequent riots, larger gatherings at pillories, at hangings, at royal processes and holidays, the latter now often perilously enlivened by fireworks' (Beattie 2001, 124 and 155). Shoemaker remarks that it is 'unlikely that constables and their parish colleagues systematically fulfilled the manifold duties with which they were burdened' and cites allegations by magistrates that they were failing to carry out 'the most basic of them'. He notes also that 'where popular support for laws was absent or divided, as was the case with the laws against vice and conventicles, constables were particularly reluctant to act'; to the unscrupulous, on the other hand, such laws created opportunities for extorting payment for 'screening' from prosecution (2008b, 220–222). Hurl-Eamon (2005, 463–464) relates actual corruption to public expectations of constables' behaviour, expectations which must have fed off stereotypes still cultivated in rogue literature, satirical ballads and plays such as Christopher Bullock's *Per-Juror* of 1717. Meanwhile the ever-expanding system of statutory rewards for apprehending and convicting offered another source of income, but also associated constables with professional informers and thief-catchers, and this may have helped erode popular support. By the middle of the eighteenth century, Saunders Welch, High Constable of Holborn and assistant to and later fellow justice of Henry then John Fielding, was complaining bitterly about the effects of declining public support on his fellow officers' ability to enforce the law: the 'necessary power of calling in aid lodged in you ... has of late years been treated with contempt by the commonalty' (1754, 6).

Welch's *Observations on the Office of Constable. With Cautions for the more safe Execution of that Duty. Drawn from Experience* was a latecomer to the genre of advice literature for officials that flourished between the late sixteenth and mid-eighteenth century. Maurizio Ascari notes how the very existence and organisation of conduct books, such as William Lambarde's *The Duties of Constables, Borsholders, Tythingmen, and such other Lowe Ministers of the Peace* (1582), assume literacy and specialisation among the various types of 'lowe and lay Ministers', and that in *Much Ado about Nothing* Hugh Oatcake and George Seacole are considered fit to be constables precisely because they can read and write (2016, 80). On the other hand, prefaces to manuals harp on the need for guidance, given on the one hand 'the large extent of the Constables Office' and, on the other 'the little skill many of you have who are called to take upon you the same Office' (Meriton 1682, A3r). The same author warned that other manuals in use at the time were 'very unsafe': William Lambarde's *The Duties of Constables,* which was still being reprinted a hundred years after its first appearance, was 'a Discourse principally of the Common Law cases, is now much alter'd by Statute since'; another was full of 'unwarrantable Authorities and gross Errors'; yet another included legislation of the Interregnum years no longer in force. Meriton no doubt hoped to sell more copies of his own manual by denigrating others, and would have had an interest in repeatedly updating himself; his seventh edition proclaimed that the sixth, published just three years earlier, had already been 'found by late Experience to be a Blind Guide, apt rather to lead thee out of the way, than to direct thee' (A2r). With the institution of tri-annual parliaments after the Glorious Revolution the rate of legislating increased, and this, together with the ever-growing bulk of case law, made it increasing difficult for the authors of these manuals – never mind the 'Parish Drudges' who bought and studied them – to keep abreast. Andrew Moreton was not exaggerating when he estimated that a year was insufficient for a constable to learn 'half his duty,' and complained that even a single term could so distract a man from his own affairs as to ruin him financially. To deal with the 'information overload' affecting legal matters (Blair 2003, *cit.* in Rudolph 2008, 198) Giles Jacob,[1] whose octavo *Compleat Parish Officer* (1720) was portable as well as cheap (it cost 1/6d), resorted to abridgement, condensation and alphabetic organisation, claiming to thus enable 'the Plebian, unacquainted with our Laws and Statutes' to act 'with Safety, without advising with other person, or consulting any other Authority, but this Treatise'.

To act 'with Safety' in this legal minefield seems to have become ever more imperative. In making arrests, especially in London, constables were exposed to threats, physical violence and prosecutions for assault, theft and false imprisonment (Hay 1989; Shoemaker 1991, 264–265; Shore 2009; Hitchcock and Shoemaker 2015, 107–121). To keep officers 'out of Danger' P.S. Gent.'s *Help To Magistrates* (1721) offered detailed, technical instruction on how to draw up testimonials for servants, how to distinguish between *ex officio* duties and

---

1 Jacob published 'dozens of law texts', among them a *New Law Dictionary* (1729) which was 'enormously influential' on both sides of the Atlantic; Rudolph 2008, 197–198. He also wrote a play, treatises on hermaphrodites and flogging, a series of literary biographies, a parody of *The Rape of the Lock* and a critique of Gay's *Three Hours after Marriage.* This last earned him a place – alongside Defoe – in the *Dunciad,* where he is revered as 'the Scourge of Grammar' and 'the Blunderbuss of Law'; https://en.wikipedia.org/wiki/Giles_Jacob.

those which required warrants, how to decide which warrants were faulty and should not be obeyed – and much more. He hoped that his book would do 'a great deal of Good: *First*, In giving Men an Insight into what they ought legally to do. And, *Secondly*, What they ought to avoid, as not warrantable' (A2r). Even so, he warned, 'For whatever the Opinion of some is, a Constable is no more a privileged Man than any other, where he exceeds the Bounds of his Office in Unaccountable Actions' (86). Some years earlier Henry Care (1703, 188) pleaded for tolerance and defended the office: since the constable was obliged by law to serve, 'it would go hard, if, for every trivial Slip, he should run the Risk of being ruined by Vexatious Suits'. As Robert Gardiner, Clerk to the Court of Common Pleas, reminded those responsible for selecting them, 'Constables have no Allowance, but are bound to perform their Office gratis', for which reason 'This Office ought not to be put upon the poorer sort ... for they are usually most ignorant and fearful, and less able to attend their office; their Necessity requiring them to mind their own Trade and Employment' (1710, 7).

Parish vestries would have found it difficult to avoid choosing from among the 'poorer sort', however, for over the previous century those of the richer sort had become increasingly unwilling to take on civic duties, preferring to pay the fine for avoiding service, purchase a 'Tyburn ticket' giving exemption, or finance men poorer than themselves to take their places (Beattie 2001, 134). By the 1720s over 100 out of 360 London constables were deputies, and by the 1750s some 90% of those elected were buying their way out. Many hired men served repeatedly, sometimes taking on posts that were paid, such as that of beadle, sometimes acting as or with the thief-takers we met in Chapter 5. In the meantime, the night watch, itself originally an unpaid obligation of local householders, had become in effect a paid office, a development Moreton supports (Defoe 1727, 30–31; Reynolds 1998, Chapter 2; Beattie 2001, 173–197). By the end of the eighteenth century, the early stages of law enforcement had been *de facto* professionalised. As we turn to the Old Bailey *Proceedings* for the early 1720s and then to Defoe's fictions of those same years, we shall be considering whether the ways in which they represented constables encouraged that 'sea-change in thinking about policing issues' (Beattie 2001, 157).

3   Constables in the *Proceedings*, 1720–1722

Between January 1720 and December 1722 constables are mentioned in reports of one hundred and five Old Bailey trials for theft and seventeen for violent theft. It is likely that more were involved in apprehending, those accused, but not as primary catchers of thieves, for they were usually called in only after a victim had identified and seized a suspect (Shoemaker 2004, Chapter 2). Several reports refer to them as taking prisoners either to a magistrate or, more frequently, since these arrests usually took place at night, to watch-houses to await the convenience of a justice. In theory the victims could have done this themselves, as did most of those who apprehended shoplifters. But in contexts in which thefts were associated with prostitution, client-prosecutors were often at a disadvantage, which is perhaps why constables were so often called in to deal with women suspected of stealing while providing sexual services. Rather than apprehend Sarah Floyd for stealing his twenty-nine pairs of scissors while he was with her in her cellar, for instance, Joseph Clemenson 'went to a Constable, and got him to go back with him to the Prisoner's Lodging' (*OBO*, t17221205-20). Mary Speerman, who 'refused to go before a Justice without a Constable' (*OBO*, 17200602-17), was probably not the only suspect who resisted victims' attempts to take them in themselves. Sometimes more than one officer was needed to make an arrest. A watchman as well as a constable seems to have been involved in taking Ann Festrop to a watch-house (t17210301-3), and two watchmen in addition to a constable in getting Mary Harvey and Ann Parker to a compter (*OBO*, t17211206-33). As we saw in Chapter 2, it took a high constable, presumably aided by subordinates, an hour to deal with abusive Sarah Wells and her violent protector (*OBO*, t17200115-47).

Testimony from officers of the crown may have swayed juries to favour client-prosecutors more than they otherwise did. At the trial of Eleanor Flemming, 'The Constable and another Evidence deposed that they were present when her husband offer'd the Prosecutor his Note for 4l. to make it up' (*OBO*, t17211o712-31), and at that of Elizabeth Hargrove 'The Constable depos'd, that he heard the Prisoner say she knew where the Handkerchief was' (*OBO*, t17211206-63). The most frequently heard of constables' contributions to prosecutions, however, were claims to having found the stolen goods on the suspect. These items would have been kept by the officers concerned and produced at trial to show that they corresponded to those listed in indictments. To this end constables searched the clothes and persons of Penelope Dye (*OBO*, t17200115-9), Mary Granger and Sarah Lawson (*OBO*, t17201012-17), Margaret Wilson (*OBO*, t17210419-60), Mary Bun and Elizabeth Mob (*OBO*, t17211206-32) and Rebecca Butler alias Neal (*OBO*, t17210301-18).

These particular women are not recorded as having resisted being searched, but Jane Behn alias Macopny gave and got a harder time of it: 'The Constable depos'd, that the Watchman putting his Finger in her Mouth, she bit a piece of it off; but squeezing her hard by the Throat, forc'd 5s 6d out of her Mouth' (*OBO*, t17220404-12). Prudent prosecutors tended to leave it to officers to carry out body searches, for even a mere touch of the arm could be construed as an assault, in law a misdemeanour but one for which damages could be awarded. Douglas Hay has shown that in eighteenth- and nineteenth-century England litigation commonly served as a means of forestalling a prosecution, settling a quarrel or obtaining revenge. Even the poor and criminal, people whose 'hard-won knowledge' had taught them 'how to work the system', brought lawsuits, assault being the offence most commonly alleged (1989, 362). Hay's findings are confirmed and applied to Covent Garden, an area of London known in the 1720s for its taverns and brothels, by Heather Shore in her study of the women who, during the Reformation of Manners campaigns against vice, used counter-prosecution to defend themselves and their livelihoods (2009; see also Hitchcock and Shoemaker 2015, 110–121).

Prosecutors of male pickpockets seem to have had needed less official help in apprehending their suspects, and been less inhibited about carrying out searches themselves (see above, Chapter 2). The same applies to prosecutors of shoplifters: only in two out of seventy-five reports is a constable explicitly mentioned as playing a part in an arrest. An officer confirmed the confession made before a justice by the possibly weak-brained James Codner (*OBO*, t172001107-12) and Joseph Lock 'charg'd a Constable' with John Scoon but searched him himself (*OBO*, t17211205-3).

Reports of trials for buying goods knowing them to have been stolen tell a different story. Careful searching of premises where the goods might have been stored would have been essential to making a charge of receiving stick. Mrs. Weaver took a constable with her to search William Reynolds's shop and directed him to open a shutter; behind it the officer found a tankard lid which he 'said ... had been taken off lately, the pin looking as if it had been filed within 3 Days' (*OBO*, t17201012-6). At another trial Henry Becket deposed 'that he was the Constable that carried Lewellin to the Roundhouse that night, and before the Justice next Day, where he denied everything; but as he was carrying him to Newgate he said if he would go back with him he would make an ingenious Confession'; Lewellin duly confessed, a search warrant was obtained and the stolen coach seats were found (*OBO*, t17201012-15). A constable named Willis tracked down via several brokers three women who were subsequently indicted for having received goods stolen by Joseph Reeves and John Scoon (*OBO*, 17220404-3).

Of the reports on robbery trials to mention constables, two refer to them in their routine roles: offering hearsay evidence (*OBO*, t17220907-15) and accompanying a prosecutor to make an arrest (*OBO*, t17210301-34). Out of the ordinary is one that tells of an officer who chased and arrested two men who had brutally assaulted and robbed the elderly Joseph Dormy and his wife on the streets of Hoxton. At the trial of Edmund Neal and William Pincher:

Richard Bays depos'd, That about 9 a-Clock at Night, he hearing Cry of Murder, and being a Headborough, ran out to be assisting to the distressed, having with him two Dogs: That coming to the Prosecutors, the Old Man was but just got up, and the Woman upon the Ground, very much abus'd, and in a bloody Condition; that inquiring which Way the Rogues were gone, the Old Man pointed, that he pursu'd with his Dogs, and that when he came up to the Prisoners, who had taken into the Fields, he found Pincher lying on the Ground, feigning himself to be drunk; that other Persons also being come to his Assistance, they bid Pincher rise, but he not doing so, they attempted to help him up, but he refus'd to rise, bidding them let him alone, telling them he was choaked, he was strangled, asking them if they came to rob him, bidding them take what he had, but not abuse him. That in the mean Time Edward Neal came up, and they having got Pincher up, they tax'd him with the Robbery committed, upon which Neal told them he knew Pincher, that he was an honest Fellow, that he did not believe be would do any such Fact. That upon this Bays being a Constable, told them, he suspected him to be his Companion, and so secur'd him also.

OBO, t17221205-5

Pincher and Neal had a previous history of 'beating People' for the unusual reason that 'the World had always frown'd upon them, and every body was happier in Life than they' (OA, 17221231),[2] and had earlier that evening assaulted and robbed one Solomon Nichols.[3] The ploy they tried on Bays, in which one robber played victim and his accomplice guaranteed his honesty, suggests that they were also practiced in tactics for outwitting law enforcers. Bays was clearly more than a match for them, both physically and in cunning; as well as keeping dogs for pursuit purposes, he proved leery of tales told by those found near crime scenes. Was he a deputy

---

2 Immediately after the Ordinary's account of Neal and Pincher comes Applebee's advertisement for the 'Just publish'd, THE History and remarkable Life of the Honourable Col. Jacques'; the condemned men's stories may have prepared buyers of the novel to find Jack's street robbery episodes all the more credible.

3 Nichols told the court 'That he went afterwards to the Hampshire Hog at Hoxton, where finding John Dickman he told him how he had been serv'd, and supposing the Persons who had robb'd him, would rob thereabouts that Night, they both went out in Search after them', and claimed to have 'assisted at the apprehending the Prisoners' (OBO, t17221205-5). Was Dickman a constable? Or perhaps known to be a thief-taker?

who had gained experience in law enforcement by serving this East London parish repeatedly?

Yet what if Pincher and Neal had *not* been staging a ploy? What sort of predicament might Richard Bays have found himself in if Pincher had, after all, been 'an honest Fellow' and the 'other Persons' who came to 'assist' had in fact been intent on robbing him? Constables did sometimes find themselves in the awkward position of holding the wrong party or having to decide between opposite versions of an event. John Thompson got Thomas Adams taken to the watch-house but the constable 'could not find ... upon the Prisoner any thing ... that the Prosecutor could swear to; and [deposed] that the Prosecutor was in Drink'; the two 'charg'd the Constable with each other' (*OBO*, t17200427-11). Flaxmore Dakins Esq. got Matthew Cheston arrested for trying to rob him at pistol point, but it turned out that the two men had been 'whipping for the Road', and that Dakins had prosecuted Cheston 'for his Impudence' (*OBO*, t17200907-41). Lower down the social scale, apprentice Edward Lee persuaded a constable to go with him to arrest William Plummer, whom he accused of stealing the peruque he had been delivering; Lee was judged to have brought a malicious prosecution, perhaps to cover up his having stolen the wig himself (*OBO*, t17220404-51). When Ann Williams prosecuted John Dorton for assaulting her and taking her gold ring, a friend of Dorton's counter-accused *her* friend of assaulting *him* and picking his pocket; although 'the Mob' took Williams's part and 'charg'd a Constable' with Dorton, the *Proceedings* journalist emphatically justified the jury's acquittal of him (*OBO*, t17220112-39).

If these verdicts were correct, we may assume that Lee and Williams were prosecuting in order to prevent others from indicting *them* and had made use of their constables' services for their own ends. Ann Parthyday's motives for calling in a constable and accusing her next-door neighbour were almost certainly venal. Two witnesses confirmed the defendant's claim that

> it was a malicious Prosecution, and that the Prosecutor arrested him for 20 s. to which he put in Bail, whereupon she said she would make a 40 l. Man of him, and swear a Robbery against him ... Phebe Peterson and another deposed that the Prosecutor made it her common practice to arrest People for small Sums to get Money of them.
>
> *OBO*, t17210301-12

Constables themselves stood to gain financially by arresting highway robbers and helping get them convicted, an activity in which they sometimes collaborated with thief-takers. Constable Richard Room and one Richard Mills apprehended mail robbers John Hawkins and George Simpson, and would have shared with informer Ralph Wilson the recently introduced statutory reward of £140 per robber (*OBO*, t17220510-3). Had Mills been brought along merely as a witness, or was he a thief-taker? At least one constable was involved in the capture of William Spigget (or Spiggot), Thomas Phillips alias Cross and William Heater. In this case the £420 reward plus the 'Money, Horses, Accoutrements, and other things which were taken from them when they were Apprehended' would have had to be shared out among many: presumably the carriers John Watkins and John Turner, whose packhorse and wagon had been held up; certainly John Merritt, who had been approached by Watkins to help find out his attackers and sounds very much like a thief-taker; possibly the boy Murrel and several others who 'dogg'd' Heater as he took the prisoners' horses to an inn in Long Acre; the innkeeper, John Rowlet, who helped set up a stake-out in his stables; 'Mr. Hill (the Constable)', and a certain John Pritchard who also participated in the capture and provided official sanction for the operation in the form of recorder's warrants obtained by Merritt (*OBO*, t17210113-43).

As we shall see, no one remotely resembling John Merritt appears alongside the constables who attempt to arrest either Moll Flanders or, more surprisingly, Colonel Jack, and in neither of their histories is there any suggestion of a pecuniary reward for apprehending and/or giving evidence against felons. Defoe's parish officers try hard to carry out their unpaid duties correctly and do so uncomplainingly, in spite of some shoddy treatment from those who call on them for help, in spite of faulty warrants and rules that would have been hard to apply in a metropolitan context, and in spite of the remarkable ability of the criminal protagonists to 'imaginatively exploit' their office (Hitchcock and Shoemaker 2015, 20). Yet, with one exception, they fail to send their thieves on to face pre-trial investigation, allowing, even facilitating, their escape from judicial process. Compared to those who appear in the *Proceedings,* Defoe's constables lead very difficult lives indeed.

4   Moll's Constables

4.1   *The Hue and Cry after Jemy*

Hue and cry, the most ancient of 'organic' strategies for apprehending felons, called for good responses from ordinary citizens and collaboration between communities (Ascari 2016, 79). It was up to the victim to alert an officer, call on

WHAT IT IS TO BE A CONSTABLE

him to raise the alarm, describe the culprit and show which way he or she had gone. Local residents were supposed to help in a pursuit as far as the parish boundary, where the task was to be handed on to those of the next parish, and so on until the hunters reached the sea (Gardiner 1710, 23–24).

This is what is meant to happen in Brickill, Bedfordshire, where Moll Flanders has come to meet and marry a prosperous City banker (185–187). Suddenly three horsemen turn up at the inn opposite, and Moll is 'frighted to Death' to see that one is her *'Lancashire* Husband', Jemy. She is relieved to see them ride off in a westerly direction, but later that evening, she and her new spouse are

> alarm'd with a great uproar in the Street, and People riding as if they had been out of their Wits, and what was it but a Hue and Cry after three Highway Men, that had rob'd two Coaches, and some other Travellers near *Dunstable* Hill, and notice had, it seems, been given, that they had been seen at *Brickill* ...
>
> MF, 147

Now 'heartily concern'd' for Jemy, Moll puts his pursuers off his trail by telling

> the People of the House, that I durst to say those were not the Persons, for I knew one of the Gentlemen to be a very honest Person, and of a good Estate in *Lancashire.*
>
> THE Constable, who came with the Hue and Cry, was immediately inform'd of this, and came over to me to be satisfy'd from my own Mouth, and I assur'd him that I saw the three Gentlemen as I was at the Window, that I saw them afterwards at the Windows of the Room they din'd in; that I saw them afterwards take Horse, and I could assure him I knew one of them to be such a Man, that he was a Gentleman of a very good Estate, and an undoubted Character in *Lancashire*, from whence I was just now upon my Journey.
>
> THE assurance with which I deliver'd this, gave the Mob Gentry a Check, and gave the Constable such Satisfaction, that he immediately sounded a Retreat, told his People these were not the Men, but that he had an account that they were very honest Gentleman, and so they went all back again ...
>
> MF, 147–148

Striking here is the enthusiasm with which the 'Mob Gentry' pursue the robbers, only to obediently turn back at the constable's countermand. Striking too is the alacrity with which Moll's affirmation of Jemy's status and honesty is referred to the officer, and how easily he is 'satisfy'd from my own Mouth'; as in the 'accused speaks' trial, direct oral testimony carries weight and character reference is decisive (Langbein 2005, 233–246). As would have been the case in court, Moll's testimonial is made all the more convincing by her assured delivery and by the circumstantial detail with which she bolsters it: she had seen the three Gentlemen arrive 'as I was at the Window', seen them later at dinner, and had–she claims–herself come 'just now' from Lancashire.

Constables' conduct books can help us understand the issues involved here. In calling off the pursuit, this officer has allowed three highwaymen to get away with a huge haul (£560 and some valuable lace), and exposed himself to a charge of permitting felons to escape, 'a Misdemeanour, for which he [a constable] may be indicted and fined' (Jacob 1720, 20). On the other hand, had he persisted and arrested a man who turned out to be a respectable landowner, he could have found himself in trouble with a social superior and incurred a £20 fine. Although in law the power of arresting felons belonged to constables *ex officio*, Welch was to advise his fellow officers that if called on to arrest persons they did not know personally they should obtain warrants from justices (1754, 17–18). That, however, would have involved delay, and constables could also be fined for not responding promptly to an alarm.

Although surviving in vestigial form in that cries of 'stop thief' or 'murder' were generally responded to (Shoemaker 2004, Chapter 2), the kind of hue and cry that relied on passing information by word of mouth fell into disuse in the eighteenth century (Herrup 1989, 71), replaced by written magistrates' warrants, newspaper advertisements and handbills that circulated widely and proved more efficacious (Styles 1989). Defoe's episode illustrates some of the weaknesses in a mechanism for catching thieves that relied on informants who could not always be trusted, and on the constable's ability to steer the difficult course between the need for rapid response, on the one hand, and extreme caution on the other.

4.2 *Rules for Searching*

In our second episode we find Moll's Governess using defence tactics of the kind Michel de Certeau attributes to indigenous peoples in their efforts to divert Spanish colonisers from their purposes:

> even when they were subjected, indeed even when they accepted their subjection, the Indians often used the laws, practices, and representations that were imposed on them by force or by fascination to ends other than those of their conquerors; they made something else out of

them; they subverted them from within – not by rejecting them or by transforming them (though that occurred as well) but by many different ways of using them in the service of rules, customs or convictions foreign to the colonization which they could not escape.

1988, 31–32

The occasion is that of the smash-and-grab attempt on a warehouse from whence Moll and her male partner have fled a hotly pursuing crowd. The young man is taken with the goods on him, but Moll, who has been operating in male disguise, manages to take refuge in her Governess's house,

> whither some quick-eyed People follow'd me so warmly as to fix me there; they did not immediately knock at the Door, by which I got time to throw off my Disguise and dress me in my own Cloths; besides, when they came there, my Governess, who had her Tale ready, kept her Door shut, and call'd out to them and told there was no Man came in there; the People affirm'd there did a Man come in there, and swore they would break open the Door.

MF, 170

The three mentions in this passage of 'the Door' – knocked on, kept shut, and liable to being broken open – call attention to the significance of this barrier separating private from public space. Had Moll's pursuers carried out their threat to break into her Governess's home they could have been accused of the misdemeanour of trespassing on – or the felony of forcible entry into – what Sir Edward Coke had called every man's 'Castle and Fortress as well for defence against injury and violence, as for his repose' (2003, I, 140). Constables, on the other hand, had *ex officio* powers to search suspected houses in order to discover felons or stolen goods and, in case of resistance, to break open those houses (Gardiner 1710, 23; 'P.S. Gent.' 1721, 92).

The Governess clearly knows the rules, but also that Moll herself would not have been protected by them: 'the house of any one is not a Castle or privilege but for himself, and shall not extend to protect any person who flieth to his house, or the goods of any other which are brought and conveyed into his house' (Coke 2003, I, 141). She now uses her knowledge to concoct what de Certeau calls a 'guileful ruse' that will stall the pursuers while apparently showing readiness to admit them:

> my Governess, not at all surpriz'd, spoke calmly to them, told them they should very freely come and search her House, if they would

> bring a Constable, and let in none but such the Constable would admit, for it was unreasonable to let in a whole Crowd; this they could not refuse, tho' they were a Crowd.
>
> MF, 170–171

The crowd cannot refuse this reasonable condition without putting themselves on the wrong side of the law. A constable is fetched and the door 'very freely open'd' to the officer, who guards it while 'the Men he appointed search'd the House, my Governess going with them from Room to Room'.

Not finding the man they think they are hunting but only a lady in *deshabille* at her needle with a little girl at her knee, the search party withdraws, offering apologies. The constable's presence has conferred official sanction on their incursion, but the time spent in fetching him has been used to allow Moll to change her clothes and stage a scene of domestic industry and innocence. In using the rules for searching to render the search itself futile, she and her Governess have successfully 'poached in' the proper space of legality and inveigled an officer of the law into presiding over a confidence trick and allowing a felon to escape detection.

4.3 A Good Substantial Kind of Man

The episode in which Defoe shows a thief most 'imaginatively exploiting the system of police' (Hitchcock and Shoemaker, 2011, 20) is the affair of the Covent Garden mercer, one to which 'there is much more than meets Moll's eye or may, at first, meet the modern reader's' (Faller 1993, 154).

Initially the attitude of the constable who has been called in to secure Moll is one of deference to the shopkeeper. He assumes that his prisoner will go to trial and that he will be giving evidence for the prosecution, as actual constables usually did, and responds to Moll's demand to know his name with a snide jest: 'I might be sure to hear of his Name when I came to the *Old Bayley*' (MF, 190). Step by step, over the series of two and three-way exchanges that follows, Moll will win the officer over to her side by making the mercer reveal, out of his own mouth, his ignorance of and lack of regard for the law, and especially for the constableship.

The mercer's first mistake is to refuse to let Moll go 'tho' he owned he could not say I was in his shop before', an admission which reveals the lack of any justification for holding her and provokes the threat that she will make herself 'amends upon him in a more legal way another time'. Worse follows as her would-be prosecutor refuses to allow her to send for 'Friends to see me have right done me' and assumes powers proper to an officer of the law:

> No, *he said*, he could give no such liberty; I might ask it when I came before the Justice of Peace, and seeing I threatn'd him, he would take care of me in the mean time, and would lodge me safe in *Newgate*; I told him it was his time now, but it would be mine by and by ...
>
> MF, 190–191

The mercer next denies Moll's request 'for Pen, Ink, and Paper', betraying a fear of a written record to which Moll responds by bidding the constable call in a porter as eyewitness. Having taken command of the situation, she stages a brilliant piece of theatre in which the mercer condemns himself out of his own mouth for violating the freedom from false arrest enshrined in Habeas Corpus:[4]

> I spoke aloud to the Master of the Shop, and said, Sir, you know in your own Conscience that I am not the Person you look for, and that I was not in your Shop before, therefore I demand that you detain me here no longer, or tell me the reason of your stopping me; the Fellow grew surlier upon this than before, and said he would do neither till he thought fit; very well, said I to the Constable and to the Porter, you will be pleas'd to remember this, Gentlemen, another time; the Porter said, *yes, Madam*, and the Constable began not to like it, and would have perswaded the Mercer to dismiss him, and let me go, since, as he said, he own'd I was not the Person ...

Defoe has the constable play an increasingly active part as the scene develops. From passively witnessing, he comes to 'not like' what he hears and to try to convince the mercer to come to terms, then to defend his independence as an officer:

> Good Sir, *says the Mercer to him Tauntingly*, are you a Justice of Peace, or a Constable? I charg'd you with her, pray do you do your Duty: The Constable told him a little mov'd, but very handsomely, *I know my*

---

[4] The Habeas Corpus Act of 1679 would have been a matter of special interest in 1722. David Hollingshead (2017, 16–17) explains that in the wake of Bishop Atterbury's plot to overthrow the king and restore the Stuart dynasty parliament had suspended the Act, and that Defoe wrote in defence of the measure: 'the "Solemnity" with which it has been undertaken ... imbues its [parliament's] decision with "Moment" and "Value," which, in turn, by Defoe's estimation, contributes to the citizenry's awareness that the Act [Habeas Corpus] "is no small Matter; no Trifle, or Thing to be trifled with"'.

> *Duty, and what I am Sir, I doubt you hardly know what you are doing*; they had some other hard words …
>
> MF, 191

Next comes physical manhandling as the journeyman tries to search Moll, who spits in his face and calls on the officer to 'take notice of my usage':

> the Constable reprov'd him decently, told him that he did not know what he did … and, says the Constable, I am afraid your Master is bringing himself and me too into Trouble, if this Gentlewoman comes to prove who she is, and where she was, and it appears that she is not Woman you pretend to …
>
> MF, 191

That constables making false arrests risked hefty fines and could also incur civil actions that could be expensive to fight had been brought to public attention in 1709, when one of a group of reforming constables attempting to arrest a woman had been killed by three soldiers. At the soldiers' trial, Chief Justice Holt ruled that 'the arrest of the woman was injurious and oppressive' and complained that 'constables nowadays make a common practice of taking up people only for walking the streets' (Shoemaker 2004, 179, 181). 'Walking the streets' is, of course, what Moll had been doing when first seized. By contrast, the two journeymen who now drag in 'the true Widow' are able to brandish material proof of her culpability: 'there's the Remnant of Sattin she stole, I took it out of her Cloaths with my own Hand', boasts Mr. Anthony. Moll meanwhile sits silently smiling, the Master turns pale, and the constable can only look to his prisoner for guidance:

> *let 'em alone Mr. Constable*, said I, *let 'em go on*; the Case was plain and could not be denied, so the Constable was charg'd with the right Thief …
>
> MF, 192

At this point the mercer tries to get out of the mess he has created only to reveal all the more clearly his ignorance of who may do what in the name of the law:

> he told me there was no occasion to go before the Justice now, I was at liberty to go where I pleased, and so calling to the Constable told him, he might let me go, for I was discharg'd; the Constable said calmly to him, Sir, you ask'd me just now, whether I was a Constable

> or a Justice, and bad me do my Duty, and charg'd me with this Gentlewoman as a Prisoner; now, Sir, I find you do not understand what is my Duty, for you would make me a Justice indeed; but I must tell you it is not in my Power: I may keep a Prisoner when I am charg'd with him, but 'tis the Law and the Magistrate alone that can discharge that Prisoner; therefore 'tis a mistake, Sir, I must carry her before a Justice now, whether you think well of it or not: The Mercer was very high with the Constable at first; but the Constable happening to be not a hir'd Officer, but a good Substantial kind of Man, I think he was a Corn-chandler, and a Man of good Sense, stood to his Business, would not discharge me without going to a Justice of the Peace; and I insisted on it too.
>
> MF, 192–193

From the start the mercer has assumed that he can order the constable about, perhaps that he is dealing with a poor man deputising for a richer parishioner like himself – a point on which Moll sets us right. As a 'good Substantial kind of Man', the corn chandler is the mercer's social and economic equal, and in knowledge of civic rights and duties he is very much his superior.[5] This Defoe drives home when the mercer rudely addresses the officer as 'Fellow' and tells him to 'go about ... [his] Business', only to receive further instruction in 'what it is to be a Constable':

> Sir ... you have broken the Peace in bringing an honest Woman out of the Street, when she was about her lawful Occasion, confining her in your Shop, and ill using her by your Servants ... I think I am civil to you in not commanding or charging you in the King's Name to go with me, and charging every Man I see, that passes your Door, to aid and assist me in carrying you by Force, this you cannot but know I have power to do ...
>
> MF, 193

Worse follows when the constable enjoins the journeyman to go with him before the justice:

---

5 As he would know from Giles Jacob (1720, 21) a constable 'may discharge any person arrested on Suspicion of Felon only, where no Felony is committed; but if a Felony be actually committed he cannot justify the discharging him, tho' he knew that the Party is innocent; but it must be done by due Course of Law, otherwise it will be an Escape'.

> THE Fellow look'd like a condemn'd Thief, and hung back, then look'd at his Master, as if he cou'd help hm, and he, like a Fool, encourag'd the Fellow to be rude, and he truly resisted the Constable, and push'd him back with a good Force when he went to lay hold on him, at which the Constable knock'd him down, and call'd out for help, and immediately the Shop was fill'd with People, and the Constable seiz'd the Master and Man, and all his Servants.
>
> MF, 193

The arrest proves a popular one with the 'Mob of about 500 People ... and especially the Women' who follow the officer and his charges to the justice, pelting the mercer with dirt and forcing him to have a coach called. So, Moll somewhat comically puts it, 'we Rode the rest of the way, the Constable and I, and the Mercer and his Man' (*MF*, 194). The pairing of the four main actors neatly expresses the odd alliance between shoplifter and officer, temporarily united against two tradesmen who have got themselves on the wrong side of the law while trying to use its representative against a thief who knows more than they do about what constables, and indeed ordinary citizens, 'ought legally to do. And ... What they ought to avoid, as not warrantable' (P.S. Gent. 1721, A2r).

5   A Faithful Officer Humiliated

In the last of our episodes, we meet a constable truly enmeshed in the intricacies of his office and discover that even a justice's warrant did not necessarily protect the officer trying to execute it. P.S. Gent. (1721, 86–89) dedicated whole chapters to the penal responsibilities that could be incurred in executing a warrant issued by a magistrate 'for a Matter out of his Jurisdiction' and/or 'where he is no Judge of the Causes', one 'not specifying the Cause', or one in which 'a Mistake by the names agreeing may run him into taking the wrong Party'.

Defoe dramatises the last of these risks in the episode that follow Jack's nightmare about constables at his door. Jack wakes from his disturbed night to learn from his brother, the Captain, that Will has been impeached by a member of their gang and is in Newgate. 'Extreamly alarmed', he prepares to leave London, but before he can do so disaster strikes:

> going cross *Rosemary-Lane*, by the End of the Place, which is call'd *Rag-Fair*, I heard one call *Jack*, he had said something before, which I did not

> hear, but upon hearing the name *Jack*, I look'd about me, and immediately saw three Men, and after them a Constable coming towards me with great Fury; I was in a great Surprize, and started to run, but one of them clap'd in upon me, and got hold of me, and in a Moment the rest surrounded me, and I was taken, I ask'd them what they wanted, and what I had done; they told me it was no Place to talk of that there; but show'd me their Warrant, and bad me read it, and I should know the rest when I came before the Justice, so they hurried me away.
>
> I took the Warrant, but to my great Affliction, I could know nothing by it, for I could not read, so I desir'd them to read it, and they read it that they were to Apprehend a known Thief, that went by the Name of one of the three *Jacks* of *Rag-Fair* for that he was charg'd upon Oath, with having been a Party in a notorious Robbery, Burglary, and Murther, committed so and so, in such a Place, and on such a Day.[6]
>
> CJ, 127–128

The constable and his helpers show scrupulous respect for the proprieties: the busy and none too respectable streets around Rosemary Lane are no 'Place to talk' of what Jack has or has not done, and they are not in any case the ones to explain. Defoe does not tell us where the proper place is, but early readers would have taken it for granted that it will be the parlour of the home of the nearest active justice.

Even though he had not actually been 'out' with the gang on the night of the fatal robbery, Jack is now certain that he is bound for Newgate and the gallows. Luckily for him the justice before whom he is brought is willing to hear his side of the story and meticulous in his respect for prisoners' rights. His rigorous cross-questioning of Jack and the constable is presented in the form of a long drawn-out 'trialogue' (Faller 1993, 150):

> the Justice ask'd me my Name; but, hold, *says he,* young Man, before I ask you your Name, let me do you Justice, you are not bound to answer

---

6 Defoe seems to have changed his mind about when Jack learned to read, for he had earlier had him tell the reader that he had done so by the age of 10 (*CJ*, 64). Giuseppe Sertoli (1999, 65) has systematically examined more disconcerting inconsistencies in the chronology of *Colonel Jack*, suggesting that they are 'segni di una scrittura in movimento, di un modo di narrare che "si fa" man mano che procede, attraverso continue modifiche, correzioni di rotta – e che lascia dietro di sé tracce evidenti, seppure enigmatiche e spesso equivoche, del suo incerto e avventuroso cammino.'

till your Accusers come, so turning to the Constable, he ask'd for his Warrant.

WELL, *says the Justice*, you have brought this young Man here by Vertue of this Warrant; is this young Man the Person for whom the Warrant is granted?

Con. I believe so, and please your Worship.

Just. Believe so. Why are you not sure of it?

Con. An't please your Worship, the People said so, where I took him.

Just. It is a very particular kind of Warrant, it is to apprehend a young Man, who goes by the Name of *Jack*, but no Sir Name, only that it is said, he is call'd Capt. *Jack*, or some other such Name. Now young Man, pray is your Name Capt. *Jack*? or are you usually call'd so?

I presently found, that the Men that took me knew nothing of me, and that the Constable had taken me up by Hear-say, so I took Heart and told the Justice, that I thought with submission, that it was not the present Question, what my Name was, but what these Men, or anyone else had to lay to my Charge, whether I was the Person, who the Warrant empower'd to Apprehend.

HE smil'd, 'tis very true young Man, *says he*, it is very true, and on my Word if they have taken you up, and do not know you, and there is no Body to Charge you, they will be mistaken to their own Damage.

CJ, 128–129

Defoe here has the justice draw attention to the difference between 'believing' that a person is the one mentioned in a warrant and being 'sure of it', indirectly reminding readers that the arrest of a person not known personally could lead to an action for false imprisonment. To avoid this, P.S. (1721, 86) advised that

> If a Warrant be brought to a Constable his safest Way is to charge the Party making the Plaint to assist him in the King's Name, and shew him the Party or Parties mentioned in the Warrant, unless himself be well acquainted with him or them, lest a Mistake by the Names agreeing may run him into an Error in taking the wrong Party.

In London, with its large and fluctuating population, constables must often have received warrants to arrest persons with whom they were *not* 'well acquainted', and unless called quickly to the scene of a crime it must have been difficult to get the 'Party making the Plaint' to identify a suspect (see Hurl-Eamon 2005, 468). In this instance it turns out that that 'Party' is

George, the gang member who had snitched on Will and is himself being held in gaol, so that the constable has had to trust the word of local men who think they know who is meant by 'a known Thief, that went by the Name of one of the three *Jacks* of *Rag-Fair*'. It is the worse for the officer that 'Hear-say' was by this time coming to be distrusted in legal as well as in other contexts (Langbein 2005, 179), but surprising that the illiterate Jack is able to spot that it is unreliable as a basis for an arrest.

No less surprising is the fact that Jack is helped by the magistrate to make out other weaknesses in procedure. The justice has drawn attention to the lack of any 'Sir name' in the sloppily worded warrant, and also reads aloud the part that includes the crucial 'something' which Jack had not heard in Rosemary Lane and which the constable had omitted when reading the document aloud: the appellative that reveals that the arrest order had been meant not for the Colonel but for his brother the Captain. The constable had clearly not registered the importance of 'Additions', as noticed by Giles Jacob (1720, 54) in warning officials that taking 'another of the same Name' but with a different title constituted a wrongful arrest.

Safe now in his knowledge of the mistake, Jack insists on his accuser being brought to confront him, and George is brought in fetters from gaol; he does not recognize Jack and says so, at which point the justice returns to grilling the officer:

> VERY good, Mr. Constable, *says the Justice*, What must we do now?
>
> I AM surpriz'd, *says the Constable*, I was at such a House, naming the House, and this young Man went by, the People cryed out there's *Jack*, that's your Man, and these People run after him, and apprehended him.
>
> WELL, *says the Justice*, and have these People any thing to say to him? can they prove that he is the Person?
>
> ONE said no, and the other said no; and in short they all said no, Why then said the *Justice*, what can be done? The young Man must be Discharg'd; and I must tell you, Mr. Constable, and you Gentlemen that have brought him hither, he may give you Trouble, if he thinks fit for your being so rash; but look you young Man, *says the Justice*, you have no great Damage done you, and the Constable, tho' he has been Mistaken, had no ill-design, but to be Faithful to his Office; I think you may pass it by.
>
> CJ, 130

Unsurprisingly, Jack has no desire to 'give ... Trouble' by suing his apprehenders but insists that they 'go back to the Place where they had insulted me, and Declare publickly there that I was honourably acquitted, and that I was not the Man ... and so we came all away good Friends, and I was clear'd with Triumph' (*CJ*, 130).

Once again, an oddly jolly conclusion. Like Moll's alliance with her constable, Jack's blossoming friendship with his apprehenders is founded on an equivocation, for he too is no innocent. He may not be guilty of the burglary and murder for which he has been arrested, but he *had* committed several highway robberies and he is lucky that – as it later turns out – George had not been one of the two who had been with him and Will that night. He is also fortunate in that George is honest enough not to accuse him falsely, as did some arrested thieves attempting to save their lives. Like those duped by Moll and her Governess, Jack's constable and his assistants end up as the thief's victims. The officer and his posse may have been 'rash' in seizing the first 'Jack' they come across, but they have been subjected to close interrogation and reproof by a magistrate, put in fear of a lawsuit and sent back to a busy commercial street to publicly confess to their community that they had wrongfully arrested a local inhabitant. For the officer, especially, the shame thus incurred would have been grim reward for being – rather too ardently – 'Faithful to his Office'.

In an interesting coda to this episode, Jack reports the justice as having complimented him on 'well managing of [his] ... own Defence', and refers us back to an earlier passage in his history: that in which he had laid claim to 'a natural Talent of talking ... to the purpose' and illustrated it by telling of an occasion on which he had been wrongly accused and 'defended ... [him] self by Argument, proving the Mistakes of my Accusers, and how they contradicted themselves' (*CJ*, 64). In the scene we have just discussed, Jack has indeed demonstrated his 'Talent of talking', but made to feel himself deficient in another respect: 'I resolv'd if it was possible I would learn to Read and Write, that I would not be such an incapable Creature, that I should not be able to read a Warrant, and see whether I was the Person to be Apprehended or not (*CJ*, 130). Years later, in Virginia, under the influence of his 'Tutor', Jack will read morally and culturally edifying books, but the first of the uses of literacy advocated in this novel is purely practical and absolutely vital for a thief: the ability to make out an arrest warrant.

6   Conclusion

In making Jack ashamed of his illiteracy Defoe pinpoints a specific manifestation of the need for information and guidance which J. Paul Hunter sees as having driven the young, urban and mobile population of seventeenth- and eighteenth-century England to learn to read (1990, Chapter 3). In 1582 William Lambarde could assume that his parish officers could read his manual and copy out testimonials (Ascari 2016, 80). A hundred or so years later many of those waiting to be tried for capital offences, among them a high proportion of skilled artisans, apprentices and journeymen, many of them migrants and all desirous of a better life, would have been among the 'new readers' for whom the print industry supplied news, ideologically orientated narratives – and guide books (Hunter 1990, Part 3; Linebaugh 2006, Chapter 3).

Constable's manuals were not, of course, written to aid the accused or those vulnerable to arrest, yet for de Certeau reading can be a form of 'poaching', 'invent[ing]' in texts something different from what they 'intended" (2011, 133). The *Old Bailey Proceedings* and the Ordinary's *Account*, though intended for a middling sort public of the kind to which potential victims, prosecutors and officials belonged, were thought to have also circulated in gaols and been used by prisoners or by their much disparaged 'Newgate attorneys' to prepare for trial (Shoemaker 2008a).[7] The guidance offered to constables by Henry Care, Robert Gardiner, P.S. Gent., Giles Jacob and others on how to 'safely' carry out their duties, could also have been read against the grain for hints on 'errors' that could be exploited to block or prevent an arrest, a search, a prosecution. In the fictional episodes we have discussed Moll, her Governess and Jack do just those things, manipulating officers of law into taking *their* sides against would-be prosecutors who have called on them for help. If early novels took over many of the functions fulfilled by what Hunter calls their 'pre-texts', among them guide books, they may also have taught a minority of readers more than their authors would have wished.

The fictions attributed to Defoe may have had other unintended effects. The constables we meet in *Moll Flanders* and *Colonel Jack* differ markedly from the feeble and corrupt stereotypes of rogue literature and satirical plays of early modern England. They may be rather credulous, but they are conscientious, honest and fair-minded men of good sense, faithful to their office and, considering the many and complex rules and regulations they were expected to apply, well-informed. If they almost always fail in the exercise of their duties, it is not so much because of personal failings but because their antago-

---

7 W.J. Sheehan (1977, 237) found that in Newgate 'Law books were ... popular reading and prisoners pored over these volumes in order to prepare the defences, often with the help of law students preparing for the bar'.

nists, driven by desperate needs, manage to identify weaknesses in the system which the 'Parish Drudge' was forced to serve with 'neither Profit nor Pleasure therein, but an inconceivable Fatigue' (Defoe 1727, 17). In offering sympathetic portraits of civic officials who, for all their efforts, prove no match for criminals, Defoe may have helped undermine an already weakening trust in amateur law enforcement and reinforced the trend towards professionalisation that, by the end of the century, would cause the traditional English constable to disappear from the streets of London.

It would be unfair to leave Defoe's constables at that however. They do *almost* always fail in their duties, but if the constable who so terrifies Moll Flanders in the first of my epigraphs to this chapter had given way to her pleadings and allowed 'an escape', his prisoner would never have moved on to the next room along the judicial corridor.

CHAPTER 7

Before the Justice

1   Introduction

The second of my chapters on the intricacies of office enters fully into the formal process of the law: preliminary, pre-trial hearings before justices of the peace. Defoe must have thought these of great interest to his readers, for he dramatises one such hearing fully in *Colonel Jack* (see Chapter 6 above), and in *Moll Flanders* two fully and another three in summary. Some of his readers would have had experience of accusing, or being accused by, someone of at least some petty crime, a few even as magistrates, others as spectators. Even those who did not may well have been curious about occasions on which ordinary citizens came into direct contact with and were examined by officers of the law who could help resolve conflicts in the community but also had the authority to send to prison and to assign certain punishments. As we shall see, the *Proceedings* are of little help in illuminating what went on at this phase of law enforcement, but they may have stimulated curiosity about how those in the dock at the Old Bailey came to be there. Before looking at contemporary sources, however, it will be useful, as in the case of constables, to briefly survey the history of the office of justice of the peace, focusing especially on the changes that were taking place during the long eighteenth century.

2   Justicing Business

'Men of ample Fortunes who administered the communities in which they resided' is how Norma Landau describes the later Stuart and early Hanoverian 'peculiarly English' model of justices of the peace, one which distinguished them from the continental European 'salaried functionaries who took office "that they may eat Bread" and governed those whom they have never seen before.'[1] Created by statute in the reign of Edward III 'to hear and determine felonies and trespasses done against the peace', the office, like

---

1 Landau 1984, 1, quoting from T. Barlow, *The Justice of Peace: A Treatise Containing the Power and Duty of that Magistrate* (London 1745, vii–viii). Stipendiary magistrates were not introduced in England until 1792.

that of the constable, was transformed over the following centuries as the powers of magistrates 'were continually extended by statute not only with the expansion of the criminal law but also with the creating of a wide range of new administrative responsibilities' (Shoemaker 2008b, 20). These would have included such sensitive issues as rating assessments, the application of settlement laws, granting alehouse licences, appointment of parish officials and binding out of pauper children as apprentices (Paley 1991, xxii–xxv). On the law enforcement front, most of a seventeenth- and eighteenth-century justice's time would have been taken up with adjudicating – either alone or in session with one or two other justices – misdemeanours. This loosely defined category included

> some property offences (theft, fraud, trespass), significant numbers of vice offences (keeping a disorderly or unlicensed alehouse, prostitution, gambling), regulatory offences (neglect of office, failure to repair highway, selling goods underweight), poor law offences (idleness, vagrancy, bastardy) and offences against the peace (riot, assault, defamation).
> SHOEMAKER 2008b, 6

Ruth Paley, editor of the sentencing notebook kept during the 1730s by the Hackney J.P., Henry Norris, comments that to read through its entries

> is to be left in no doubt of the unrelenting tedium of a justice's criminal business, made up as it was of an apparently interminable succession of assaults, occasionally enlivened by a few broken windows, the theft of the washerwoman's laundry or the arrival of an unlicensed pedlar.
> 1991, xvii

Paley estimates Norris's justicing business to have taken up between one and a half and three days a week. In making himself available to complainants and performing his duties meticulously, he was unusual, one of only six very active members out of a commission of seventy-eight (Paley 1991, xxx). The flight from office which affected the constabulary during the long eighteenth century hit the magistracy, especially that of London, even more severely. Although large numbers of new justices were nominated at intervals, many of those nominated neglected to take out the writ of *dedimus potestam* that authorised them to act, and of those that did, many simply neglected to attend sessions or listen to complaints (Beattie 1986, 59–60 and 2001, 102). Shoemaker finds that of those on the London and Middlesex commissions in the late seventeenth and early eighteenth centuries 'only a fraction ... actually heard judicial business' (2008b, 70). By the late 1720s the whole of the City's judicial business was being dealt with by just three magistrates, and when the last of the three died, in 1737, a rotation system was hurriedly set up, in effect giving birth to the first regular magistrates' court (Beattie 2001, 108).

Beattie suggests a number of reasons for the withdrawal by London's merchant class from services they had provided for centuries (2001, 98–102). They may have been reluctant to associate in sessions with political antagonists, while crowded court calendars, more intense parliamentary service, and the growing complexity of commercial and financial dealings were demanding more of their time and attention. Their increased wealth and polite lifestyle may also have 'so widened the social divide that the task of dealing with the petty conflicts of the poor, with misdemeanors and minor thefts, became more distasteful to aldermen as well as time-consuming'. Then again,

> the work of the magistrates may have become more complex, perhaps more difficult, or uncomfortable ... Rewards and pardons introduced complexity, and forced magistrates to make more choices and to become more engaged in the details of offences than in the past: the corruption and malicious prosecution that massive rewards gave rise to could only have made the work of magistrates nastier and messier.

Fear of litigation may also have been a factor. De Veil's posthumously published *Observations on the Practice of a Justice of the Peace* (1747) warned 'such GENTLEMEN as design to Act for *Middlesex,* or *Westminster*' against a whole series of pitfalls, among them adjudicating cases in which he had no authority:

> *Old Bailey Solicitors* &c. make it their Business to entangle him in Difficulties, and do very often bring Matters before him in a most courteous Manner, and use the most plausible Arguments, to induce him to act in a Thing, which they at the same time know is only cognizable in the *Courts in Westminster-Hall*: But whenever they prevail, they immediately cause an Action to be brought against the Justice for concerning himself, where he had no Jurisdiction.
> 3–4

A manual of 1730 cited by Landau (1984, 354) warned metropolitan justices that 'though Men of Commanding Fortunes may be above the Lawes, we have

Instances of some others, in the Commission, who have had Actions brought against them and have paid very dear for their mistakes'.[2]

Even when there was no design to entrap, justices must often have been perplexed as to the right course of action:

> Many apparently straightforward entries actually raised quite difficult issues. The most obvious one was the classification of an offence. It was the justice's duty to effect reconciliation wherever possible, except in cases of felony, for compounding a felony was, in itself a serious crime. Unfortunately the difference between a felony and a misdemeanour was not always obvious.
> PALEY 1991, xxviii

The distinction was crucial, for in dealing with misdemeanours justices were allowed wide discretion and could and did exercise their personal preferences. Shoemaker found that his seventy-one active J.P.s could be divided into 'three ideal types' according to how they dealt with petty crime. 'Mediating justices' tended to encourage accuser and accused to settle out of court, while 'law and order' justices tended to encourage accusers to prosecute by indictment, or to consign defendants directly to houses of correction for immediate punishment, while 'social control justices … used the judicial system to attempt to reform the morals of the lower classes', either by binding over or committing to a house of correction (2008b, 228–231).[3] Henry Norris clearly belongs to the first type, for his 'main con-

---

2 Like those for constables, justices's manuals proliferated from the sixteenth century on. Paley suggests that Norris may have used William Nelson's *The Office and Authority of a Justice of Peace* or Nathaniel Blackerby's *The Justice of the Peace his Companion* (1723). According to Norma Landau (1984, Chapter 11) the standard advice book for Elizabethan and early Stuart justices had been William Lambarde's *Eirenarcha* (1581); this was ousted by Michael Dalton's *Country Justice* (1619). From 1755 the authoritative manual was Richard Burn's *The Office of the Justice of the Peace and Parish Officer*, which Landau sees as having replaced the late Stuart 'patriarchal' model justice as natural leader of his community with a 'patrician' one of a distant governor, 'merely part of the legal apparatus'. Justices would also have sought advice from their clerks, who drew up warrants, recognisances and documents consigning suspects to prison.
3 On the frequency with which early modern magistrates, especially those appointed for the City of London, exercised summary justice and committed accused persons directly to Bridewell, see Dabhoiwala 2006.

cern ... was to persuade the parties concerned to make up their quarrel or to compound the offence' (Paley 1991, xxxi). Similarly, in County Durham, the Reverend Edmund Tew dealt with over 1,000 cases between 1750 and 1764, but only twenty-one of these came to trial (Morgan and Rushton 2000). Instead D'Oyley Michel and Isaac Tillard, two Middlesex justices whom we shall run into a little later, advocated 'commitment to houses of correction over other procedures'.[4]

Strictly speaking, felonies could not be dealt with in any of these three ways. John Beattie (1986, 270–271) explains:

> How they were to proceed against accused felons was still largely governed in the eighteenth century by statutes of 1554 and 1555 that together required them to take depositions of the victim and his witnesses in writing and to examine the accused and reduce his statement also to writing. At the conclusion of this enquiry, the magistrate was required to grant the accused bail or commit him to jail. ... The Tudor magistrates were not being asked to act impartially and judicially, to investigate and dispose of the case as they thought the facts warranted, committing some accused to trial and discharging others. Indeed they were clearly forbidden to discharge anyone brought before them accused of committing a felony. All suspects were to go on to trial, and the magistrate's task was to ensure that they got there and that the strongest evidence of their guilt would be contained in the depositions and examination that they were required to send in to the court. In the Marian procedure the magistrate was more a policeman than a judge; he was charged to assemble a prosecuting brief that would stiffen and supplement the case presented orally by the victim-prosecutor in court. He was not actually forbidden to report information that was in the prisoner's favor, but nor was he expected to search for such evidence 'as maketh against the king,' in Michael Dalton's phrase.

In theory the prohibition on discharging those accused of felonies remained in place until well into the eighteenth century, but in practice, Beattie shows (1986, 274), 'a remarkable change' was taking place in this period:

---

[4] Shoemaker 2008b, 231n; but see also 226, where Michel is included among mediating justices and 70, where Tillard is grouped with reforming justices who prosecuted vice cases by recognisance.

the magistrate's examination ceased being simply a means of assembling the best evidence against the prisoner and took on some of the characteristics of a judicial hearing. Magistrates began to feel more obligation to makes some assessment of the evidence being presented and to assume more right to dismiss the charges when they thought the case too weak to justify a trial.

By the 1750s Henry Fielding was asserting justices's right to dismiss, but some were assuming it in practice a good deal earlier. In the 1730s Henry Norris discharged three men accused of horse-stealing, and in the case of a woman accused of another capital felony 'was clearly instrumental in persuading the prosecutor to drop charges' (Paley 1991, xxviii–xxix). Sir Richard Brocas, Lord Mayor of the City of London for the year 1729–1730, dismissed over half of the ninety-two felony charges brought before him between that date and his death in 1737, 'most commonly in cases in which the accused had been charged merely on 'suspicion' of committing the offence' (Beattie 2001, 106). Brocas did not throw out *all* charges made on suspicion, so Beattie deduces that

> There must, therefore, have been a hearing – a form of enquiry into the nature and strength of the evidence that supported the prosecutor's belief in the defendant's guilt. And it is clear that such an enquiry, such testing of the evidence, allowed defendants to bring testimony of their own to counter the suspicion they were under. It is the holding of an enquiry – an enquiry that might end in defendants under suspicion being discharged or sent to trial – that seems to be new, going as it did far beyond the procedure envisaged by the Marian legislation and beyond the practices followed in the 1690s.

It is not possible to compare Brocas's record directly with those of the four aldermen who held the office of Lord Mayor between 1720 and 1722,[5] and the *Proceedings* throw little light on what went on at the pre-trial stage, but that little, read alongside some of the many justices's working documents that have survived and been digitalised for the *London Lives* archive, allow us

---

5 Their terms of office fall within the twenty-three-year period for which the charge books are missing.

glimpses of early 1720s justices examining informants and defendants according to patterns rather different from those imagined by Defoe.

3   London Magistrates at Work, 1720–1722

Of just under two thousand reports of cases heard at the Old Bailey between 1720 and 1722, only one hundred and fifty-four explicitly mention justices, usually as part of the phrase 'before the justice'. Victims who wanted to press charges were not obliged to take their complaints to magistrates; they could go directly to the grand jury or a sitting court to get indictments drawn up and arrest warrants issued, but during the time needed to get this done a suspect could escape (Paley 1991, xvi). Eighteenth-century readers of the *Proceedings* would have assumed that even where justices were not mentioned most of those indicted would have come to the Old Bailey via that route. They would also have known that the very fact of a trial taking place meant that the justice had not discharged the accused, exercised summary jurisdiction, merely bound her or him over to keep the peace or be on good behaviour, or mediated a settlement between accused and victim. They would assume that the magistrate had carried out his statutory obligation to 'examine all suspected felons brought before them, together with their accusers, and to provide written summaries of these examinations to the clerk of the court' (https://www.londonlives.org/static/PS.jsp).

Many of these summaries have survived and can be usefully compared with the reports on the Old Bailey trials for which they served as preparation. These manuscripts would not, of course, have been publicly accessible in the 1720s, but some of the hearings they document – especially those held in the Guildhall by the Lord Mayors of the City – were open to those interested. This section looks at a few of the justices' working documents relating to men and women charged with picking pockets and shoplifting between January 1720 and December 1722. Although they do not offer a solid basis for comparison with what happens before justices in Defoe, for they tell us nothing about magistrates discharging prisoners or taking one of the softer options open to them, they do offer insight into what his thieves fear so dreadfully as they are dragged before justices, and what their sterner prosecutors would have been hoping for.

For three of these cases, we can draw fairly clear outlines of what took place during pre-trial examinations. On 7 September 1720, 'Henry Emmery of St. Andrew Undershaft, was indicted for privately stealing 4 pair of Pistols value 14 l. a Musquetoon, value 1 l. and other Goods, out of the Shop of Francis Smart, on the 2d of June last' (*OBO*, t17200907-16). At the trial Smart, at that time gunmaker to the Hudson's Bay Company,[6] 'deposed that his Shop had been robb'd several times', so he may have been eager for a conviction and probably complained in those terms to D'Oyly Michel when he took Emmery before him on 27 July 1720. It is not stated that he was accompanied by the two witnesses he produced in court: Charles Biew, the Southwark pawnbroker who had lent Emmery twenty-five shillings on 'two pair of ... [Smart's] Pistols',[7] and Robert Garrard, the apprentice or journeyman who identified 'the Pistols produced in Court' as 'his Master's (the Prosecutor's) and lost out of his Shop'. The only record of the hearing to survive is the 'Examinacon and confession' of Emmery himself, 'Who Saith that about five weeks agoe he did feloniously Steal out of the Shop of Frances Smart Gunmaker living in Leaden Hall street London One pair of Pistols capt with Silver value five Pounds or thereabouts' (*LL*, LMSLPS150310090). The confession is signed by Michel and by 'Emery', and witnessed by 'Fran Smart' and by 'Pidgeon'. The latter was almost certainly acting as clerk to Michel and was probably an attorney;[8] it would have been he who made the summaries and sent them to the clerk of the court, and who also drew up a *mittimus* for the constable who was to take Emmery to gaol to await trial.

When it came on, about six weeks later, Smart, Biew and Garrard must have repeated their evidence, and Emmery's succinct confession, which the *Proceedings* misleadingly describe as 'very full', was 'read in Court'. The accused man apparently did not retract his confession in court and is reported by the journalist to have had 'nothing to say for himself'. If he had been very alert or had had legal advice, he might have pointed out contradictions in the prosecution case: he had confessed to stealing only *one* pair of pistols, not to the *two* pairs Smart said he 'heard of' at the pawnbrokers, never mind the

---

6 In October 2001 'A Fine And Rare Pair Of 16-Bore Flintlock Fowling-Pieces' signed 'F. Smart. Londini. Fecit' and dating from about 1715 was sold at Christie's for £10,575; guns apparently came from 'the family armoury of the Earls of Dunmore, Dunmore Park, Stirlingshire'; the second Earl, John Murray, was one of the commanders of the British army at the siege of Vigo in 1719; https://www.christies.com/en/lot/lot-3103161e.
7 Biew's pawnshop, the Katherine Wheel, was in Blackman Street, 'the southern portion of the main thoroughfare in Southwark, which is now commonly referred to as the High Street or Borough High Street' (Rothwell, 2022).
8 The 'Examinacon and Confession' of Thomas Bates taken before Samil Perry, another Middlesex justice, was 'Attested by R Pidgeon' on 23 January 1719 (*LL*, LMSMPS501750021), and on 12 May 1722 'Mr. Pidgeon Sollicitor' spoke for an absent prosecutor (*LL* LMSMPS502-030008).

BEFORE THE JUSTICE 133

*fou*r listed – together with 'a Musquetoon ... and other Goods' – in the indictment. Henry Emmery was found guilty and, along with nine others, sentenced to death, a result Smart must have known was likely when he chose to accuse him of a felony before a justice. But then he would also have known that most death sentences were not carried out, and since Emmery's name does not appear in any Ordinary's *Account*, he may have received some kind of pardon.

My second example reveals the background to the trial held on 13 January 1721 in which coachman William Howard prosecuted Peter de Plosh for privately stealing on 16 December 'a pair of Gloves, a Hat, an Iron Tobacco-Box and 3 s. 9 d. in Money, from ... [his] Person ... as he lay asleep on a Butcher's Stall between 2 and 3 a Clock the Morning' (*OBO*, t17210113-5). Howard's first witness must have been a constable: 'Werrey deposed that the Prisoner was a Common Disturber was making a Noise in the Street, had threatned to set his Uncle's House on Fire, and he was sent for to secure him, who threatning him, he search'd him for fear he should have any Pistols in his Pocket, and found the Prosecutor's Box there.' The second was evidently one of the J.P.s sitting with the judges on the bench: 'The Justice deposed that one Tyler confest before him that the Prisoner and himself pickt a Man's Pocket on a Butcher's Stall in Bishopsgate-Street, and that the Prisoner was brought before him for threatning to set his Uncle's House on Fire.' The justice in question must have been Isaac Tillard, like Michel a Middlesex magistrate living in Tower division (*LL*, LMSMPS501920042). He may have used his power of summary jurisdiction to confine de Plosh to a house of correction, as was his habit (Shoemaker, 2008, 225, 231, 270). De Plosh was not accused of a felony until 31 December, when William Tyler, a Brick Lane weaver, told Justice Tillard on oath that 'on ~~Sunday~~ Saturday the 17th day of this Instant December'[9] he had been with de Plosh from 7 o'clock in the evening until 2 or 3 in the morning, that they had seen a man sleeping on a butcher's stall and that de Plosh had 'goe to him and Search his Briches

---

9   This date differs from the one indicated in the indictment as it was reported – 16 January – which in 1720 fell on a Friday. I tend to think Tyler was right, but in the – as yet lawyer-free trial – such discrepancies, even if noticed, would not have helped the accused. On 23 January 1719 James Stratton had been examined by City justice Sir John Fryer, and informed him 'on Oath' that 'one whose name he understands now is Thos Butler, abt Clark abt Smith' had picked his pocket eighteen months earlier (*LL*, LMSLPS150310029); at his trial Butler called attention to the fact that the date of the theft sworn to before the justice differed from that in the indictment, but he was nevertheless convicted and sentenced to death (*OBO*, t17200303-30).

Pockett and as soon as ever he had done it told him the Said William Tyler he had taken out of the Said mans Pockett two pence half Penny and an Iron Tobacco Box Showing the Same unto him' (*LL,* LMSLPS150320005). From this it appears that, contrary to Tillard's deposition at trial, Tyler did *not* confess to taking any active part in the theft or to sharing in any of the miserable pickings taken from the sleeping man's pocket. The more valuable items listed in the indictment make their appearance only on 4 January, when William Howard gave Justice Tillard his sworn version of what happened that night (*LL,* LMSLPS150320007), a version which is compatible with Tyler's – *except* for the addition of the extra money, the gloves ('value Six pence') and the silver-laced hat ('value at two shillings and six pence'), additions which pushed the total value of the articles stolen up to nearly seven shillings and made the theft a capital offence. On the same day Tillard issued recognisances obliging Howard, Charles Boon, William Tyler and his wife Mary to appear 'at the next General Gaol Delivery of Newgate and prosecute and give Evidence with Effect against Peter de La Plosh'. Howard and Boon were bound over on sureties of £40 each; the Tylers seem to have been in prison already ('pred TextorSun Penalimprisnamt'), which suggests that the couple had been apprehended for some other felony and that William had accused de Plosh in order to earn himself immunity from prosecution (*LL,* LMSLPS150320009).

No one comes out of this story well. De Plosh may have been a hooligan, and his uncle, the constable and the J.P. were no doubt glad to have him off the streets of Bishopsgate, but the transportation sentence he received was hardly justified by his theft of two-pence halfpenny and an iron tobacco box. Howard almost certainly perjured himself in beefing up the quantity and value of the things taken, and worse still, so did Justice Tillard in deposing that Tyler had confessed at examination to taking part in the theft; the *Proceedings* do not mention Tyler as giving evidence, but he may have done, perhaps tailoring his story to earn his immunity.

The case City magistrate John Lade Esq. had to prepare for the Old Bailey in January 1722 was also messy. On the 14th of the month John Syddal (spelt 'Siddal' in the *Proceedings*), a cutler trading on London Bridge, brought before him Thomas Yeomans and Sussannah Court. Lade's clerk recorded Syddal as swearing that he had been robbed of 'six groce of Bath Mettall Rings and four dozen of Belt Locks', that he suspected Yeomans, 'a seaman like man' and believed Court, who had been 'pretending to buy a Thimble', to have been 'privy to the stealing thereof' (*LL,* LMSLPS150330009). The woman would have been the 'Susan Coats Spinster, alias Barret, Widow, alias Winter, Wife of Reynolds Winter', who with Sarah Smith had been stopped when trying to sell zinc-copper alloy rings to a Mr. Wass.[10] Examining the two of them, Justice Lade had it recorded that Yeomans claimed to have found the rings, while Court denied having been in the shop, but owned to going with Smith 'to Export the Rings to sale and farther saith not but refuse to signe this Examination' (*LL*, LMSLPS150330009). Lade bound Syddal over to prosecute both on the £40 surety of Francis Clark (*LL*, LMSLPS150330017). By the time the trial came on, however, Yeomans had got his indictment dropped by 'discovering' Susan Coats's husband. On 30 January he was back before Lade 'being duly Examined at his own request' and confessing 'upon his oath' that 'He and Reynold Winter now a prisoner, in Newgate' had robbed Syddal's shop and also that they had together stolen 'from John Waterson in Cannon Street London a chints Gowne a Sarsnet Lining aquited Petticoat and a Pair of Stocking and that Winter sold them to a woman in the mint' (*LL*, LMSLPS150330027).[11] Waterson ('Waters' in the recognisance), a silk dyer who had 'had the Goods to clean', was the same day bound over to prosecute Winter only (*LL*, LMSLPS150330018). At the Old Bailey on 28 February Yeomans testified against his partner on the two indictments. Susan Coats was acquitted, but her husband was found guilty and executed; though a young man he went to his death in very poor health, perhaps as a consequence of having spent well over six weeks in Newgate in the depths of winter (*OA*, 17220314).

The documents that most often survive among the working papers for the early 1720s are confessions. In addition to those mentioned in earlier chapters,[12] on 23 June 1722, Griffith Jones confessed before Justice Sir William Stewart to having picked a gentleman's pocket of a handkerchief the previous evening (*LL*, LMSLPS150330063). Since Stewart was Lord Mayor at the time, Jones would have been examined in the Guildhall, and at trial ten days later would have found his examiner looking down on him from the bench (*OBO*, t17220704-52). Similarly unlucky was Hannah Conner, who

---

10 It is possible that Sarah Smith had avoided being arrested for receiving by informing on Yeomans and Coats: in court she 'depos'd, that Yeomans left the Rings at her House, and Coats desir'd her to go with her to sell'em' (*OBO*, t17220228-8). She also, according to Yeomans, sold on the 'Two Callico Gownes one Petticoat Two Childrens Frocks' that he, Francis Jackson and William Browne stole 'out of a yard … in the parish of Lambeth' (*LL*, LMSLPS150330027).

11 At the trial Yeomans deposed instead that they sold them in Rag Fair – another discrepancy (*OBO*, t17220228-8).

12 Those of Elizabeth Eves before Justice Paul Margaret, in which she named William Reynolds as receiver (*LL*, LMSLPS150310095; *OBO*, t17201012-6), and that of Ann Nichols, who admitted to multiple shoplifting before Sir John Fryer on 27 November 1721 (*LL*, LMSLPS150320101).

was taken before Sir John Fryer during his mayoralty and confessed to stealing a silver tankard (LL, LMSLPS150310116); at her trial Conner retracted her confession but was not believed (OBO, t17201207-6). Another confession to shoplifting was that heard by alderman and sometime Tory M.P. for London, Sir William Withers. Before him 'Elenor Jones (als Evans)' confessed 'voluntarily' that 'the severll: bundles of Silk, & haire twist, then producd & weight, Eight pounds, ware by her at severall times taken felloniously out of the Shopp of John Everringham ... [and] sold at Severll: times, to one Christian Rowlscone' (LL, LMSLPS150310028) In spite of discrepancies and muddled dates, Elenor Jones is evidently the 'Alice Jones, alias Evans' prosecuted for stealing twist in March 1720, and 'Christian Rowlscone' (later 'Rowlstone') must be the 'Mr. Rawlinstone a Broker the back side of St. Clements' to whom Elenor/Alice was offering her latest pickings when the prosecutor (here spelled 'Everingham') caught up with her (OBO, t17200303-4). Jones's confession does not seem to have been read out in court, which was just as well for Rawlinstone; he had told her, Jones had claimed, that

> She must bring her some more bundles of Twist & then she Should be paid the other mony: in persuance whereof She felloniously took divers bundles of twist out of the Shopp of one Dll: Wattson, a Quaker wch. bundles ware produced at the same time ... but Wattson being a Quaker refused to prosecute.
>
> LL, LMSLPS150310028

As with Sarah Smith and Thomas Yeomans in the Reynolds Winter case, neither prosecutor nor examining magistrate seem to have thought it worthwhile building a case against this receiver, even though he clearly not only knew that the twist he bought was stolen but withheld payment to his supplier, thereby forcing her to risk her neck by stealing more. Fryer, on the other hand, went to some trouble to strengthen the prosecution of Mary Coates, Ann and Mary Thatcher, who had received stolen shirts and linen from John Scoon and Joseph Reeves; in addition to the confessions of the two principals (LL, LMSLPS150330037), he took sworn testimony from their lodger, Mary Thornton (LL, LMSLPS150330038; OBO, t17220404-3). Daniel Farmer, the 'Broker in Chick Lane', who also bought some of the shirts, was for some reason not prosecuted; perhaps, like Rawlinstone, he turned evidence?

In our very limited sample of justices' working documents relating to those accused of felonies between January 1720 and December 1722, we have come across no hint of 'testing of the evidence, [such as] allowed defendants to bring testimony of their own to counter the suspicion they were under'; rather we have seen magistrates doing what they were supposed to do by law: ensure 'that the strongest evidence of ... guilt' would be contained in the depositions and examination that they sent in support of the testimony given orally in court (Beattie 1986, 270). Yet we have also seen justices exercising discretion by omission, leaving to go free at least one shoplifter who had been accused on oath, and three who, although not formally charged, were clearly guilty of receiving. In two instances we also see them acting in defence of the accused. When Evan Scipiers first went before a justice to charge with picking his pocket Katherine Waters, the woman who had been looking after his dying wife, 'It appeared that he was so drunk ... that he would not give him his Oath that Night, but bid him come again the next Morning when he might better know what he did'. Scipiers must have done just that – or gone to a less scrupulous justice, for Waters did go to the Old Bailey, where she was acquitted (*OBO*, t17200907-27). Another magistrate intervened from the bench in favour of Alice Peak, a chandler accused of picking the pocket of a soldier whom she counter-accused: 'The Justice deposed, that the Prosecutor when before him owned that he took the Prisoner's Apples, and beat her, and offer'd her a Crown to make his Peace.' The jury acquitted her (*OBO*, t17211011-25), but the poor woman seems to have died, perhaps murdered, two weeks later.[13] Of its nature, the documentation discussed would not include examinations concluding with the accused being discharged or reconciled to their accusers, but it is by no means impossible that some London magistrates were doing in the early 1720s what we know Henry Norris and Sir Richard Brocas did at the end of the decade: using their own judgement and releasing suspected felons. If that is so, some of the decisions taken by Defoe's justices of the peace would have been the more credible to his early readers.

4   Justices in *Moll Flanders*

4.1   *A Justice Satisfied*

In the previous chapter we left Moll's Governess in her house, where she has foiled a search party's attempt to find the 'man' they had pursued from the scene of a break-in. The search had 'appeas'd the Mob pretty well', Moll tells

---

[13]   Her death seems to have resulted either from having been savagely beaten and thrown downstairs by Christopher Atkinson (a bailiff?) or, according to an apothecary, 'from other Hardships, as Cold and want of necessaries' (*OBO*, t17211206-9).

us, but evidently not completely: seizing on a scapegoat in the person of her Governess, they carry her 'before the Justice' (*MF*, 171).

As was customary, the accusers speak first and do so on oath: 'Two Men swore that they see the Man, who they pursu'd, go into her House'. Presumably this indicates their intention to prosecute the Governess as an accessory, defined in Dalton's *Country Justice* (1715, 398) as one who 'knowing that another hath committed a Felony, do feloniously or voluntarily receive or harbor him, or relive, assist, comfort or Aid him'. Defendants, on the other hand, were at trial forbidden to make sworn statements so as to prevent perjury, and although there was no such prohibition at pre-trial, Edmund Bohun (1693, 152) advised justices to make every possible effort to avoid putting an accused person on oath:

> When the Defendant appears, read the Complain to him, and ask him what he saith to it; and if he confess it, then there will need no Proof; if he deny it, endeavour to find out the Truth, as far as is possible without Oaths to avoid Perjury, by cross examining of all Parties, and if the Truth can be found out, the pains is well spent, but if it cannot, Oaths must be given.

This defendant, however, is determined to make use of all possible means of strengthening her defence. She responds to the two men indignantly, offers to swear and suggests an alternative narrative which explains away the prosecutors' testimony without contradicting it:

> My Governess rattled and made a great noise that her House should be insulted, and that she should be used thus for nothing; that if a Man did come in, he might go out again presently for ought she knew, for she was ready to make Oath that no Man had been within her Doors all that Day that she knew of, and that was very true indeed; that it might be indeed that as she was above Stairs, any Fellow in a Fright might find the Door open, and run in for shelter when he was pursued, but that she knew nothing of it; and if it had been so, he certainly went out again, perhaps at the other Door, for she had another Door into an Alley, and so had made his escape and cheated them all.
>
> *MF*, 171

Like the plausible scenarios used by Defoe's thieves to deflect suspicion, the Governess's hypothetical story incorporates elements of verifiable detail – such as the existence of a door into the alley – that make it, as Moll comments, 'indeed probable enough'.[14] The justice seems to think so too, but to make sure, and perhaps to convince her accusers to desist, 'satisfied himself with giving her an Oath, that she had not receiv'd or admitted any Man into her House to conceal him or protect or hide him from Justice: This Oath she might justly take, and did so, and so she was dismiss'd' (MF, 172). The string of alternatives in the wording of the oath – 'receiv'd or admitted', 'to conceal ... or protect or hide' – is a typically legalistic linguistic device intended to cover all possibilities. What it does not cover is the possibility that the fugitive admitted may be not just 'any Man' but also 'any Woman'. The gender bias inherent in the formula allows the Governess to swear without technically committing perjury and thus, like the imaginary 'Fellow' she suggests might have escaped her through her back door, manage to 'cheat ... them all'.

4.2 Trifling with Justice

Moll's 'poor Partner in this Mischief' proves less adept at getting himself off the hook. He still has two pieces of stolen silk upon him when caught by his pursuers, who do not hesitate to consign him to formal process of law:

> he was carried away before my Lord Mayor, and by his Worship committed to *Newgate*, and the People that took him were so willing, as well as able, to Prosecute him, that they offer'd themselves to enter into Recognisances to appear at the Sessions, and persue the Charge against him.
>
> MF, 172

Earlier we came across actual prosecutors putting up £40 each for recognisances, so the shopkeepers' offer reflects their determination to punish a theft from a fellow trader, and their ample financial means. Their choice of justice would also have been significant for Londoners among Defoe's early readers, who would have known that 'my Lord Mayor' would have been available for several hours a day and several days a week:

---

14   Relevant here are two casuistical issues explored by G. A. Starr (1971, 131). First, can one be guilty of lying without uttering a single untruth? And secondly, can one be guilty of lying through speaking literal truths?' The traditional answer had been 'emphatically affirmative' but the Governess here – like Moll elsewhere – 'speaks and acts on the assumption that ... [it] should be answered in the negative'. Many of Moll's negotiations with those who try to enforce the law could usefully be analysed in the light of casuistical reasoning.

it was ... widely understood among those who might occasionally have need of a magistrate's services, including constables and watchmen, that the lord mayor was regularly to be found in the Guildhall ... the City of London had in place by the late seventeenth century what no other jurisdiction in the metropolis yet had: the germ of an established magistrates' court that did not depend entirely on the whim of a magistrate, but had a permanent life and a public character.

BEATTIE 2001, 94.

The young man's captors clearly know where best to go to find an active and authoritative justice, and they are rewarded by their captive's being immediately 'committed to *Newgate*'.

The prosecution process comes to a halt, however, when the thief avails himself of the accomplice-pardoning provision of the Shoplifting Act of 1699. The difficulties involved in bringing these deals to fruition are illustrated by Moll's account of her partner's futile attempts to fulfil his side of the bargain. To earn his immunity, he would have had to confess, taking a risk that at first promises success, but then rebounds, with disastrous consequences:

he got his Indictment deferr'd, upon promise to discover his Accomplices, and particularly, the Man that was concern'd with him in this Robbery, and he fail'd not to do his endeavour, for he gave in my Name who he call'd *Gabriel Spencer*, which was the Name I went by to him, and here appear'd the Wisdom of my concealing my Name and Sex from him, which if he had ever known I had been undone.

HE did all he cou'd to discover this *Gabriel Spencer*; he describ'd me. he discover'd the place where he said I Lodg'd, and in a word, all the Particulars that he cou'd of my Dwelling; but having conceal'd the main Circumstances of my Sex from him, I had a vast Advantage, and he never cou'd hear of me ...

THIS turn'd to his Disadvantage, for having promis'd Discoveries, but not being able to make it good, it was look'd upon as a trifling with the Justice of the City, and he was more fiercely persued by the Shopkeepers who took him.

MF, 172

Moll here reminds us how carefully she had covered her own tracks, but also reminds us of how hard it must have been – especially for one shut up in Newgate – to trace someone who preferred not to be found in what was by now Europe's most populous city. We might also understand the frustration of the shopkeepers, who put up good money in order to nail their culprit only to be sent on a wild goose chase after the mythical Gabriel Spencer. If they now pursue the young man on to trial 'more fiercely' than ever, it is because he has got them and the City's chief magistrate involved in fruitless immunity negotiations.

4.3 An Ancient Gentleman in Bloomsbury

Our next hearing, that which follows the affray in Covent Garden, is complicated by the fact that in the course of the events leading up to it, four different charges have been brought and a lawsuit threatened. The mercer has accused two different women with the same theft, the journeyman has been charged by Moll with false arrest (or assault), and both by the constable with breaking the peace. Perhaps it is because he is hoping for a wise and experienced magistrate to sort out this judicial mess that the takes his charges to 'an Ancient Gentleman' – but why the Bloomsbury address? To Defoe's early readers the area north of Holborn, on which the fourth Earl of Southampton had built his magnificent piazza and palace in the mid-seventeenth century, and which the Russell family were to develop into the great Bedford estates, would have signified growing wealth and rising social status. Covent Garden, on the other hand, once 'London's socially most prestigious parish' was by the early eighteenth century known for its brothels and gaming houses, and had 'started its long slide towards becoming one of the worst slums in the metropolis' (Shoemaker 2008b, 292–295). We may imagine the constable anxious to get his charges away from a dodgy neighbourhood, and the ancient gentleman's horror as five hundred or so of the lower sort, mud-slinging women prominent among them, arrive outside his imposing new house demanding to know 'which is the Rogue? Which is the Mercer?' (*MF*, 194).

The hearing begins with a 'summary account of the Matter' from the constable, and Moll being bidden to speak next. Unable to avoid naming herself, she opts for '*Mary Flanders*', patches together a plausible identity as the widow of an American planter (something not too far from the truth), bolsters her story with 'some other Circumstances … which he cou'd never contradict', and plays on the old gentleman's sympathies by stressing how 'very much frighted' she had been when rushed on by the furious journeyman. The constable then gives a more detailed relation of 'his Case; his Dialogue with the *Mercer* about Discharging me, and at last his Servants refusing to go with him, when he had Charg'd him with him, and his Master encouraging him to do so; and at last his striking the Constable, and the like' (*MF*, 194–195).

Master and journeyman have little to say in their defence. The mercer makes 'a long Harangue of the great loss they have daily by Lifters and Thieves; that it was easy for them to Mistake'. The journeyman's excuse that 'other of the Servants told him, that I was really the Person' would have rung false to careful readers, and feeble to all. Since there is no one to swear that Moll is guilty of anything, never mind a felony, the justice can do what the constable could not, namely discharge her, which he does, 'very courteously'.

He then turns his attention to her erstwhile accusers:

> he was very sorry that the *Mercers* Man should in his eager pursuit have so little Discretion, as to take up an innocent Person for a guilty Person; that if he had not been so unjust as detain me afterward; he believ'd I would have forgiven the first Affront; that however, it was not in his Power to award me any Reparation for any thing, other, than by openly reproving them, which he should do; but he suppos'd I would apply to such Methods as the Law directed; in the meantime he would bind him over.[15]
>
> MF, 195

Defoe's early readers would have understood from this that the justice means to issue a recognisance requiring the mercer to put up a surety which would be forfeited if he misbehaved, essentially a means of keeping tabs on him until Moll can 'apply to such Methods as the Law directed'. As Shoemaker has shown,

> like informal mediation ... recognizances appear to have frequently facilitated informal settlement of disputes. Although the recognizance technically postponed the hearing of the dispute until the defendant appeared before sessions, in practice the experience of being bound over often encouraged defendants to reach informal settlements with their prosecutors before sessions.
>
> 2008a, 95–98

---

15 There is some confusion here. It was indeed the mercer's man who 'took an innocent Person for a guilty Person', but it was the mercer himself who 'detain[ed] her afterward'; both actions would have been considered 'Affront[s]' so both men are to be 'openly reprove[d]', but the 'him' who is bound over must be the mercer.

It is this mechanism that Moll now exploits – to the tune of at least £200. She is naturally anxious not to come to the attention of 'the People at *Hick's-Hall*' (which is where the Middlesex County quarter sessions adjudicated offences against the peace), or of those at the Old Bailey, but in order to make anything out of the master she must begin a 'Prosecution in Form'. This turns out to be one of the kind Norma Landau (1999, 535) has described as 'entrepreneurial', one never intended to end up in court: 'When eighteenth-century prosecutors brought indictments for assault, riot, or other non-felonious offenses against the person, their goal was not punishment of the defendant ... but instead the extraction of payment, or less frequently, apology from the defendant.' With the aid of 'an Attorney of very good Business, and of good Reputation', much dressing up and protracted haggling, Moll extracts both. The mercer apologises,[16] and hands over '150 l. and a suit of black silk Cloathes ... he paying my Attornies Bill and Charges, and gave us a good Supper into the Bargain. ... HE treated us handsomely indeed, and paid the Money chearfully enough; so that it cost him 200 l. in all, or rather more' (*MF*, 198).

The journeyman receives harsher treatment:

> as to the Breach of the Peace committed by the Journeyman, he [the justice] told me he should give me some satisfaction for that, for he should commit him to *Newgate* for Assaulting the Constable, and for Assaulting of me also.
> ACCORDINGLY he sent the Fellow to *Newgate,* for that Assault ...
> *MF*, 195

The disparity between his treatment of man and master reveals this ancient Bloomsbury gentleman to be the type of justice who helped the rich mediate conflicts but imposed strict controls on the poor (Shoemaker 2008b, 233). He has assumed that the journeyman will not be able to make bail, an assumption confirmed when his 'Case' comes up:

> the *Mercer* beg'd very hard for him, told me that he was a Man that had kept a Shop of his own, and been in good Business, had a Wife and several Children, and was very poor that he had nothing to make satis-

---

16   Although not, as she had initially demanded, in the form of 'an Advertisement of the particulars in the common News Papers' (*MF*, 198). Donna Andrew 1998) has found newspapers being used to publish apologies from the mid-century on, but for Defoe to make Moll Flanders credibly demand it in 1722, the practice must date from earlier.

faction with, but he should come to beg my pardon on his Knees, if I desir'd it as openly as I pleas'd ...[17]

MF, 198

As there is 'nothing to be got by him', Moll sees that she will lose nothing by behaving 'generously'; when the 'poor Fellow' is brought into the jolly supper to cringe before her, she condescends to forgive him, and desires that he withdraw 'as if' ... [she] did not care for the sight of him" (*MF*, 198–199).

As Faller notes (1993, 155), the 'as if' is ambiguous. Obviously, the phrase indicates a feigned distaste for the man, but ... [is] Moll feigning forgiveness, also?' Like the whole of the long, complex Covent Garden-Bloomsbury episode, it resists 'simple' construing:

> A great deal more is at stake here than the getting and giving up of money, and one can't quite measure who wins, who loses, and to what extent justice had been done, in only these terms. The constable, the magistrate, and even the mob raise the idea of a very different kind of justice – as does Moll, too, though only to exploit it.

4.4   *A Full Hearing in Foster Lane*

Similar doubts are raised by the episode we turn to next, which takes us back into the busy heart of the City. It is Christmas Day, and in Foster Lane, a street connecting St Paul's with the Guildhall and known in the eighteenth century for its goldsmiths, Moll is seen going into an empty shop, and is seized by an 'officious Fellow' who has been watching from over the way. The smith is 'fetch'd home from some Neighbouring Place', and the usual 'great Crowd' gathers to hear the three-cornered debate that follows. Moll insists that she had entered intending to buy, a claim the neighbour justifiably laughs off. The master dithers:

> Mistress, you might come into the Shop with a good Design for ought I know, but it seem'd a dangerous thing for you to come into such a Shop as mine is, when you see no Body there, and I cannot do Justice to my Neighbour, who has been so kind to me, as not to acknowledge he had reason on his Side; tho' upon the whole I do not find you attempt'd to

---

[17] Ironically, the mercer has risked following the failed shopkeeper in his slide into poverty, for the £500 in damages plus charges initially demanded had threatened to 'be the ruin of his Business and Shop' (*MF*, 197).

take any thing, and I really do not know what to do in it: I pressed him to go before a Magistrate with me, and if any thing cou'd be prov'd on me, that was like a design of Robbery, I should willingly submit, but if not I expected reparation.

MF, 212

The smith's dilemma – how can he 'do Justice' both to his neighbour and to a lady who may be a genuine customer – is congenital to a law enforcement system dependent on community action. If he lets the suspect go, he risks offending the man who has tried to protect his property and losing his vigilante services; if he prosecutes, he risks unpopularity and/or having to pay the 'reparation' Moll threatens.

This time, there is no need for a constable to carry the contending parties before a magistrate. The shop is so close to the seat of City government that it is not surprising that there happens by 'Sir *T.B.* an Alderman of the City, and Justice of the Peace, and the Goldsmith hearing of it goes out, and entreated his Worship to come in and decide the Case' (*MF*, 212). What does Defoe assume here? At the very least, some familiarity with the administrative and judicial governance of the City, each of whose twenty-six wards was represented by an alderman elected for life from among its wealthiest residents (from 1710 on they had to possess property worth at least £15,000). Since this particular one is also a justice, he must also have been one of the most senior members of Common Council (Beattie 2001, 87, 91–92), and in addition he is a baronet. As Loveman (2023, 427) explains, however, in supplying his initials, Defoe also invites his readers to reap 'the reward of recognition and what looks like a sly bit of wit at the expense of a man famous for failure of judgement': Sir *T.B.* is no doubt the merchant Sir Thomas Bludworth, who served as alderman from 1663 to 1682,[18] and as Lord Mayor for the year 1665–1666. Bitterly criticised for his inaction during the Great Fire, Budworth was, according to Defoe's *Tour through the Whole Island of Great Britain*, still remembered and unforgiven seventy years later 'for the implacable Passion he put the People of London in, by one 'rash Expression ... : (*viz*) *That it was nothing, and they might Piss it out*'.

The Foster Lane smith evidently does not share this memory. In having him intercept Sir *T.B.* and entreat his help, Defoe suggests that he knows and respects him, and is confident that he will be ready to act in his judicial capacity.

---

18   Loveman (2023, 427) also notices that 'Moll's oblique chronological references dates the episode to Christmas Day 1673'.

As an outsider and as a woman, Moll will be at a disadvantage in this well-to-do, cohesive business community, and need all her tactical ability to convince the alderman of her innocence. Fortunately for her, the styles of storytelling adopted by her potential prosecutors are to her advantage: 'GIVE the Goldsmith his due, he told his Story with a great deal of Justice and Moderation, and the Fellow that had come over, and seiz'd upon me, told his with as much Heat and foolish Passion, which did me good still, rather than Harm' (*MF*, 212).

Come her turn to speak, Moll offers a circumstanced tale supported by material evidence. She has come recently down from the north intending to buy half a dozen spoons to match those she has in the country, and 'by great good Luck' she has in her pocket an old silver spoon to serve as a pattern.[19] Claiming that on entering the smith's shop she had knocked with her foot and called out 'to make the People hear', she then ventures into the hypothetical with a cheeky lesson on how to make a proper citizen's arrest:

> if he really had a mind to have done his Neighbour any Service, he should have stood at a distance, and silently watch'd to see whether I touch'd any thing, or no, and then have clap'd in upon me, and taken me in the Fact: That is very true, *says Mr. Alderman* ...
>
> *MF*, 213

Nudged into enquiring further, Mr. Alderman cross questions the neighbour, catches him out in what he thinks is a contradiction and, closing his 'full Hearing', gives it 'as his Opinion, that his Neighbour was under a mistake, and that I was Innocent, and the Goldsmith acquiesc'd in it too, and his Wife, and so I was dismissed'.

A coda to the episode reveals the alderman to be less naïve than this 'Opinion' suggests, but even so he is no match for Moll. She is about to depart when he stops her: '*hold Madam*, if you were designing to buy Spoons I hope you will not let my Friend here lose his Customer by the Mistake'. The 'Customer' readily agrees, and when the smith produces matching spoons, ostentatiously takes the necessary thirty-five shillings from a purse containing 'near 20 Guineas':

---

19 William Ray (1990, 81) cites this as one of the many occasions on which Moll negotiates herself out of trouble or obtains her ends through 'an ongoing process of narrative negotiation'. Ray's concept of narrative negotiation applies to many of the interactions discussed in this book.

> WHEN Mr. *Alderman* saw my money, *he said*, well Madam, now I am satisfy'd you were wrong'd, and it was for this Reason, that I mov'd you should buy the Spoons, and staid till you had bought them, for if you had not had Money to pay for them, I should have suspected that you did not come into the Shop with an intent to buy, for indeed the sort of People who come upon these Designs that you have been Charg'd with, are seldom troubl'd with much Gold in their Pockets, as I see you are.
>
> MF, 213

Moll here uses the probatory weight of physical things to convince the justice, who forgets that the value of such evidence is only as solid as the story behind it (Welsh 1992, Chapter 1). In taking her gold as irrefutable proof of respectability and honesty, Sir *T.B.* also betrays the prejudice that assumes thieves to be invariably penniless. To the reader, on the other hand, Moll confides that she 'never went without such a Sum about me, what ever might happen': like her habitually smart attire and gold watch, the twenty guineas are part and parcel of her favourite disguise as 'gentle woman'. She is not, however, satisfied with a verdict reliant merely on props:

> I SMIL'D, and told his Worship, that then I ow'd something of his Favour to my Money, but I hop'd he saw reason also in the Justice he had done me before; he said, yes he had, but that this had confirm'd his Opinion, and he was fully satisfy'd now of my having been injur'd; so I came off with flying Colours, tho' from an Affair, in which I was at the very brink of Destruction.
>
> MF, 213–214

Once again, Defoe has allowed a woman all his readers know to be guilty to pull the wool over the eyes of a magistrate, and perhaps jogged in some of his contemporaries' memories of Bludworth's misjudgment at the time of the Great Fire. In her defence, Moll has deployed logical and empirical proofs with a sophistication worthy of a lawyer,[20] certainly sufficient to outwit not

---

20   Beth Swan (1998) sees in Moll a 'Felon as Lawyer', but this is slightly misleading since it suggests that she appropriates a role proper to a professional advocate. It would be more accurate to say that, like all felons of her time, she argues on her own behalf with a skill in rhetoric that, as lawyers took over the role of defending, is no longer attributed – or

only the ordinary citizens who apprehend and accuse her, but the crown officers appointed to decide what will happen next.

4.5   Fix'd Indeed

The last of the scenes in which Moll negotiates with a justice of the peace comes only three days later, and is narrated succinctly:

> when I came to the Justice, and pleaded there that I had neither broken any thing to get in, nor carried any thing out, the Justice was enclin'd to have releas'd me; but the first sawcy Jade that stop'd me, affirming that I was going out with the Goods, but that she stop'd me and pull'd me back as I was upon the Threshold, the Justice upon that point committed me, and I was carried to *Newgate* ...
>
> MF, 214–215

There is nothing automatic about this justice's decision to commit Moll to gaol to await trial. Although inclined to discharge her, he is by the Tudor statutes impeded from doing so by the maid's objection, one which, by his use of 'affirming', Defoe suggests she has made on oath. Yet Sir *T.B.* had persisted with a 'full Hearing' in spite of an accusation by an eyewitness, something this justice does not do. Nor does he take the course followed by the ancient Bloomsbury gentleman, and bind the defendant over to give her and her potential prosecutor an opportunity to reach a settlement. Moll had already offered to pay the silk dealer 'for the two Peices, whatever the value was, tho' I had not got them, and argued that as he had his Goods, and had really lost nothing, it would be cruel to pursue me to Death, and have my Blood for the bare Attempt of taking them' (*MF*, 214). Her appeal for mercy had prevailed with the mistress and might have done so with the master if he had been encouraged to come to terms by a mediating justice. Then again, and as she had earlier with the master, mistress and constable, Moll calls attention to the fact that she had not 'broken any thing to get in'. Although in theory housebreaking was 'the Intent to commit some Felony, whether the intent be executed or not' (Jacob 1729, cited by Starr 1976, 402), among those actually tried for housebreaking in the early 1720s only one was convicted for entering a house with *intent* to steal, and even then for

---

allowed – to the accused; on the 'lawyerisation' of the trial and the 'silencing' of the defendant, see Langbein (2003, especially 258–284), and on the nineteenth-century novel's restitution of access to the stories of the accused, Schramm, 2000.

a misdemeanour rather than a felony.[21] Even a strict 'law and order' justice might have used his summary powers to commit Moll on grounds of trespass to a house of correction, where she could have been forced to hard labour or received a whipping, as does the 13-year-old Captain Jack when sent to Bridewell for his part in kidnapping and nearly murdering a child (*CJ*, 69–70).[22] Early 1720s readers might not have been surprised to read of a magistrate choosing none of these compromise solutions and adhering to the provisions of the Tudor statutes, but they may have been puzzled to read of one acting unhesitatingly solely on the word of a female servant; her employer, the man who will inevitably act as prosecutor, takes no active part in the hearing and does not seem to have been invited to do so. Defoe may have been in a hurry to at last show the law triumphing and get Moll committed to Newgate, where we shall meet her in the next chapter.

5 Conclusion

Overall, how does Defoe represent his justices of the peace? Certainly, neither in the grotesque, satirical manner of say, Christopher Bullock, or of his own satires of the 1690s,[23] but then again, his justices are not the idealised magistrates of early modern law books. They are, as Loveman (2023, 428) remarks, 'diligent office holders … yet … despite fulfilling their duties conscientiously, fail in detecting or deterring crime.' My impression is that in imagining these justices at work, Defoe was trying to to create characters believable to readers he assumed to know something about what being a magistrate in the early eighteenth-century London entailed, and interested in reading about how they might deal with tricky cases. In *Moll Flanders* and *Colonel Jack* Defoe presents us with justices facing a range of situations that, like those recorded

---

21 'John Carter, alias Whalebone … indicted for a Misdemeanour in entering the Dwelling House of Thomas Tapping on the 9th of this Instant May, with an Intent to steal his Goods … Guilty. Fined 10 l. and to undergo 4 Months Imprisonment' (*OBO*, t17210525-63). See also John Barter, who was 'indicted for a Trespass in endeavouring to break open the House of John Allen, with an intent to steal … Acquitted' (*OBO*, t17200427-19).

22 The title pages and illustrations of eighteenth-century chapbook editions of *Moll Flanders* (such as Defoe 1750) show her being whipped at a cart's end, and suggest that a popular audience might have considered corporal punishment appropriate for a woman like Moll; many thanks to the anonymous referee of my 2016 essay for drawing my attention to these texts.

23 On Defoe's attacks on magistrates for laxity and class bias in applying the vice laws in these satires and in the *Review*, see Bauer (1982).

in Henry Norris's notebook, are 'apparently straightforward' but 'actually ... [raise] quite difficult issues'. The one before whom Moll's Governess is taken must choose which of two stories to believe but has no hard evidence on which to base his decision; the 'man' the shopkeepers claim to have seen has disappeared, and the alternative explanation offered is pure hypothesis. His final decision is based on a legal truth-testing device – an oath – not generally recommended for testing a defence, and in this case rendered nugatory by its gender bias. The Lord Mayor has instead to deal with a thief caught at the scene of the crime with the goods upon him, but legal process is blown off course by the young man's attempt to take advantage of recent legislation intended to encourage informers. The ancient Bloomsbury gentleman has a whole tangle of conflicting charges to sort out, and ends up setting free a professional thief, nearly costing a prosperous mercer his business, and consigning to gaol an over-zealous employee. Sir *T.B.*, the most sophisticated of the series, has to decide whether a suspect's intentions had been felonious or not, and in spite of careful testing and cross-examination, falls for material 'proof' of innocence and makes what the reader knows full well to be the wrong decision. Moll's last justice makes the right one, but only because forced to do so by a procedure imposed by very old statutes that were already being pushed aside as magistrates began enquiring into evidence presented by defendants as well as by accusers. In Chapter 6 we saw another justice negotiating a solution which frees a young man we know to be guilty of highway robbery, and forcing a conscientious constable to make public apology for a mistake caused by lack of precision in the warrant he had done his best to serve, and by his – quite understandable – ignorance of which of the 'Jacks of Rag Fair' is which.

I do not think Defoe means us to greatly blame these justices for their erroneous decisions. They are neither stupid nor careless in carrying out their tasks, which they do more scrupulously that did some of the real justices of the early 1720s. They are ready to listen to both sides of the story they must decide on – perhaps readier than the Marian legislation permitted – and they do their best to fulfil their conflicting obligations, to both keep the peace in their communities while enforcing an extremely strict judicial code. On the whole, Defoe seems to have preferred to show them failing in the second of their duties rather than in the first.

PART 3

Proper Places of the Law: Newgate, the Old Bailey and Beyond

∴

CHAPTER 8

Newgate: From Committal to Indictment

> The Fortunes and Misfortunes of the Famous Moll Flanders &c. Who was born in NEWGATE …
>
> MF, title page

⋯

> IT is true. that the orginal of this Story is put into new Words … the Copy which came first to Hand, having been written in Language, more like one still in *Newgate*, than one grown Penitent and Humble, as she afterwards pretends to be.
>
> MF, 3

⋯

> MY True Name is so well known in the Records, or Registers at *Newgate*, and in the *Old-Baily,* and there are some things of such Consequence still depending there, relating to my particular Conduct, that it is not to be expected that I should set my Name, or the Account of my Family to this Work …
>
> MF, 9

⁘

1   Introduction

The title, preface and opening words of Defoe's first crime fiction frame its protagonist, 'author' and the text itself as products of London's most notorious prison, a prison whose 'Records, or Registers' hold secrets that must never be revealed until, perhaps, after the narrator's death. About Moll's family we find out more when she meets her transported mother in Virginia, and learns that the association with Newgate goes back at least two generations:

she had fallen into very ill Company in *London* in her young Days, occasion'd by her Mother sending her frequently to carry Victuals and other Relief to a Kinswoman of hers who was a prisoner in *Newgate*, and who lay in a miserable starving Condition, was afterwards Condemned to be Hang'd, but having got Respite by pleading her Belly, dyed afterwards in the Prison.

MF, 71–72

By a process of accumulation dear to Defoe,[1] numerous references to Newgate as both origin and destination of thieves, as a place of suffering in itself and as antechamber to the gallows or exile are scattered through the second half of the book, building up to a climax when Moll is finally 'carried to *Newgate*':

that horrid Place! my very Blood chills at the mention of its Name; the Place, where so many of my Comrades had been lock'd up, and from whence they went to the fatal Tree; the Place where my Mother suffered so deeply, where I was brought into the World, and from whence I expected no Redemption, but by an infamous Death: To conclude, the Place that had so long expected me, and which with so much Art and Success I had so long avoided.

MF, 215

No longer a virtual place, heard about, remembered, imagined and anticipated but, except for the occasional visit to an imprisoned colleague, in physical terms 'so long avoided', Newgate is now a material and social reality within which Moll is 'fix'd indeed'. Into its dystopic community of 'hellish Noise... Roaring, Swearing and Clamour ... Stench and Nastiness', she is soon assimilated:

like the Waters in the Caveties, and Hollows of Mountains, which putrifies and turns into Stone whatever they are suffer'd to drop upon; so the continual Conversing with such a Crew of Hell-Hounds as I was ... had the same common Operation upon me, as upon other People, I degenerated into Stone; I turn'd first Stupid and Senseless, then Brutish and thoughtless, and at last raving Mad as any of them were; and, in short, I

---

[1] Marta Bardotti (1990) notes numerous instances in her reading of *A Journal of the Plague Year;* see, for example, 83–85.

became as naturally pleas'd and easie with the Place, as if indeed I had been Born there.[2]

MF, 218

Since, of course, Moll *had* been 'Born there', early readers might have thought that her story will end as did the brief biographies of criminals told by the Newgate ordinaries – with an account of their behaviour at the place of execution. But as Faller (1987, 201) remarks, 'Defoe's novels ... [differ] from actual criminal biography in ways both obvious and highly subtle. They are longer, and leave their protagonists unpunished.' Moll will not die an infamous death, and neither will her highwayman husband, Jemy, who joins her in gaol. This chapter throws light on aspects of the time they spend in Newgate that belies her claim to have become 'naturally pleas'd and easie with the Place'. Unlike the 'poor Jenny' who is so resigned to her fate that she can sing and dance her way to the gallows (*MF*, 216), Moll, with the help of her Governess, does her level best to get herself released before trial, and the less enterprising Jemy has a way of de-railing his prosecution more or less forced on him. If that 'continual Conversing' reduces inmates to stone from a moral point of view, from a practical one, lines of communication within the prison's walls and with the outside world are essential to their efforts. Before turning to Defoe's fictional prisoner, however, we may look briefly at life in early eighteenth-century Newgate, calling on the *Proceedings* for glimpses of actual prisoners exploiting the holes in its porous physical and judicial fabric.

2   Newgate Traffic

The prisons of early modern England were not purpose-built but adapted out of structures erected for other purposes. The towers and passageways of the

---

2 Richetti (1998, 62) offers interesting insights on the 'intensely figurative language' of this passage: 'For once, the scene controls her discourse and resists the mapping of contours that has been her signature, as in the rendering of the London streets, for example, in her days as a thief. Defoe's peculiar strength as a narrator fits Moll's personality: he renders the relationships of persons and objects rather than their integrity and depth as individual substances ... all this changes, at least temporarily, in Newgate, where shifting surfaces yield to stasis and the experience of depth.' As we shall see, however, the 'bustling' Governess takes over Moll's 'mapping' role, offering 'scattered, improvised resistance to a diffused and inefficient social necessity'.

City's 'new' north-western gate had been used to confine prisoners from the twelfth century on. Re-built in 1423 by Lord Mayor Richard Whittington but destroyed in the Great Fire of 1666, Newgate was slowly being re-erected during Defoe's lifetime (Kalman 1969; Grovier 2009). Its imposing exterior, a five-storey 'Tuscan' facade with seven allegorical statues depicting Justice, Mercy, Truth, Liberty, Peace, Plenty and Concord, was belied by its notoriously chaotic, unsanitary and disease-ridden interior. Overcrowding was endemic, and worsened towards the end of each eight-week sessions cycle, intensifying the ever-present danger of typhus. During the 1690s the authorities were on occasions forced to simply pardon batches of prisoners and let them go free (Beattie 2001, 48–50, 364).

Early modern prisons were never meant for long-term incarceration, but to hold debtors until they paid off their creditors, and those accused of felonies until they came to trial at the courthouse next door and, if condemned, returned to it until sentence was carried out. Lacking the correctional functions required of the modern penitentiary, Newgate did not subject prisoners to strict surveillance, regimentation and isolation, although at least one reformer was advocating 'classification and separation of inmates' right at the beginning of the eighteenth century.[3] The day-to-day running of the prison was left largely up to the prisoners themselves: beds, candles and liquor were sold on by senior prisoners acting in partnership with the keepers, while meaner tasks were performed by the newly arrived.[4] Accused and condemned felons were lodged together but separately from debtors, and in theory men were separated from women. But the prison was run as a business, and the only strict form of segregation was based on a prisoner's ability to pay (Beattie 1986, 300; Grovier 2009, 97–101).[5] The poor slept on the floor in the common side wards –

---

[3] Dr. Thomas Bray wrote his 'Essay towards the Reformation of Newgate' in 1701 but it was published only a hundred and fifty years later (Dixon 1849); see also Kalman 1969, 56 and, on Bray, Halliday 2007, 59–60. Famously, Michel Foucault (1991, Part 2, Chapter 2) traced the development of new models of punitive imprisonment from late sixteenth-century Flanders through late eighteenth-century England and America. Following Foucault, John Bender (1987, 61) saw the seed of the penitentiary idea as having been emblematically sown in *Moll Flanders* in that Defoe's narrative 'oscillates between points of view that imply surveillance and enclosure. On the one hand … readers enter the mental world of a single character and fictionally view reality as a network of contingencies dependent on observation, on the other … readers ally themselves with the controlling power of an omniscient narrator.'

[4] For a fuller description of life in eighteenth-century Newgate, see Sheehan 1977.

[5] As Lois Chaber points out (1982, 216), Moll avoids the condemned hole and obtains 'a dirty little chamber to myself' only 'by the help of money'.

dark, cold and dirty – while those who could afford to pay lodged in the better ventilated, illuminated, heated and furnished 'master's side', and the most affluent in the small but expensive 'press yard' that was technically part of the keeper's lodging. The author of *The History of the Press-Yard* (1717, 2–3) reported that the fee for admission to this 'Mansion of the Miserable' had 'been of late Years fix'd to twenty guineas' and the weekly rent at 'Eleven Shillings each, per Week'. Income from rents and from taphouse sales enabled governors and keepers to recoup with profit the expenses incurred in buying their offices, as did fees exacted from prisoners on arrival and on discharge, for lighter leg irons, for visits from outside the prison, including overnight stays, and sometimes – allegedly – for allowing escapes.

Newgate was therefore a prison that could, at a price, easily 'accommodate randomness and licence' within its walls, but also – again at a price – allowed and even encouraged 'traffic' with the world outside (Bender 1987, 11, 44).[6] It seems to have been easy to escape from, and some prisoners were allowed out to beg, and perhaps go thieving.[7] Journalists came to collect stories, as Defoe may have done in 1721, and their publications, like the *Proceedings* and Ordinary's *Account*, stimulated the public to go sightseeing, especially to gawp at the condemned during chapel services on the eve of hanging days.[8] It was normal for family, friends, neighbours and whores to come in to supply food, clothing, psychological, emotional and sexual comfort, and to help with preparation for trial.

This brings us to an aspect of Newgate that has not been much remarked upon: its role as a legal arena, a space in which judicial process could be carried forward, or delayed and even blocked. Defoe certainly thought that the Ordinary made it his business 'to extort Confessions from Prisoners for private

---

6   Monika Fludernick (2023, 191) sees the early modern prison as 'a mirror image of society at large', and notes that, at least in Elizabethan times, 'as many trades were exercised there as they were outside the prison walls'.
7   Near the end of her history, Moll Flanders recalls from her 'long Conversation with Crime, and with Criminals' a memory of 'one Fellow, that while I was a Prisoner in *Newgate*, was one of those they called then *Night-Flyers* ... who by Connivance was admitted to go Abroad every evening, when he play'd his Pranks, and furnish'd those honest People, they call Thief-Catchers with business to find out the next Day, and restore *for a Reward*, what they had stolen the Evening before' (*MF*, 254).
8   The day before his execution, Richard Cecil told the Ordinary 'That he desir'd to receive the Sacrament in private, without being incommoded by the Number of Strangers, who are gazing upon the Prisoners, during the Divine Service, as has always been the Custom of the Chapel' (*OA*, 17201026).

Ends, or for the farther detecting of Offenders' (*MF*, 226).[9] Then again, as a holding pen, the prison enabled prospective prosecutors and thief-takers to view prisoners and identify suspects, a detective practice encouraged by means of advertisements in handbills and newspapers (Styles 1989). Some may have been called in by prisoners hoping to avoid a trial by 'discovering' accomplices and accessories.[10] Joseph Smith, reported by the Ordinary to have been 'desirous, before he Left the World, to make all the Discoveries he could', seems to have received some of his victims in prison: 'I am inform'd, that he ... confest that he did or knew of the Robbing the Jews Synagogue; which Confession he made to the Jews, who on Tuesday last apply'd themselves to him' (*OA*, 17200815).

Other frequenters of the prison would have been so-called '*Newgate* Sollicitors' who came to check on the details needed to draw up indictments correctly (*Directions for Prosecuting Thieves* 1728, 3), those mentioned in the *Great Grievance* of 1699 as members of the 'Body Politick or Corporate' that defended shoplifters, and perhaps law students helping prisoners make sense of law books (Sheehan 1977, 237). Visitors may have provided more concrete assistance. In a single Old Bailey session – that of January 1720 – eight out of the forty-nine on trial for some kind of property crime called on people to speak for them; they, or someone on their behalf, must have made the necessary arrangements beforehand.

There were also shadier methods of influencing judicial process, methods that would have involved intermediaries in negotiations with prosecutors and their witnesses. 'Preventing Evidence to be given against a Criminal' was punishable by imprisonment and a large fine (Jacob 1729, cited in Starr 1976, 400), but those facing the prospect of the gallows would hardly have been deterred by that. Edward Arnold deposed that John Bartholomew Earl had threatened to swear a robbery against him if he did not withdraw from his prosecution of Francis Buxton for riot, assault and battery, and Buxton himself that William Saunders, who had got a forged affidavit sworn to, 'said he had got it nicely done, and if he would not give him 5 guineas for it, he would send him out of the World' (*OBO*, t17210301-62). At five guineas the services of Saunders came relatively cheaply. Fifty guineas was the price Richard Browne was accused of

---

9   On the profits made by eighteenth-century prison chaplains from the sale of *Accounts*, see Rachel Franks (2016). On Defoe's feud with Paul Lorrain, Ordinary of Newgate from 1698 until his death in 1719, see Singleton (1976); on attacks on Ordinaries from competing writers of criminal lives and other sources, Linebaugh (1977, 254–256).
10 The relevant statutes stipulated that the informants be 'out of prison' when offering to turn evidence, but I have the impression that this condition was not always satisfied.

'offering Mr. Smith ... to stop a Prosecution against Mr. Parker' (*OBO*, t17211011-8). Thomas Bishop, who had been 'peacht' by his accomplice, John Boon, for his part in mugging Sarah Reed, must have been awaiting trial in Newgate when he, or someone for him, contacted a relative of the snitch; at his trial Michael Boon (brother to John?) deposed that Bishop had admitted his part in the robbery but 'told him that if he would deny it at the Old Baily the Prisner would be at all Charges, and he (*J. Boon*) should be well rewarded'(*OBO*, t17200303-23).[11] When Robert Hunter and George Post came to the bar to be sentenced, they admitted to having deployed two perjured witnesses in their defence, but told how 'one Strickland came to them to Newgate, and told them that there was no other Way for them to come off; and accordingly procured the said Persons' (*OBO*, t17210712-53). Hunter and Post were probably referring to the William Strickland who, with Elizabeth Ashworth, perjured themselves (to no avail) in favour of William Burridge (*OBO*, t17220228-30; see also *OA*, 17220314).

We know about these attempts to block or pervert the course of justice because they failed; surely others were successful. Fifty-one trials for theft of one kind or another between January 1720 and December 1722 ended in aquittals because 'no Evidence' appeared in court; were these all cases of spontaneous *pentimenti* on the part of prosecutors, or had some absences been arranged? And how proof against tampering was the institution to which we now turn? Grand juries have since disappeared from the British judicial system, their functions having been taken over by magistrates' hearings; but throughout the eighteenth century their role was crucial in that it was this body that determined whether or not an accused person should be sent for trial or not (Beattie 1986, 318–319).

3 Indictment

At the beginning of every Old Bailey sessions the grand juries for the City of London and for Middlesex would meet – the former at the Guildhall and the latter at Hicks Hall – to declare the bills of indictment (formal accusations of felonies) either 'true' (*vera*), in which case the prosecution went ahead, or 'we do not know' (*ignoramus*), in which case the accused would be discharged at

---

[11] Those who instigated prosecutions would have been all the happier to default if someone was willing to cover 'all Charges', especially the hefty bonds (recognisances) which prosecutors and witnesses stood to lose if they did not turn up at trials.

the end of the trial sessions. Beattie (2001, 52) describes the kind of men chosen to serve on London grand juries in the 1690s, many of them repeatedly:

> For the most part they were drawn from the upper ranks of the London rate-paying population. Eighty per cent of grand jurors in the 1690s were men in the prosperous wholesale or retail trades – including linen drapers, mercers, haberdashers, and merchants of all kinds. They were also widely experienced in other aspects of the government of the City …

Unlike their modern counterparts, who are expected to have no 'prior knowledge or an interest in the outcome' and to make a judgement 'entirely on the basis of the evidence they hear in court', eighteenth-century jurors (both grand and petty) were seen as having been fitted for their judicial role by their experience in local administration: 'Neither the personal requirements of a particular prosecutor nor the broader needs of the society would have been seen as illegitimate influences on their decisions' (Beattie 1986, 403).

The bills of indictment on which grand jurors deliberated would have been drawn up by clerks – until 1737 in Latin – on the basis of the calendars of prisoners in gaol, recognisances and information taken by magistrates, and sometimes in consultation with prosecutors (Beattie 1986, 333). According to early modern law books they were to record 'the names of the accused; his or her occupation or status; place of residence; the place where the crime was committed; the date on which it was committed; the nature of the offence; the name of the victim' (Sharpe 1999 [1984], 53).[12] Even the most apparently neutral of these particulars could have predisposed a grand jury, and if the bill was found true, the petty trial jury to whom the indictment would be read at arraignment stage.[13] In her analysis of trial discourse, Elisabetta Cecconi (2019, 71) found that in the *Proceedings* 'the honorific title "Mr." is used to refer to witnesses and prosecutors and it is rarely applied to defendants'. Unless determined by change of a woman's marital status or alternative spellings, aliases

---

12   In his study of early modern assize records, J.S. Cockburn (cited in Sharpe 1990, 54) demonstrated the omissions, inaccuracies and deliberate falsifications that make them largely useless as historical evidence. Writing from a different perspective and with special reference to accused women, Mary Jo Kietzman (1999, 680–681) argues that the 'legal fictions' used by clerks in order 'to counter … women's attempts to evade the law by maximizing their accountability … in effect generated more loopholes through which the inventive subject could slip'.

13   I rely here on the versions of indictments with which each report in the *Proceedings* begins.

would have suggested criminal precedent and an intent to evade identification. Two or more accused together, especially if one of them had been charged with receiving, would have suggested to readers that the accused were members of 'confederations' or 'gangs', and rung alarm bells. Parishes of residence and trades (if indicated) would carry associations of higher or lower socio-economic status. Most important for what was to come, however, would be the way the crime was described and the values placed on the goods stolen. The capital legislation of the 1690s and after differentiated among many types of thefts according to the values of goods, location, time of day and manner of the theft, and assigned specific punishments accordingly. Distinctions among types of theft were, however, often not clear cut. Grand larceny, for example, involved

> the theft of goods of the value of one shilling or more, but without any aggravating circumstances such as assault, breaking and entering, stealing 'privately', or taking from specific individuals, such as employers, or specific locations, such as a house.
> https://www.oldbaileyonline.org/about/crimes#grandlarceny

Few convictions for grand larceny resulted in death sentences (six out of two hundred and ninety in my sample). But it would only need the goods stolen to be valued at forty shillings and for it to be claimed that they had been taken from one of a number of 'specified places', including a warehouse, lodging house or dwelling house, for a capital sentence to be more likely; thirty-four of the one hundred and sixty-eight found guilty of this offence in 1720–1722 were given death. As we have seen, the snatching of a silk handkerchief on the street might be described in such a way as to make it either private (and thus pickpocketing) or as putting in fear (and thus highway robbery). Both would in theory have been non-clergyable but trial juries were more likely to avoid exposing pickpockets to death sentences than they were street robbers.

As Beattie (1986, 333) concludes from a comparison of commitment calendars with indictments, some prosecutors reduced their charges at indictment stage so as to prevent fatal outcomes. Others would have been less squeamish, or would at least have wanted to get their suspects before juries and give evidence against them, if only to avoid forfeiting hefty recognisances. It was certainly cheaper to pay the clerk's fee, which at Hicks Hall in 1726 seems to have been 3s 4d. for 'Drawing the Indictment for Felony & Robbery' but only 2s for 'a single felony' (Beattie 2001, 390). This scaling of fees would support the contention by the 'Person of Quality' who published

A Guide to English Juries in 1682 that it was in the interests of 'covetous' clerks to aggravate charges:

> When the Clerks draw an Indictment, Information, &c., they'l not only alledge and insert in it in the very Fact, &c. one is accused of, but craftily, and full of Art stuff it and load it, into the bargain, with several fictitious and sleigh allegations of their own, to swell up, and aggravate the matter; as Circumstances of Malice, or design, &c. in the Party when did the Fact, spoke the words, &c. So that sometimes from a Mouse, a Mountain; ... This usual way of wording Indictments, is so notorious, dangerous, hurtful and grievous, that it several times, and in all Ages has been complained of by all Persons whatsoever, except the Clerks and Prosecutors themselves ...
>
> 79–80

The *Guide* was still being offered for sale in our period – it was advertised in the *Proceedings* for January 1720 – so it is likely that suspicions about the comportment of administrative staff were circulating in the second decade of the eighteenth century. Beattie (2011, 283n) suggests that this may help account for grand juries' having thrown out a higher percentage of indictments than they had in the last decades of the previous century. In September 1733, the City grand jury devoted the whole of its presentment to corruption with the system, charging that

> many of the bills of indictment brought to them in the grand jury room were frivolous or malicious and that they had been concocted by men in league with magistrates' clerks as a way of generating fees, and – though they made this charge orally and not in their presentment – as a way of profiting from the rewards on offer for the conviction of certain kinds of offenders. The grand jury accused the clerks, 'Newgate Sollicitors' ... and 'informing Constables' of engaging in what amounted to a conspiracy.
>
> BEATTIE 2001, 398

Were the grand jurors themselves above corruption? G. A. Starr (1976, 401) called attention to a report in Abel Boyer's *The Political State of Great Britain* for February 1721 (xxi, 190–191) that 'a bill for preventing the corruption of jurors was introduced in the Commons early in 1721', and notes that Defoe welcomed it warmly in his *Appleby's Journal* article of 10 March 1722: 'As for the Corruption of Juries ... we have a Law lately pass'd, which, it is hoped, will remove all Complaints of that kind'.[14] Whether or not such a law actually passed and whether it applied to grand as well as to petty jurors, and irrespective of Defoe's authorship of the article in *Appleby's*,[15] it would seem that maladministration in legal procedure was topical in the early 1720s. Early readers of *Moll Flanders* may not have been surprised to read of jury manipulation as one of several tactics tried by the Governess as she tries to prevent her protégé's trial from coming on.

4 Preventing Trial in *Moll Flanders*

4.1 Tampering with Witnesses

Moll's claim that once consigned to Newgate she 'expected no Redemption but by an infamous Death' is belied by the fact that she wastes no time in getting help from the woman who had solved so many of her problems in the past (Swarninathan 2003, 14–15). 'THE same Night' that she is committed to gaol, she sends word to her Governess, who springs into action:

> THE next Morning, she came to see me, she did what she cou'd to Comfort me, but she saw that was to no purpose; however, as she said, to sink under the Weight, was but to encrease the Weight, she immediately applied her self to all the proper Methods to prevent the Effects of it, which we fear'd; and first she found out the two fiery Jades that had surpriz'd me; she tamper'd with them, persuad'd them, offer'd them Money, and in a Word, try'd all imaginable ways to prevent a Prosecution; she offer'd one of the Wenches 100l to go away from her Mistress, and not to appear against me but she was so resolute ...
>
> MF, 217

The sum the Governess offers is enormous – way above the £40 reward offered by the state for convicting on the charge Moll is to face – and especially tempting to a woman like this 'Wench'; Defoe is careful to let us know that she is 'but

---

14 G.A. Starr (1976, 401) adds: 'I cannot account for D.'s optimism, since the only relevant statute passed in this session (9 Geo.I.c.8.s.11) added no new legislation; it merely noted the problem and extended former statutes for another seven years.'

15 Maximilian Novak (2012) convincingly re-attributes to Defoe many of the articles in *Appleby's* contested by Furbank and Owens.

a Servant Maid at 3 l. a Year Wages or thereabouts', yet 'she refus'd it and would have refus'd it, as my Governess said she believ'd, if she had offer'd her 500 l' (*MF*, 217). Nor will she allow her fellow servant to be swayed:

> Then she [the Governess] attack'd tother Maid, she was not so hard Hearted in appearance as the other; and sometimes seem'd enclin'd to be merciful; but the first Wench kept her up, and chang'd her Mind, and would not so much as let my Governess talk with her, but threatn'd to have her up for Tampering with the Evidence.
>
> *MF*, 217

Defoe suggests no reason for this humblest of servant's refusal of the equivalent of thirty-three years' wages in order to bring a (failed) thief to trial on a capital charge, but what with her alacrity in fetching the constable without waiting to be sent, her uppity blocking of the justice's inclination to let Moll go, her rejection of the bribe, and now her threat to have the woman up for tampering, she and her fellow servant 'might just be the most moral people in the book' (Faller 1993, 165).

The maid's zeal is certainly not shared by her employers, on whom the Governess next tries her arts of persuasion. The mistress is inclined to compassion, but her husband rejects the Governess's blandishments for pecuniary reasons: 'the Man alledg'd he was bound by the Justice that committed me, to Prosecute, and that he should forfeit his Recognizance.' If he had given £40 bonds to guarantee that not only he, but also the two maids, would give evidence at trial, the sum he stands to forfeit would have been, at £120, high indeed. The rule was not always enforced, however, as is implied by the fact that in December 1721 the Old Bailey bench thought it necessary to specify that 'All persons that have not attended the Court in the Trials of those Prisoner who they are bound to Prosecute, are to have their Recognizances Estreated' (*OBO*, s17211206-1).[16] Defoe shows how the ordinance could be circumvented:

> My Governess offer'd to find Friends that should get his Recognizances off of the File, as they call it, and that he should not suffer; but it was not

---

16   King (2000, 43–44) has shown that about one tenth of prosecutors in his Essex sample dropped out before trial and suggests that courts were lenient about forcing payment for fear of discouraging prosecutions.

possible to Convince him, that could be done, or that he could be safe any way in the World, but by appearing against me ...
MF, 217

The 'Friends' who could disappear recognisances are presumably clerks whose palms may be greased, so this passage implies a shared assumption that the Guildhall bureaucracy was amenable. The prosecutor's timidity, however, blocks off this line of escape, and Moll despairs: 'I was to have three Witnesses of Fact, against me, the Master and his two Maids, that is to say I was as certain to be cast for my Life, as I was certain that I was alive' (MF, 217). Then, somehow or other, 'by the indefatigable Application of my diligent Governess ... no Bill [is] preferr'd against ... me the first Sessions' (MF, 218), and she gains another five weeks' grace, but no hope of an acquittal:

> I had a Crime charg'd on me, the Punishment of which was Death by our Law; the Proof so Evident, that there was no room for me so much as to plead not Guilty; I had the Name of old Offender, so that I had nothing to expect but Death in a few Weeks time, neither had I myself any thoughts of Escaping ...
> MF, 219

Moll's future is not quite as closely determined as this passage suggests. We do not yet know what this 'Proof so evident' is, whether she really is known to the court by 'the Name of an old Offender'.[17] Indeed, as Gladfelder notes (2001, 129) we are never told under what name she is known at all, to the court or any one else.[18] As for the 'Crime charg'd on me', this crucial information will only emerge when the grand jury gives its verdict. The news that it will soon do so sends Moll into 'Fits, and Swoonings, several

---

17 Written records of persons tried at the Old Bailey were kept only from 1715, when William Thomson, Recorder for the City of London, introduced registers for the purpose (Beattie 2001, 431–432).
18 As Gladfelder goes on to point out (129–130), Moll constantly resists the 'closure and inescapability of a True Name ... any single immutable name exposes Moll to discovery, arrest, and imprisonment' – indeed, to a death sentence. Mary Jo Kietzman (1999) has convincingly related Moll's recourse to 'serial subjectivity' to that of actual women thieves, such as Mary Carleton, the 'German Princess'. I am less convinced by Kietzman's claim that 'Defoe resolves Moll's story by replacing serial subjectivity with a proto-psychological model' – that of a unified subject who accepts accountability for her past actions (701).

times a day', but as usual she soon returns to the practical business of outsmarting judicial process:

> I sent for my old Governess, and she, *give her her due,* acted the Part of a true Friend, she left me no Stone unturn'd to prevent the Grand Jury finding out one or two of the Jury Men, talk'd with them, and endeavour'd to possess them with favourable Dispositions, on Account that nothing was taken away, and no House broken, &c.
>
> MF, 221

We are not told which stones the Governess does turn in her attempt to prevent the bill of indictment being found true, or whether her endeavours entail anything other than the usual mitigating arguments. In any case, unfortunately for Moll, the 'one or two' amenable jurors are 'over-ruled by the rest', who evidently harken to the prosecution witnesses: 'the two Wenches swore home to the Fact, and the Jury found the Bill against me for Robbery and Housebreaking, that is, for Felony and Burglary' (*MF*, 222).

The equation of housebreaking, a daytime crime, with the nocturnal one of burglary, is a mistake that may have been commonly made. The jurist William Blackstone was to criticise the whole concept of burglary as 'apt to create some confusion' (cit. in Beattie 1986, 162), and although fifty-seven out of seventy-two early 1720s indictments for burglary were careful to specify that the house had been entered 'in the Night time', the *Proceedings* reporter did not always manage to keep the distinction clear in his mind.[19] The doubling-up of offences in Moll's bill would not in itself have surprised eighteenth-century readers, in that prosecutors unsure of being able to convict on a more serious charge would often pair it with a lesser one as a fallback option.[20] But what has motivated this timid, but so far not vindictive prosecutor, to couple what might have been classed as grand larceny with housebreaking/burglary? Would Defoe's early readers have remembered that there

---

19   The *Proceedings* for 7 December 1720 reported that Dorothy Hellom had been indicted 'for breaking open the House of William Mills in the Day Time' and for 'breaking the House of Samuel Caldicut in the Day Time', but nevertheless recorded the verdicts as referring to 'Burglaries' (*OBO*, t17201012-29).

20   Shelley Tickell (2018, 154–155) remarks on the use of such 'hedging strategies' by prosecutors who, 'in concert with those who legally advised them, including officials responsible for drawing up indictments', brought charges under both the draconian 1691 Shoplifting Act and the rather less severe 1713 Act to punish theft from houses.

was a statutory £40 reward for getting convictions for the latter but not the former, and suspected that he had been persuaded to aggravate his charge by the 'covetous' clerks denounced in the *Guide to English Juries*?[21]

As we shall see, Moll will later object strongly to the burglary component of her indictment, but at grand jury stage she has no opportunity to do so, for defendants were not heard. She takes the finding as having sealed her fate, and so do her fellow inmates, whom she sees 'shake their heads, and say they were sorry for it'. A keeper even comes to Moll 'privately ... and ... with a Sigh', advises her that her trial is to come on in two days' time, and that she should 'prepare for Death':

> for I doubt you will be Cast, and as they say, you are an old Offender; I doubt you will find but little Mercy; They say, *added he,* your Case is very plain, and that the Witnesses swear so home against you, there will be no standing it ... indeed, *Mrs. Flanders,* unless you have very good Friends, you are no Woman for this World.
>
> MF, 222

The role of 'very good Friends' whose influence in high places enables them to save the lives of condemned criminals will become clear in Chapter 10. For Moll now the pace of judicial procedure is accelerating. Defoe has the solicitous keeper mark the days: news that her bill has been approved arrives on a Wednesday and she will be 'tried a *Friday*'; in between, on the Thursday, she will be taken from the prison to the courthouse next door to be formally accused and required to plead. Before following Moll on to that stage, we turn back to events that will complete our picture of how, in Defoe's representation of it, legal process might be successfully frustrated from within Newgate.

4.2 *Jemy in the Press Yard*

Moll is going through the most stone-like, 'harden'd Part of ... [her] Life' when she is called back to feeling and thinking by a 'sudden Surprize'. She is told one night – for the prison grapevine is remarkably efficient – that three highwaymen have been captured after a fight with the 'Country People', and are next morning to be moved from their dank cellar 'into the Press-Yard, having given Money to the Head-Master of the Prison, to be allow'd the liberty of the better Part of the Prison'. Along with other women prisoners, Moll places herself so

---

[21] See Clayton and Shoemaker (2022, 107) on the effect of rewards in increasing victims' propensity to bring prosecutions for crimes involving forcible entry.

as 'to see these brave topping Gentlemen', and she is amazed to recognise in the first man to come out the *'Lancashire* Husband' she had saved from the hue and cry at Brickill (*MF*, 220). Overwhelmed with remorse for her part in forcing Jemy to take the road, Moll grieves

> Day and Night for him, and the more so, for that they told me, he was the Captain of the Gang, and that he had committed so many Robberies that *Hind*, or *Whitney*, or the *Golden Farmer* were Fools to him; that he would surely be hang'd if there were no more Men left in the Country he was born in; and that there would be abundance of People come in against him.
>
> *MF*, 220–221

As so often, Defoe draws attention to the importance of money, and not only in getting Jemy a better lodging. If, three months later, the expected 'abundance of People' has not appeared it is because Jemy and his comrades 'found means to Bribe or buy off some of those who were expected to come in against them, and they wanted Evidence for some time to Convict them' (*MF*, 232). Eventually the prosecutors

> made a shift to get proof enough against two of them, to carry them off; but the other two, of which my *Lancashire* husband was one, lay still in Suspence ... yet it seems they were resolv'd not to part with the Men neither, not doubting but a farther Evidence would at last come in; and in order to this, I think Publication was made, that such Prisoners being taken, any one that was robb'd by them might come to the Prison and see them.[22]
>
> *MF*, 232

These prosecutors are alert to the usefulness of print in getting convictions (Styles, 1989); with £40 on the heads of Jemy and his one surviving comrade, it would have been well worth the cost of publicising their presence in Newgate.

Moll makes cheeky and imaginative use of this law-enforcement strategy. Claiming to be one of those who had been robbed on the road and thus po-

---

22   Here Defoe has Moll state that two witnesses were required for a conviction; as noted by Starr (1976, 404), following Giles Jacob and others, the two witness rule applied only in treason cases.

tentially the long-awaited witness, she dresses in her best, muffles up her face and goes incognito to look at the two highwaymen, afterwards saying publicly 'that I knew them very well. *IMMEDIATELY* it was Rumour'd all over the Prison, that *Moll Flanders* would turn Evidence against one of the Highway Men, and that I was to come off by it from the Sentence of Transportation.' Defoe allows us to glimpse here the interesting possibility that Moll could have got herself a free, unconditional pardon by providing the testimony needed to hang her husband. He then takes the plot in another direction. When Jemy expresses a desire to see the informer, Moll is permitted to go to him in the press yard, where she is left by the compliant keeper to 'talk with him alone, yes, yes, as much as I pleas'd'. There follows a tearful agnition scene and a long exchange of bowlderised personal histories which results in Jemy offering to 'deliver [her] or ... die in the attempt' (*MF*, 234). No such heroics follow. As we shall see, Defoe will deliver his protagonist from Newgate by legal means, but in order for that to happen she will need first to be tried, convicted and condemned to death.

5   Conclusion

Defoe certainly intended his readers to be horrified by his picture of Newgate as reducing its inmates to unfeeling, unthinking stone-like objects. But in the interstices of the powerful theme of debasement, his prison accommodates forms of irrepressible vitality. Information, money and people circulate within the walls of the prison, and between it and the world outside, opening up opportunities to give a slip to the forces pushing its inmates on along the corridor of judicial procedure, some of which probably in fact succeeded. Moll's Governess runs almost the whole gamut of these possibilities, first trying with the help of a huge bribe to convince the prosecution witnesses to make themselves scarce, then offering to corrupt clerks so that the prosecutor himself will not lose out by withdrawing, and finally trying to get an *ignoramus* verdict directly out of the grand jurors. Jemy adds to the repertoire, successfully bribing enough prosecution witnesses to delay his trial, and later, as we shall see, relying on 'friends' among the great and mighty to avoid one altogether.[23] Defoe invites us to take cognisance of loopholes in this phase of law

---

23   Kate Loveman (2023, 432) remarks that 'in contrast with Defoe's early pamphlets, there is no inveighing against corruption ... the fact that justice can be bought is treated by all – Moll, Jemy, Moll's ally the Governess and her gaoler – as an obvious and accepted fact:

enforcement, the 'cracks ... in ... surveillance' his thieves and their helpers try, and sometimes manage, to exploit in their desperate attempts to save their necks.

---

the system is not broken, this is how it functions'. I would add that the absence of explicit moralising about their attempts to pervert the course of justice does not mean that Defoe intended that his readers too take them for granted.

CHAPTER 9

The Old Bailey

1   Introduction

This chapter takes us into the most clearly organised and 'readable' of the law's 'proper' places (de Certeau 1988, 3): the purpose-built courthouse known as the 'Sessions House' or more usually as the 'Old Bailey'.[1] Like the prison to which it was adjacent, it had been rebuilt after the Great Fire of 1666. Its upper level, which housed a dining room for worthies, was supported by Doric columns between which sat the judges in their scarlet robes, together with the current Lord Mayor of the City of London (who acted as president), the Recorder, and 'several of his Majesty's Justices of the Peace for the City of London, and County of Middlesex'. Beneath the bench there would have been a table for lawyers, clerks and the journalist on whose shorthand notes the *Proceedings* would be based. Privileged observers and officials occupied balconies on either side of the bench, while the twelve jurors, probably wearing gowns, sat in partitioned spaces to the left and right. In the walled-off area of the courthouse yard the accused waited their turns to speak from the dock, where their voices were amplified by a sounding board and faces illuminated by a mirrored reflector directing light from the windows so that the jury could, as directed by the clerk to the court, 'Look upon the Prisoner, you that have been sworn, and hearken to his cause' (Beattie 2001, 271). Others too would have been looking and hearkening, but also heckling, cheering and taking an active part in the theatre of the trial. The front of the ground floor of the courthouse was left open in order to reduce the risk of typhus infection from 'gaol fever' (typhus) and provide room for waiting litigants, witnesses, officers of the law and the crowd of spectators whose presence legitimated the court's proceedings as open to all (King 2000, 255).

To this highly organised space there corresponded procedures which, although less strictly enforced than in a modern courtroom, established who was to speak, when and to what purpose (Beattie 1986, 344). Not least of the constraints derived from the speed needed to get through fifteen or more trials a day: 'Where criminal trials before a jury are today measured in days and

---

[1] https://www.oldbaileyonline.org/static/The-old-bailey.jsp.

weeks, if not months, a trial in 1700 would be measured in minutes, only occasionally in hours, never in days' (Beattie 2001, 259–260). There would have been little or no time for reflection or consultation; participants had to keep their wits about them and express themselves clearly and concisely.

Other ways in which trials of Defoe's time differed from today's need to be kept in mind if we are to read the *Proceedings* and Moll's account of her day in court without too many anachronistic expectations.[2] Rules of evidence were only just beginning to be formulated, defendants were not yet presumed innocent until proved guilty and they were forbidden the help of counsel:[3]

> The prosecution was required to provide evidence that the prisoner was guilty of the charge laid. But if any assumption was made in court about the prisoner himself, it was not that he was innocent until the case against him was proved beyond a reasonable doubt, but that if he *were* innocent he ought to be able to demonstrate it for the jury by the quality and character of his reply to the prosecutor's evidence. That put emphasis on the prisoner's active role. He was very much in the position of having to prove that the prosecutor was mistaken. And for the most part he had to prove it on his own and by his immediate replies to the charges, rather than through a lawyer. In this fundamental way the 'old' form of the trial … was very different from its 'modern' successor. Partly as a consequence, trials differed in other important ways too: in the judge's role, for example, in the way that evidence was introduced and assessed; and in jury practice.[4]

This chapter is structured according to the four phases of this lawyer-free 'altercation' or 'accused speaks' form of the criminal trial: arraignment, at which the prisoner was formally charged and required to plead; the hearing of the evidence; jury deliberation and verdict; and sentencing. Each of these

---

2 Ann Campbell (2019) describes her teaching experiment in staging a version of Moll's trial conducted according to the adversarial, prosecution vs. defence format familiar to us from legal dramas made for television and film. The exercise was intended to help students 'discern connections between the twenty-first and eighteenth centuries … while maintaining a focus on historical and cultural specificity'.

3 In practice defence lawyers were being tolerated in some courts, including the Old Bailey, from the 1730s, although they were not allowed to address the jury until the nineteenth century; Lemmings 2011, 119–120.

4 Beattie 1986, 341–342; see also Langbein 2005, 167–177 and, for a different view, Whitman 2008 reviewed by Gallanis 2009.

sections is divided into two sub-sections: the first of each pair outlines what was supposed to take place and what – according to the *Proceedings* – actually did take place during a selection of trials held between January 1720 and December 1722, while the second discusses Defoe's representation of the corresponding stage in *Moll Flanders*. Since Moll goes on trial for felony and burglary, my sample for this chapter consists of reports of the forty-six trials for burglary with intent to steal held at the Old Bailey between January 1720 and December 1722.[5]

2   Arraignment

2.1   *Arraignments 1720–1722*

On the morning of the first day of each Old Bailey sessions the 'prisoners' – as they are always termed in the *Proceedings* – would have been brought from Newgate into the courtroom, where they would have been called to the bar in batches of perhaps a dozen 'to acknowledge their identity by holding up a hand when they heard their name, and to plead to the indictment, guilty or not guilty, when the substance of the charge was read to them' (Beattie 1986, 335–336). In keeping with the principle of defendant unpreparedness (Langbein 2005, 62–63), this would have been their first opportunity to learn exactly what they had been charged with. In theory they could, with the help of counsel, make objections based on 'submissions of law' but few did so (Langbein 2005, 26; Beattie 1986, 412–413); if any of those charged with burglary in the early 1720s objected, it was not reported. None refused to plead. The only two who pleaded guilty as charged would have been set aside for sentencing later.[6] Guilty pleas in capital cases were actively discouraged by judges, 'because it meant that they had to sentence the prisoner to death without having the information a trial might provide upon which they might base a reprieve and a recommendation of mercy' (Beattie 1986, 336). The rest, including six who had confessed before a justice of the peace and would hear their confessions read in court,[7] must have pleaded 'not guilty'. They would then have been asked how they would be tried, a purely formal question 'to which the

---

5   I exclude Arthur Gray, accused of burglary with intent to rape (*OBO*, t17211206-10).
6   Francis Griffith (*OBO*, t17200427-10); John Trantrum (*OBO*, t17211011-46).
7   Samuel Boice (*OBO*, t17201207-38); Mary Kelley (*OBO*, t17210830-27); Jonah Burgess (*OBO*, t17220112-9); Joseph Tomlinson (*OBO*, t17220112-24); Alice Leaky (*OBO*, t17220112-36); Mary Cope (*OBO*, t17220404-21 and t17220404-22). John Webb's confession in the Round House was also reported in court (*OBO*, t172220704-41).

only acceptable answer was "by God and my Country"'. The *Proceedings* journalist clearly took it for granted that every prisoner said what was expected of her or him and did not waste space by recording these or other preliminaries: the swearing in of the jurors, any challenging of jurors by defendants, and the clerk's second reading of the indictment for the benefit of the jury.

2.2   *Arraign'd, as They Call'd It*

Defoe takes more trouble over the arraignment of Moll Flanders:

> WELL there was no Remedy, the Prosecution went on, and on the *Thursday* I was carried down to the Sessions House, where I was arraign'd, as they call'd it, and the next Day I was appointed to be Try'd. At the Arraignment I pleaded not Guilty, and well I might, for I was indicted for Felony and Burglary; that is, for feloniously stealing two Pieces of Brocaded Silk, value 46l. the Goods of *Anthony Johnson*, and for breaking open his Doors; whereas I knew very well they could not pretend to prove I had broken up the Doors, or so much as lifted up a Latch.
>
> MF, 223

Moll's phatic 'Well' here eases readers into the formalities of the courtroom, the interposed 'as they call it' acknowledging that the term 'arraign'd' may be as unfamiliar to them as it – together with other items of legalese such as 'appointed', 'indicted', 'feloniously' – had previously been to her.[8] Then, speaking in her colloquial idiom, she justifies her plea with a characteristic touch of righteous indignation ('I pleaded not Guilty, and well I might') and, showing off her knowledge of legal technicalities, such as the fact that even lifting up a latch could be interpreted as breaking a house, confidently asserts her ability to prove her innocence, at least of that component of the charge.[9]

The felony component of Moll's indictment – about which she has nothing reassuring to tell us – includes two significant details new to her, and to us. Defoe surely chose the name of her prosecutor for its ordinary Englishness: there must have been many thousands of Johnsons in eighteenth-century London, and probably a hundred or so Anthony Johnsons. On the other hand, this particular Anthony Johnson's description and evaluation of the goods stolen distinguishes both him and the woman he is accusing from run-of-the-mill

---

[8] Beth Swan (1997, 151) compares the language Moll uses here with that used in an indictment for assault and theft of 1753.
[9] Jacob 1729, quoted in Starr (1976, 402).

victims and defendants. Silk accounted for only a small proportion of the textiles stolen in eighteenth-century London (Tickell 2018, 99); the brocaded or embossed variety, multi-coloured and often threaded with gold and silver, would have been imported from Italy and been destined to grace the bodies and houses of England's wealthiest. The nature, quality and value of this prosecutor's stock places him in the top rank of London wholesalers, and signals to readers that he is a merchant of substance. His standing would have counted high with the propertied men on the jury and the even more prosperous gentlemen on the bench. The quality of the goods also identifies Moll as threatening a trade of key importance to the City. Johnson might have been less popular with the 'disorderly crew' crowding the yard,[10] but even there a choosy silk thief would perhaps not have aroused the sympathy that might have been generated by humbler burglars who stole clothes, bedlinen and household items.

As we saw in Chapter 8, Moll's indictment has been framed in terms that expose her to a savage penalty: a verdict of guilty of burglary would guarantee a death sentence, whatever the value of the goods stolen, or indeed whether they were actually stolen at all, since breaking into a house with *intent* to steal was enough to hang a convict. Even without breaking, stealing goods worth forty shillings or more from specific places – including dwelling houses and warehouses – was a capital crime. But how strictly the statutes were applied would have to a great extent depended on the jurors, and they would have been aware of the likely consequences of their decisions. As we turn to the 'brief contest of stories' that follows (King 2000, 223), we shall need to remember that, in giving testimony, witnesses too would be taking account of how it might affect verdicts, and therefore also sentences.

3 Altercation

3.1 *Burglary Trials 1720–1722*

Lacking any preliminary address by counsel, the 'altercation' or 'accused speaks' form of the trial was opened directly by the *'partie pursuivant'*, described by Sir Thomas Smith as 'all those who were at the apprehension of the prisoner, or who can give … evidence against the malefactor' (cit. in Langbein 2005, 13). During its early years, the *Proceedings* could not, for reasons of space, include more than a small proportion of the testimony given,

---

10   Martin Madan, *Thoughts on Executive Justice* (1785), quoted in King 2000, 253–254.

and some record none at all. In the fuller reports, prosecutors are invariably the first to speak. A few told how they took suspects red-handed. Thomas Partington deposed that his wife had fetched him home from a neighbour's house between eleven o'clock and midnight, and that he had found 'the Door open, and the prisoner by the Bed side. He seiz'd the prisoner, who pretended to be drunk, and let fall the Goods'. In support of this, 'Mrs. Partington depos'd, she was sure she latch'd the Door when she went out and staid but 3 or 4 Minutes before she return'd with her Husband' (*OBO*, t17220704-5; see also t17210301-42). Most prosecutors had had to track their burglars down after the fact, and would sometimes take with them parish officers who could safely arrest, search and later supply credible testimony in court. James Creech deposed that he suspected Joseph Harrison, and 'immediately got a Warrant, and found all the China, and one of the Pieces of Tiking hid at length in the Prisoner's Bed, he having ript his own Bed to put them into it'. The finding of the goods was confirmed by John Phillips and a Mr. Jones, who was evidently a constable. At the trial Jones referred what the arrested man had told him on the way to the justice:[11]

> The Prisoner when he took him denied that he broke open the Door, saying that he went in at the Cellar Door, having taken away the Key of it beforehand; and in expectation of Favour told them where he had pawn'd the other piece of Tiking to a poor Woman, which they found accordingly.[12]
>
> *OBO*, t17201207-14

Harrison must have regretted his tip-off about the 'poor woman'; she must have been the Ann Price who in court confirmed that he had asked her to pawn the goods for him.

As with other categories of property offender, retailers often testified against accused burglars, some telling how they played an active part in discovering them. When Charles Palmer tried to sell Simon Parsons three coach

---

11   Justice John Lade, whom we met in Chapter 8, took Creech's sworn statement and Harrison's examination, which he refused to sign; LL LMSLPS150310118.
12   Constables also deposed against Samuel Dely alias Deling (*OBO*, t17200303-5), Joseph Smith alias Smithson, alias Horton (*OBO*, t17200303-18), William Withall, alias Harris (*OBO*, t17201012-13), William Courtney (*OBO*, t17211011-18) and Jonah Burgess (*OBO*, t17220112-9). Watchmen deposed at the trials of John Webb (*OBO* t17220704-41); Thomas Justus (*OBO*, t17220228-29), John Webb and Thomas Crib (*OBO*, t17220704-54), and Simon Jacobs (*OBO*, t17221010-23).

glasses and seven seats, Parsons 'apprehended him on Suspicion, and advertised the Goods: by which means Sir John found them again' (*OBO*, t17220907-44; see also t17200303-39). Jeweller John Body got an excellent response to the advertisements he distributed among goldsmiths when his house on London Bridge was robbed by an enterprising family who had climbed up from the Thames and got away with '40 Gold Rings, value 25 l. and other Goods, to near the value of 200 l.'. One pawnbroker's assistant, and three women who acted as pawnbrokers' go-betweens, deposed that they had been offered Body's rings and necklaces by Elizabeth Wayland, her mother, Sarah Pool and sister, Susan Dyer. One of the intermediaries also described how 'about 5 in the Morning, March 29. she met Wayland in Red-Lyon-street, South-Wark, with a great Bundle in her Apron, very wet and draggled, tho' it was then a fair Morning' (*OBO*, t17220704-45).

Harrison, Palmer and a further eight defendants belonged to the category of usual suspects comprised of servants and ex-servants targeted by the 'Theft from Houses Act' of 1713.[13] Other domestic employees testified in support of their employers' accusations, deposing that they had made sure that the house was securely locked up and that next morning they had found a door or window forced (*OBO*, t17200303-19), had seen defendants take something (*OBO*, t17220404-11), or caught them at the scene of the crime. Against James Appleton alias Appleby alias John Doe, Mark Pinkly, servant to Thomas Wedhal, Esq, deposed that

> coming to his Masters Chambers which he had left shut in Grays Inn, he found the Chamber door open, and the prisoner coming out; that Nicholas a Porter then came to his Assistance, and they carried him to the Lodge; that they mist 3 Wigs, 2 of which with a pair of Shoes they found at the Stocks, and Richard Jones standing by them.
> *OBO*, t17220228-15

Pinkly's testimony was confirmed by that of Jones himself, who again gave evidence against Appleton at the next trial to come on (*OBO*, t17220228-16). Another sixteen early 1720s burglary prosecutions relied on testimony from accomplices trying to earn themselves immunity, and perhaps a share in the

---

13   Samuel Dely alias Deling (*OBO*, t17200303-5), Samuel Boice (*OBO*, t17201207-38), Samuel Dexter (*OBO*, t17210712-11); Mary Kelley (*OBO*, t17210830-27); Alice Leaky (*OBO*, t17220112-36); Walter Herbert (*OBO*, t17210113-3); Mary Cope (*OBO*, t17220404-22); John Boat (*OBO*, t17220704-57) either were or had been servants to their prosecutors.

£40 reward available for convicting burglars. William Downing may have made a lot of money that way. In four separate burglary trials he got James Harvey and Joseph Smith convicted (*OBO*, t17200303-40; t17200303-18), and David Lazenby twice (*OBO*, t17200303-18; t17200712-29). Downing had also accused John Best and got him arrested, but the report on Lazenby's second trial states that Best died in Newgate.

As in highway robbery cases, accomplices often acted against burglars in tandem with professional thief-takers. Jonathan Wild was certainly behind the prosecution of John Harris (*OBO*, t17201012-23), and probably that of Thomas Smith alias Newcomb (*OBO*, t17220510-16), obtaining guilty verdicts – and presumably shares in rewards – on the basis of testimony from William Field and William Falkner respectively. In two trials (*OBO*, t17200303-19 and t17200303-47), Wild himself took the stand, giving detailed testimony which would have impressed readers of the *Proceedings* with his detective skills and familiarity with receiving networks. He apparently did not, however, wholly convince the juries, which in each case concluded that the offence 'did not appear to be a Burglary ... and found him [the accused] Guilty of Felony only'.

This was by no means an unusual decision, but one that the reports would not have led readers to predict. William and Mary Smith 'own'd the Fact', and William Robinson of Wapping is one of sixteen who are not credited with making any reply at all to their prosecutors.[14] William Robinson of Fulham is explicitly dismissed as having 'had nothing to say' (*OBO* t17200907-48), John Vaughan, Walter Shelton and Mary Freeman as 'saying nothing material in their Defence' (*OBO*, t17220112-28). Given the days, perhaps weeks, even months they would have spent in Newgate before coming to trial, it is, as Beattie (1986, 350) comments,

> hardly surprising that men not used to speaking in public who suddenly found themselves thrust into the limelight before an audience in an unfamiliar setting – and who were for the most part dirty, underfed

---

14 William Isaac and George Mathews (*OBO*, t17200303-39); William Robinson of St John at Wapping (*OBO*, t17200303-47); John White of St.Botolph without Bishopsgate (*OBO*, t17200427-14); Richard Trantum (*OBO*, t17200712-7); Robert Mayo (*OBO*, 17200907-36); John Harris (*OBO*, t17201012-23); John White of St Katherine Coleman (*OBO*, t17210301-16); William Williams (*OBO*, t17211011-13); Alice Leaky (*OBO*, 17220112-36); James Appleton (*OBO*, 17220228-15 & 16); Ann Smith and Sarah Hains (*OBO*, t17220404-11); John Greenland (*OBO*, t17220704-5); John Webb (*OBO*, t17220704-41); Charles Palmer (*OBO*, t17220907-44); Simon Jacobs (*OBO*, t17221010-23).

and surely often ill – did not usually cross examine vigorously or challenge the evidence presented against them.

Defendants who had wanted to plead guilty but been persuaded not to would indeed have had little or nothing to say (Shoemaker 2008, 567). Yet reports like those on Robinson, Vaughan, Shelton and Freeman may well be inaccurate (568), and as for those that say nothing explicit about defence evidence, 'negative inferences are hazardous. We cannot safely infer that something was not happening at these trials solely because the pamphlets do not report the happening' (Langbein 2005, 85). Although forced by lack of space to omit and summarise, the printers did not do so randomly:

> on average, accounts of trials resulting in acquittals were shorter than those resulting in convictions ... By omitting many details of acquittals, the *Proceedings* focused attention on cases where defendants were convicted, thus conveying the message that criminality would be punished ... Even in trials that led to convictions, much of the witness evidence was summarized or omitted. By disproportionately omitting evidence for the defense, convictions were made to appear more justified than they had appeared in the courtroom ... When the defense case was more substantial, reports were still often significantly abridged, much more so than was the case for the evidence for the prosecution.
> SHOEMAKER 2008, 567–568

Reports on early 1720s burglary trials follow this pattern. No defence testimony is recorded for fourteen of the twenty-nine trials that ended in acquittals,[15] or for most of the twenty-three that resulted in partial verdicts.[16] With a few exceptions, the rest devote to defences only a fraction of the space allowed prosecution testimony. Yet if the *Proceedings* 'were to have any claim to com-

---

15 The journalist states merely that 'the Evidence not being sufficient' or 'not affecting' the defendant, the jury acquitted Edward Katharine (*OBO*, t17200303-52); Stephen Delforce (*OBO*, t17200303-53); Samuel Wafer and Thomas Griffith (*OBO*, t17200427-10); John Whalebone and John White (*OBO*, t17200427-13); James Sands and William Hobbs (*OBO*, t17200427-46); John Taylor (*OBO*, t17210113-7); Mary Williams and John Daffey alias Mosely (*OBO*, t17210301-45); Isaac Josephs (*OBO*, t17210525-4) and Thomas Tinsty (*OBO*, t17220704-60); George Matthews (*OBO*, t17200303-39).
16 Of Susannah Elliot (*OBO*, t17211011-24), for example, the journalist wrote that 'there being no Evidence to prove the Burglary, the Jury found her guilty of Felony only'.

prehensiveness' and 'represent the court as an accessible and impartial source of justice' (Shoemaker 2008, 567), some defences had to be reported in detail. It is with these that the rest of this section is concerned.

The report on the trial of John Brocken is unusual in that it represents an evenly balanced contest of stories:

> Barbara Macdonnel deposed, that being to rise early the said Morning she left a Lamp burning: about 2 a Clock hearing a Noise she drew the Curtain back, and saw the prisoner with his Body half in at the Window, taking the Money out of her draw, but being surpris'd and afraid she did not then lay hold of him, but when he was gone, arose in her Shift ran to the door and cry'd out stop Thief. She saw the Prisoner plainly, knew him very well, and was positive she was rob'd by the same Man that then stood at the Bar. The Circumstance of the lamp was confirm'd by another Witness.

Macdonnel paints a vivid picture of the scene in what must have been her bedroom or sleeping space: one rich in circumstantial details (the burning lamp, the curtain, the man's body half in at the window), and coloured by her initial surprise and fear, then by her courage and promptness in going after the intruder still 'in her Shift'. The jury might have been convinced by her, the reader is made to feel, but if so, was apparently then swayed by Brocken's defence. This included an alibi, allegations of inconsistency and of an attempt at bribery, and testimony from more than one character witness:

> The prisoner in his defence call'd his Comrade, who swore he lay with him from 8 that Night to 9 next Morning; and prov'd by other Witnesses that the Prosecutor had said that the person that rob'd her was a short Man; that the prisoner was tall, and that the Prosecutor had offer'd Money to a Woman to swear against him. Several appear'd to his Reputation. Not Guilty.
>
> OBO, t17211206-23

No other defendant in my sample is reported as offering such a complex defence, but carter John Wilson, accused by Philip Constable of breaking his lock early one morning, offered a plausible, alternative version of what he had been doing:

> The Prisoner pleaded that he came to Town on his Master's Business, and by his Order, with his Cart and Horses with Gardening for Stock-

Market, which having deliver'd, as he was going for a Load of Dung to an Inn next the Prosecutor's House, just as he came against his Door the Prosecutor came out and seiz'd him. His Master deposed he sent him to Market as aforesaid, and order'd him to bring Home a Load of Dung from the said Inn.

OBO, t17200115-4

Philip Constable is made to tell his side of the story in only forty-two words, and since he had 'seiz'd ... him [Wilson] by the collar' while the alleged breaking of the lock was still in progress, his account comes to a halt before any offence is stated to have been actually committed. Wilson's counter-story is almost twice the length (eighty-two words), includes concrete details, projects the ethos of a conscientious working man and is confirmed in all particulars by his employer, so his acquittal comes as no surprise.

The July 1722 jury had to decide on a more complicated case. The forty-first trial of the sessions saw apprentice glazier John Webb 'indicted, for that he (with Thomas Crib, now at large)' had broken into two houses and stolen four casements. Eyewitness testimony from the night watch is reported in detail and Webb, who confessed in the watch house, was found guilty of felony (*OBO*, t17220704-41). Thomas Crib must have been arrested within a day of this hearing for just thirteen trials later in the same sessions he was confronted with evidence 'the same as in the Trial of Web' (here rechristened Thomas), but offered an innocent explanation of how he came to be carrying the stolen windows. His story would have been all the more convincing in that it explained away the watchman's testimony without contradicting it:

> the prisoner in his Defence, said, that as he was sitting at his Master's (Hain's a Joiner) Door, Tom Web, whom he knew was a Neighbouring Glazier's Apprentice, came to him, and said, Tom, my Master sent me to fetch home some Casements to day, but I have neglected it, prithee go and help me? He went, found the Casements standing against the Wall, took one up, and carried it to Web's Master's Shop. The Jury acquitted him.
>
> *OBO*, t17220704-54

The report gives the impression of a naive young man speaking frankly, relaying the exact words of his fellow apprentice's request for help. So completely does the writer enter into Crib's point of view that in the penultimate sentence he drops the indirect-speech tag by which he usually distances himself from witnesses' statements: instead of the usual 'he said that he went etc.' the journalist affirms directly that 'He went'.[17]

Other alternative explanations for possession of stolen goods are made to sound less plausible. *A propos* of china and cloth found in his lodgings, Joseph Harrison is stated to have 'denied the stealing the Goods and said that a Man brought them to him (t17201207-14)', while William Smith apparently claimed that he 'brought the Goods home to his Wife, telling her he found them in Houndsditch' (*OBO*, t17200030319). In some instances the reporter openly adopts the prosecutor's point of view, a reminder that as yet the burden of proof lay with the defendant. John Lee, allegedly found with Sir Charles Wager's 17 Muscovy Ducks 5s 4 Geess 3s 2 Turkies 3s 31 Hens and 4 Cocks 'said he was Drunk and a Man hired him to carry them, but could not prove it' (*OBO*, t17211206-37).

Only nine defendants besides Brocken are reported as having called character witnesses, with varying results. The 'several' called by Thomas Justus may have got him his acquittal, in spite of a night watchman having testified against him (*OBO*, t17220228-29), but David Lazenby, a master silk weaver who was also able to call several to his reputation, was found guilty (*OBO*, t17200712-29). Reports on other trials may have omitted to mention character witnesses so as not to cast doubt on guilty verdicts (Shoemaker 2008, 570). The importance of reputation is reflected in the *Proceedings*' tendency to call disapproving attention to failures to produce any. William Withall alias Harris is noted as having 'denied the Fact, but called none to his Reputation' (*OBO*, t17201012-13), while Mary Jones could neither prove her story 'nor call any to her Reputation' (*OBO*, t17200303-7). Modern readers may feel sorry for Henry Hawks, who 'called several to his Reputation; but none appeared' (*OBO*, t17210301-42), yet one suspects that the journalist intended ridicule.[18] John Blackstone 'called his Master to his Reputation, who deposed that he had served him 4 Years of his Time, and had not robbed him', but what might have been a useful defence was scuttled by a question from an unidentified source: 'being ask'd whether he was with him till he was apprehended, said he had been gone from him some time' (*OBO*, t17200115-25).

---

17   Verbatim testimony appears only from around 1712, and then mainly 'in trials which were thought to be salacious, amusing, or otherwise entertaining'; https://www.oldbaileyonline.org/static/Publishinghistory.jsp#a1678-1729; also Shoemaker 2008, 566.

18   See also Samuel Dely alias Deling, who called 'one Edward Smith to his Reputation, with whom he was Servant 7 Years ago' (*OBO*, t17200303-5), and William Courtney, whose witness 'deposed, that his Father and Mother were very honest, as was the Prisoner formerly, but had lately fallen into ill company' (*OBO*, t17211011-18).

Blackstone was contending with an accomplice witness whom he denied knowing. Joseph Smith alias Smithson, alias Horton, on the other hand, knew his accuser all too well. William Downing, he claimed, had 'been condemn'd for his Life, and been pardon'd by King George and that he Swore against him now to save his own Life' (*OBO*, t17200303-18). Smith was probably right about this, but it did not help him.[19] On the other hand, John White of St. Botolph, accused of three burglaries and another theft by Isaac De-la-Mee, was acquitted 'for want of better Evidence' (*OBO*, t17200427-14), and William Lock's attempt to implicate Simon Jacobs in his gang's burglary of a poor Frenchman's cellar is stated to have failed because of Lock's 'Scandalous Character' (*OBO*, t17221010-23).[20]

We are not told how the court learned of these evidences' bad reputations, but one can imagine that known impeachers came in for a good deal of abuse from the crowd in the Old Bailey yard. Trials were often less orderly than would appear from the *Proceedings*. Beattie speculates that prisoners and jurors intervened often and noisily enough to have 'led to a certain amount of chaos' in the courtroom (1986, 344), and Shoemaker suggests that the *Proceedings* occlude challenges to witnesses by weaving their responses into the single narrative line (2008, 566). Among the few interruptions registered in early 1720s reports on burglary trials is the probing question that caused Downing to falter in his testimony against Lazenby (*OBO*, t17200712-29),[21] and the one put to Walter Herbert who, having owned to a burglary, was 'askt after what manner he committed it'; the explanation he gave must have damned him in the eyes of the jury (*OBO*, t17210113-3). The question put to John Blackstone's master about whether the prisoner was still in his service was surely aimed at eliciting damaging information, which it did.

---

19 Four years earlier a William Downing had been accused of privately stealing a valuable sword; the trial and witnesses told how he had tried to bribe and scare off evidences for the prosecution (*OBO*, t17161010-8). Downing was sentenced to death for this theft but appears in no Ordinary's *Account* and presumably obtained a pardon under the royal proclamation pardoning acts of piracy committed before 5 January 1718. Later in the March 1720 sessions, James Harvey pointed to a venal motive, saying 'that Downing had been twice condemned and swore against him now for the Reward' (*OBO*, t17200303-40).

20 For other instances of accomplice evidence being rejected by juries, see *OBO*, t17210301-16, t17220112-31 and t17220404-43.

21 'being ask'd whether the Window was open, he said it was so Dark that he could not tell: and the Prosecutor deposed that his Man told him it was shut when he went out.'

Any or all of these questions could have come from the bench. Unlike the judge who presides over modern Anglo-American felony trials while allowing barristers to unfold the evidence, an eighteenth-century judge was

> fully engaged in getting the prosecutor to tell what he had lost or how he had been harmed, why he suspected the prisoner, how the prisoner had been apprehended, what he had said when examined by the magistrate, and so on, and then in taking each witness through his story in the same way.
> BEATTIE 1986, 343

The traditional justification for forbidding counsel for the defence was that judges protected defendants' rights, something they tended to do when malice was suspected or victims were thought to have brought their misfortunes upon themselves. On the other hand, 'examples of judges' hostility to prisoners would not be hard to find ... sallies and judicial witticisms ... clearly calculated to weaken a prisoner's defense and to influence the jury' (Beattie 1986, 347). There were powerful ideological reasons to avoid publicising such interventions:

> their overriding concern appears to have been to present trials as simple confrontations between the victim and the accused and judges' attempts to influence the jury undermined that story. Moreover, such judicial partisanship appeared to contradict the principle established through hard struggle during the Restoration, of jury independence from interference by the judiciary. Without resorting to coercion, eighteenth-century judges continued to give a strong steer to juries in some cases, but these interventions (whether successful or not) were not reported in the *Proceedings*.
> SHOEMAKER 2008, 571

Defoe, on the contrary, brings the role of Moll's judge into the limelight, fully exploiting the narrative and dramatic potential of the altercation trial.

3.2 *Courage for My Tryal*

> ON the *Friday* I was brought to my Tryal, I had so exhausted my Spirits with Crying for two or three Days before, that I slept better the *Thursday* Night than I expected, and had more Courage for my Tryal, than indeed I thought possible for me to have.

WHEN the Tryal began, and the Indictment was read, I would have spoke, but they told me that the Witnesses must be heard first, and then I should have time to be heard. The Witnesses were the two Wenches, a Couple of hard-Mouth'd Jades indeed, for tho' the thing was Truth in the main, yet they aggravated it to the utmost extremity, and swore I had the Goods wholly in my possession, that I had hid them among my Cloaths, that I was going off with them, that I had one Foot over the Threshold when they discovered themselves, and then I put tother over, so that I was quite out of the House in the Street with the Goods before they took hold of me, and then they seiz'd me, and brought me back again, and they took the Goods upon me: The Fact in general was all true, but I believe, and insisted upon it, that they stop'd me before I had set my Foot clear of the Threshold of the House; but that did not argue much, for certain it was, that I had taken the Goods, and that I was bringing them away, if I had not been taken.

BUT I pleaded that I had stole nothing, they had lost nothing, that the Door was open, and I went in seeing the Goods lye there, and with Design to buy, if seeing no Body in the House, I had taken any of them up in my Hand, it cou'd not be concluded that I intended to steal them, for that I never carried them farther than the Door to look on them with the better Light.

MF, 223–234

Defoe's narration of Moll Flanders's hearing would have been credible to his early readers in that most of its features might have been selected from among those reported in the *Proceedings*. The indictment having been read, a pair of the prosecutor's servants swear to having seen a thief leaving the premises, to have grabbed her and found stolen property on her; the accused denies their allegations and offers an innocent explanation of her presence at the scene. Moll apparently resembles many of her actual counterparts in calling none to her reputation, and since she has repeatedly lamented her lack of 'Friends', we would not expect her to produce any now; readers familiar with the importance of reputation in deciding a verdict may, however, have found her lack of community support ominous.

Where Defoe's narrative differs strikingly from the reports is in making an accused woman speak out so clearly and strongly. That we are meant to be impressed by Moll's boldness is clear, for she surprises even herself by her 'Courage for ... [her] Tryal'. We surely admire her eagerness to answer the charges before it is her turn, and notice the precision with which she rebuts the witnesses' claim that she was already in the street when seized; the wenches have indeed 'aggravated' the truth, if not 'to the utmost extremity'.

Our reactions are, however, complicated by Moll's weaving asides to the reader into her address to the court, and by statements that contradict what she had told us earlier. We may doubt the claim that Moll had hidden the damask among her clothes, for she has told us nothing of this. Likewise, although we must accept as sincere her belief that the maids had stopped her before she had 'set ... [her] Foot clear of the Threshold', her admission (to us) that she had been intending to make off with the silk reveals this to be a disingenuous quibble. On the other hand, both the hiding of the silks and the position of her feet when the maids grab her are material circumstances which would have rendered the theft an accomplished deed rather than one in progress and of uncertain outcome. Although, according to the law books of the time, this should have made no difference to the verdict, Johnson's having 'lost nothing' might have softened the jury's attitude, just as it had that of the mistress, the justice of the peace and one or two grand jurors. Moreover, unlike those actual counterparts who swore to having locked and barred the premises, Anthony Johnson's maids make no attempt to prove breaking and entering, never mind that the episode had taken place 'in the night time'. Counsel for the defence, had Moll been allowed one, might have made more of these points than she does.

Moll's innocent explanation of what she was doing in Johnson's house, however, blatantly contradicts her earlier statement (to us) that the building she had entered was 'not a Mercer's Shop, nor a Warehouse of a Mercer, but look'd like a private Dwelling-House, and was it seems Inhabited, by a Man that sold Goods for the Weavers to the Mercers, like a Broker or Factor' (MF, 214). Her claim that she had been intending to buy, familiar to us from the Foster Lane episode, would have been met with scepticism by tradesmen on her jury, and made them receptive to the judge's sarcastic comment:

> THE Court would not allow that by any means, and made a kind of a Jest of my intending to buy the Goods, that being no Shop for the Selling of any thing, and as to carrying them to the Door to look at them, the Maids made their impudent Mocks upon that, and spent their Wit upon it very much; told the Court I had look'd at them sufficiently, and approv'd them very well, for I had pack'd them up under my Cloaths, and was a going with them.
>
> MF, 224

This bantering would be anything but funny to Moll, whose main defence it effectively destroys, and by giving space to the judge's hostile interference and to the maid's jeering exploitation of it, Defoe may have awakened in some readers concerns about judicial impartiality and jury independence.

In this respect, in giving Moll a strong voice, and in making female domestic servants the protagonists of a prosecution, his narration may be truer to what actually took place during early eighteenth-century trials for common property offences than were the *Proceedings*. By highlighting the reasoning and speaking skills of both witnesses and defendant it realises the model of the 'altercation' or 'accused speaks' trial more fully than do the succinct and less than vivid official reports. Moll registers her own and others' speech only indirectly, yet she makes us aware of the orality and agonistic nature of the trial, referring continually to people speaking aloud and in various registers: aggravating, swearing, insisting, arguing, jesting, mocking. The account renders the trial as a noisy back-and-forth verbal struggle in which the contenders vie to convince those listening that theirs is the true version of the facts, while the judge, contrary to the orthodoxy of the time but perhaps consistently with common practice, intervenes heavily on the side of the prosecution. What will her jury make of all this?

4   Verdict

4.1   *Burglary Verdicts 1720–1722*

In the early eighteenth century it was customary for the Old Bailey jury to leave the courtroom at the end of every batch of hearings with a list of defendants' names and, in a room reserved for the purpose, briefly discuss their verdicts. Their deliberations remain shrouded in mystery and, like much else that took place behind the scenes – and still does – they may have been all the more impressive for that. Decision-making would, however, have been speedier than it is today, if only because the jurors would have been making up their minds as the trial went on, and would have followed guidance from judges, from their foremen and the more experienced among them. It is in any case likely that London jurors

> shared assumptions and understandings of the law and the assessment of evidence and character. The juries … in this period were very different from their modern counterparts in that they were more socially cohesive. Many jurors must have known one another and may have

served together at previous sessions. They were also more knowledgeable at the outset about the law, about the tasks they were asked to perform, and the options open to them. For juries made up of employers and masters, of men experienced in civic affairs as well as the ways of the court, making judgements about men and women who were not unlike their servants and employees was natural and familiar activity.

>   BEATTIE 2001, 273–274

On the jurors' return to the courtroom, each prisoner would have been asked to stand and acknowledge her or his name before receiving the verdict. Of those indicted for burglary between January 1720 and December 1722, fourteen would have heard themselves declared guilty,[22] thirty-one not guilty,[23] and at least twenty-nine guilty of 'Felony' or 'Felony only'.[24]

---

22 Joseph Smith alias Smithson, alias Horton (*OBO*, t17200303-18); Francis Griffith (*OBO*, t17200427-10); David Lazenby (*OBO*, t17200712-29); William Withall, alias Harris (*OBO*, t17201012-13); Richard Cecil (*OBO*, t17201012-19); John Harris (*OBO*, t17201012-23); Walter Herbert (*OBO*, t17210113-3); William Cryer (*OBO*, t17210301-42); William Courtney (*OBO*, t17211011-18); Jonah Burgess (*OBO*, t17220112-9); James Appleton alias Appleby alias John Doe (*OBO*, t17220228-16); Thomas Smith (*OBO*, t17220510-16); Charles Palmer (*OBO*, t17220907-44); John Trantrum (*OBO*, t17211011-46).

23 John Wilson (*OBO*, t17200115-4); John Wellbone (*OBO*, t17200115-18); John Williams (*OBO*, t17200115-38); Mary Smith (*OBO*, t17200303-19); George Matthews (*OBO*, t17200303-39); Edward Katharine (*OBO*, t17200303-52); Stephen Delforce (*OBO*, t17200303-53); John Whalebone and John White of St Botolph (*OBO*, t17200427-13 and t17200427-14); James Sands and William Hobbs (*OBO*, t17200427-46); Samuel Wafer and Thomas Griffith (*OBO*, t17200427-10); John Gambol (*OBO*, t17200602-7); John Taylor (*OBO*, t17210113-7); Mary Williams and John Daffey alias Mosely (*OBO*, t17210301-45); Isaac Josephs (*OBO*, t17210525-4); John Brocken (*OBO*, t17211206-23); Isaac Gerrard, and Ann Cawderoy (*OBO*, t17211206-49); Samuel Smith (*OBO*, t17211206-71); Richard Feast (*OBO*, t17211206-72); James Jackson (*OBO*, t17220112-31); Thomas Justus (*OBO*, t17220228-29); John Smith (*OBO*, t17220228-49); Mary Hipsly (*OBO*, t17220404-22); Samuel Addis (*OBO*, t17220510-28); Thomas Crib (*OBO*, t17220704-54); Thomas Tinsty (*OBO*, t17220704-60); Simon Jacobs (*OBO*, 17221010-23).

24 John Blackstone (*OBO*, t17200115-25); Samuel Dely alias Deling (*OBO*, t17200303-5); William Smith (*OBO*, t17200303-19); James Harvey (*OBO*, t17200303-40); William Robinson of St John at Wapping (*OBO*, t17200303-47); Richard Trantum (*OBO*, t17200712-7); Robert Mayo (*OBO*, t17200907-36); William Robinson of Fulham (*OBO*, t17200907-48); Joseph Harrison (*OBO*, t17201207-14); Samuel Boice (*OBO*, t17201207-38); John White of St Katherine Coleman (*OBO*, t17210301-16); William Giles (*OBO*, t17210301-41); Laurence Waldren (*OBO*, t17210301-52); Mary Kelley (*OBO*, t17210830-27); William Williams (*OBO*, t17211011-13); Susannah Elliot (*OBO*, t17211011-24); John Lee (*OBO*, t17211206-37); Joseph Tomlinson (*OBO*, t17220112-24); Alice Leaky (*OBO*, t17220112-36); Susan Ranse (*OBO*,

Of the convictions, three would have been made automatic by defendants' guilty pleas or confession in court. How were the other ten selected for verdicts with potentially fatal consequences? Only Jonah Burgess was accused of breaking property and none of stealing property valued at more than £20.[25] While awaiting execution, three – Joseph Smith, Harris and Appleton – admitted to the Ordinary of Newgate that they had committed at least one previous offence (*OA*, 17200413, *OA*, 17201026, *OA*, 17220314), so they may have been known to be old offenders even if not all of them had been previously convicted (Smith and Harris had). At least four of the successful prosecutions had been organised by men with professional experience (thief-taker Wild in the cases of Harris and Thomas Smith, lawyers in those of Joseph Smith and David Lazenby). Palmer and Herbert had been indicted by baronets, and Cecil was alleged to have been intending to take property 'belonging to some of the Nobility, and others'; he had also been harmed, he declared on the scaffold, by reports that he had 'affirm[ed] that he wou'd be the Death of two Persons in the House of Mr. Windel' (*OA*, 17201026). Rumours, perhaps amplified by ballads, broadsheets and newspaper reports, surely circulated like wildfire around Newgate, the Old Bailey, the taverns and coffee houses of the City, and like grand juries, petty juries were not required to attend only to what they heard in court.

Reasons for many 'not guilty' verdicts emerge clearly from only a few reports. 'Joseph Tomlinson, a little Boy' was acquitted on the two of his four offences that came 'within the late Act of Grace', while no one positively identified John Brocken as the person who reached into Barbara MacDonnel's chest. Mary Smith's husband was present at the time of her alleged offence, so she was considered not responsible for her actions.[26] The acquittals of John

---

t17220228-13); Richard Stanborough alias Hall (*OBO*, t17220228-43); Mary Cope (*OBO*, t17220404-21); Ann Smith, Sarah Hains (*OBO*, t17220404-11); Mary D'arbieau (*OBO*, t17220404-43); Richard Hunt (*OBO*, t17220404-48); John Greenland (*OBO*, t17220704-5); John Webb (*OBO*, t17220704-41); Elizabeth Wayland, Susan Dyer; Sarah Pool (*OBO*, t17220704-45). The non-capital sentences imposed on William Isaac (*OBO*, t17200303-39), John Vaughan and Walter Shelton (*OBO*, t17220112-28) John Appleton (*OBO*, t17220228-15) and John Boat (*OBO*, t17220704-57) suggest that these five too were found guilty of felony only.

25 The only who one seems to have harmed his victim, Samuel Dely, got a partial verdict, as did Elizabeth Wayland, her mother and sister, who netted jewellery valued at 'near £200'.

26 'Coverture ... was a legal doctrine in the English common law in which a married woman's legal existence was considered to be merged with that of her husband, so that she had no independent legal existence of her own. Upon marriage, coverture provided that

White of St. Botolph and Simon Jacobs are explicitly attributed in the reports to the bad reputations of the prosecution witnesses. John Williams and Samuel Addis were acquitted because 'no Evidence' appeared against them', Isaac Gerrard and Ann Cawderoy because 'the only Evidence having escaped from New Prison, no other sufficient Evidence appearing'.

The largest single group of acquittals, however, are laconically attributed to 'the Evidence not being sufficient'. This formula, which concludes reports on thirteen defendants,[27] implies that the prosecutor did come to court and presented *some* evidence, but infuriatingly does not tell us what. As long as justices of the peace were obliged by the Marian statutes to send all those accused of felonies to trial, it was perhaps inevitable that many court cases would rest on weak evidence. Poorly supported indictments should have been thrown out by the grand jury, but this did not happen frequently enough, the *Times* complained later in the century (King 2000, 238). Prosecutors who wished to back out of legal process without losing their recognisances may have put in an appearance at court but deliberately thrown their cases away by testifying doubtfully (King 2000, 240). Others may have simply been ineffective as orators. The author of *Directions for Prosecuting* (1728, 5) claimed that it was widely held among his target audience that 'they cannot be brought into Court without being introduced by a Sollicitor, nor be heard if they do not speak his Language', while in fact 'nothing pleases the Judges more, than to hear Truth told with the utmost Simplicity and Plainness'. 'Every prosecutor', he went on, 'is not expected to be a Lawyer, 'nor is their Wisdom or Strength of Judgement the Case, but their Truth and Honesty, which, when they make appear, they are sure of Justice'.[28] Yet 'Truth and Honesty' are not so easy to 'make appear' as the author implicitly admitted when he reproved prosecutors for coming to court

---

a woman became a *feme covert*, whose legal rights and obligations were mostly subsumed by those of her husband.' https://en.wikipedia.org/wiki/Coverture.

27 Edward Katharine; Stephen Delforce; Samuel Wafer, Thomas Griffith; James Sands, and William Hobbs; John Whalebone and John White of St Botolph; John Taylor; Mary Williams and John Daffey alias Mosely; Isaac Josephs; Thomas Tinsty.

28 The author is here applying to the prosecution the traditional argument that artlessness is the best proof of innocence; Beattie (2001, 264) quotes William Hawkins as declaring in his influential *Treatise of the Pleas of the Crown* (1716–1721) that 'it required no manner of Skill to make a plain and honest Defense'. Defoe would have known very well that, on the contrary, a great deal of skill is needed to make 'a plain ... case' that would convince the public; on Defoe's conscious rhetoric and his use of plain or 'low' style, see Curtis 1993.

with Fear and Trembling, intimidated as if they were to be committed to a Jail; which Surprise frequently runs them into such Errors and Mistakes, that if the Judges were not to draw the Circumstances of the Fact from them by a mild and Gentle Method, and patiently bear with a tedious and round-about Tale, what with Confusion, Circumlocution, and Tautology, the Prosecutor would fill his Evidence so full of Intricacies and Incoherencies, as would give the Advantage to the Prisoner, if he was ever so guilty.

13

The *Proceedings* are even less helpful with the large group of defendants acquitted of burglary but found guilty of theft. As already noticed, according to the law books even the lifting up of a latch qualified a theft as burglary, and prosecution witnesses often testified to much more than that. At the trial of William and Mary Smith 'Sarah Godfrey deposed that she lockt and bolted the Door over Night, and that her Mistress lighted her while she did so; that in the Morning she found them open; that the Lock of the Back Door was broke and the Yard-Door Wrencht' (*OBO*, t17200303-19). William Downing explained precisely how 'the Prisoner, himself, and one Richard Shephard broke open the House by boring and cutting the Door, and opening the lower Bolt with a Rake they found in the Garden, went in and took the Goods' (*OBO*, t17200303-40). The 'Felony only' verdicts on these offenders flagrantly ignored such testimony, and beg questions about how, if the thieves did not break anything, they had entered the buildings they robbed. These jury decisions would have been influenced less by the evidence heard in court than by factors now considered extraneous or inadmissible, such as gossip or string-pulling, or by reluctance to expose large numbers to mandatory death sentences. The practice of mitigating the effects of capital statutes by 'jury nullification' was endorsed and encouraged by judges and was central to a discretionary law enforcement system (Green 1985, 273–276). Beattie (2001, 343) argues that even the drafters of the 'Bloody Code' statutes did not intend that they be strictly applied, but rather used to terrify by executing a few felons while allowing most to be saved by discretionary mechanisms, of which conviction for a lesser offense was one.

Another, and one resorted to with increasing frequency during Defoe's lifetime, was the 'down charging' of the property stolen (Green 1985, 276). Several reports in our sample indicate as integral parts of verdicts values of goods lower than those mentioned in indictments. John Greenland, charged with stealing a 'Sheet, value 18 d. and other Things', was found 'Guilty of Felony to the value of 10 d' (*OBO*, t17220704-5), a sum just below the one shilling threshold which distinguished petty from grand larceny. The same verdict was passed on William Isaac, found guilty of taking tallow valued by his prosecutor at four shillings (*OBO*, t17200303-39). Five shillings was the value above which clergy had in 1691 been disallowed from the several property crimes, including burglary. It must have been to bring Thomas Wedhal Esq.'s £6 estimate of the value of his wigs down below that limit that a barber was called in – it is not stated by whom – to testify that they were worth only four shillings (*OBO*, t17220228-16). Forty shillings was the limit above which any 'Theft from a specified place', including a dwelling house, had been excluded from clergy in 1713. Robert East is reported as having had stolen from his house by servant Alice Leaky 'a Gold Ring, value 6 s. a Suit of Pinners, 6 s. 4 Guineas in Money, and other Things'; the jury ignored the four guineas and found Leaky 'Guilty of Felony to the value of 39s.' (*OBO*, t17220112-36). Were these down-charging verdicts intended to clear the way for the judges to sentence the convicted to lighter penalties? Will Moll Flanders benefit from some such 'pious perjury'?

4.2   *Small Comfort*

Moll's refers her verdict briefly and bitterly: 'IN short, I was found Guilty of Felony, but acquitted of the Burglary, which was but small Comfort to me, the first bringing me to a Sentence of Death, and the last would have done no more' (*MF*, 224). The jury's dismissal of the burglary charge is consistent with Moll's version of what happened, since from the moment of being taken she had pre-emptively denied that she had broken anything, and during her hearing no evidence of forced entry has been offered. The burglary component of Johnson's indictment is founded on even weaker evidence than were most of those heard at the Old Bailey in the early 1720s. If the prosecution of Moll Flanders for that offence resembles any of those mentioned in the *Proceedings* it is those so poorly supported that the journalist has nothing to report but that 'the Evidence not being sufficient the Jury Acquitted them' (*OBO*, t17210301-45).

As regards the theft of the damask, on the other hand, the jury has evidently credited the maids' testimony and followed the judge's lead in rejecting Moll's claim that she had been intending to buy. They do not, however, appear to have modified the enormous £46 price tag Johnson had placed on his brocaded silks, and have thus left her saddled with a felony which, if considered as either grand larceny or theft from a dwelling house of goods worth more than forty shillings, would have attracted a capital sentence. Moll evidently assumes it will, and her bitter comment that the 'Guilty of Felony' verdict will in any case 'bring ... me to a Sentence of Death' draws attention to the failure of the current penal code to discriminate among types of theft. Yet, as we shall now see, readers of early 1720s *Proceedings* would have expected judges to make up for that failure by assigning non-capital punishments.

5 Allocutus

5.1 Sentencing 1720–1722

Not recorded in the *Proceedings* but presumably respected by the Old Bailey court in the eighteenth century is the *allocutus*, the moment when a defendant found guilty is asked whether there is any reason why judgment should not be passed according to the law.[29] It would have been at this stage that some condemned women would have 'pleaded their bellies' and been examined by a panel of matrons selected from among the ladies present; those judged to be bearing a live foetus would be reprieved and, in most cases, subsequently pardoned.[30] Also respited were those who qualified under a general pardon, such as that covering offences 'committed before the 24th of July last [1721]'.[31]

The *Proceedings* for 1720–1722 record no other reason for staying judgement, but it does not follow that the none was offered. Desperation must surely have driven some of those convicted to at least reiterate claims that they had found or been given the goods, had been drunk or possessed by the Devil at the time of the theft, or been mistakenly or maliciously accused. They might also have pleaded with the judges to take into account youth, old age, necessity or that this was their first offence, traditional excuses that during the eighteenth century, Dana Rabin finds, were 'enriched by a vocabulary of mental incapacity' (2004, 25). Some would surely have expressed penitence or simply begged for mercy. In omitting to mention any, the *Proceedings* avoided disquieting its readers by drawing attention to pleas rejected or ignored by the bench (Shoemaker 2008, 570). The punishment summaries which conclude the legal business of each sessions merely list the

---

29   *Law Dictionary* (https://thelawdictionary.org/allocutus/)
30   A total of eighteen women found guilty on various counts were 'respited for pregnancy' between January 1720 and December 1722, but none of the sixteen accused of burglary seems to have claimed to be with child.
31   Mary Bostock (*OBO*, t17210830-4) had been sentenced to death for 'Theft from a Specified Place' but was respited for this reason and later given a conditional pardon; since two of Joseph Tomlinson's thefts were 'within the late Act of Grace, he receiv'd the Benefit of the same' (*OBO*, t17220112-24).

convicted under headings according to severity of sentence, giving the impression that they had been assigned automatically, and in a context drained of emotion. The tone of the judgement summary for the January 1720 sessions (OBO, s17200115-1) is typically and bleakly perfunctory and bureaucratic:

> The Tryals being over, the Court proceeded to give Judgment as followeth; Receiv'd Sentence of Death, 11.
> Mary Jones, Jane Griffin, Penelope Dye, William Child alias Giles, Richard Rowe, Hannah Holstock, Thomas Bartram, John Smith, Richard Evans, Mary Hughes, and Sarah Wells.
> Burnt in the Hand, 1.
> Elizabeth Baker, formerly Convicted.
> To be Transported, 18.
> Margaret Norris, Elizabeth Phillips, Edward Busby, Joseph Bryan, John White, Sarah May, Mary Helson, Joseph Spavin, Mary Selby, Elizabeth Smith, Charles Cross alias Williams, Jane Kidgell, John Blackstone, Johanna Radwell, Elizabeth Rigby, Margaret Wilson, Eliz. Pool, and Ann Nichols alias Ireland.
>
> The Six Women Pleaded their Bellies, and a Jury of Matrons being impannelled, found Mary Jones with Quick Child; and the other Five, Not with Quick Child.

How would those in my three-year burglary sample have been distributed? All of the thirteen men found guilty as charged received the sentence of death that had been made mandatory by the Tudor statute disallowing benefit of clergy for this offence. In stark contrast, *none* of those found guilty of 'Felony only' were condemned to death. From this we must infer that *all* their offences had been considered clergyable larcenies, irrespective of the value of the goods stolen. Their judges would then have been free to choose among a range of punishments: they could sentence convicts to be branded, to be whipped, either in public or privately, to undergo a spell of incarceration in a house of correction, or to be transported. This last option had only very recently become available, for until just four years before the publication of *Moll Flanders*, convicts could not be sentenced directly to transportation. Early in 1718, however, due largely to the efforts of William Thomson and a handful of London MPs, parliament passed the 'Felon's Act', more familiar to us as the 'First Transportation Act'. Often perceived as providing a less drastic alternative to hanging, the statute clearly stated that its intention was to provide a more effective alternative to branding, whipping and imprisonment, punishments that had come to be considered by many – including Thomson himself and probably Defoe – as too light and too quickly forgotten:[32]

> Any person or persons ... convicted of grand or petit larceny, or any felonious stealing or taking money or goods and chattels, either from the person, or the house of any other, or in any other manner, and who by the law shall be entitled to the benefit of clergy, and liable only to the penalties of burning in the hand or whipping, (except persons convicted for receiving or buying stolen goods, knowing them to be stolen) it shall and may be lawful for the court before whom they were convicted ... if they think fit, instead of ordering any such offenders to be burnt in the hand or whipt, to order and direct, That such offenders, as also such offenders in any workhouse, as aforesaid, shall be sent as soon as conveniently may be, to some of his Majesty's colonies and plantations in America for the space of seven years
>
> 4 Geo. I c.11 (1717)

Comparing punishments handed down to convicts before and after the passing of this act, Beattie found that it made little difference to the treatment of those convicted of burglary, housebreaking or street robbery, who continued to be condemned to death almost as before. However, the new law, made more easily applicable by the subsidies authorised in 1720, quickly revolutionised the punishments meted out to less serious offenders: in the early sessions after the Act came into force virtually all were sentenced directly to transportation (Beattie 2001, 437).[33] This is confirmed by Ashley Rubin, whose statistical analysis suggests

---

[32] Thomson argued that burning and whipping allowed convicts to return to the environment from which they had been plucked, whereas it was the 'intent of ye law to prevent theire doing further mischiefe, which they generally doe, if in theire power by being at large after a conviction for stealing' (quoted in Beattie 2011, 442). As we shall see, in *Colonel Jack* Defoe supports this view, but as already noticed in Chapter 7, illustrations to chapbook editions of *Moll Flanders* suggest that, for some, whipping was still considered an appropriate punishment for women like her.

[33] Defoe would have been interested in the dispute that took place at the Old Bailey in 1720 or 1721 about the limitations imposed by the Act on the sentencing powers of the court, and that forced the Recorder to clarify that 'there remained a Discretionary Power in the Court whether they wou'd transport, Burn or whip'; Beattie 2001, 439 and n.

> a limited role for transportation in replacing capital punishment ... [and] that the official adoption of transportation tightened the mesh of the criminal justice system ... After 1718, thousands of individuals who previously would have been released from custody with a fine, a lashing or branded flesh instead endured seven years of hard labor in a foreign land, if they survived the hazardous sea voyage there.
>
> 2012, 844

The sentencing of thieves found guilty of 'felony only' in the years immediately before and after the passage of the first Transportation Act fits this picture. Between April 1715 and April 1718 one of the twenty receiving that verdict were sentenced to death, one to a whipping, and eighteen to be branded. From his position on the Old Bailey bench, Thomson was in a unique position to make sure that, once transportation procedure had been streamlined and made easily workable, thieves were not set 'at large', at least not for many years, and especially not on their home ground. Between January 1720 and December 1722 only two, the boy Joseph Tomlinson and Alice Leaky, were ordered to be burnt in the hand: all the rest, from Samuel Mayo with his six-pennyworth worth of pins to the Wayland women with their £200 worth of silver and jewellery, were sentenced directly to one and the same punishment: seven years' hard labour in the colonies. As we shall see, Moll Flanders will eventually join them on the other side of the Atlantic, but by a much more tortuous route. Rather than sending her into exile directly, Defoe first puts her through a gruelling ritual.

5.2 The Dreadful Sentence

> The next Day, I was carried down to receive the dreadful Sentence, and when they came to ask me what I had to say, why Sentence should not pass, I stood mute a while, but some Body that stood behind me prompted me aloud to speak to the Judges, for that they cou'd represent things favourably for me: This encourag'd me to speak, and I told them I had nothing to say to stop the Sentence, but that I had much to say to bespeak the Mercy of the Court, that I hop'd they would allow something in such a Case, for the Circumstances of it, that I had broken no Doors, had carried nothing off, that no Body had lost any thing; that the Person whose Goods they were was pleas'd to say, he desir'd Mercy might be shown, which indeed he very honestly did, that at the worst it was the first Offence, and that I had never been before any Court of Justice before: And, in a Word, I spoke with more Courage than I thought I cou'd have done, and in such a moving Tone, and tho' with

> Tears, yet not so many Tears as to obstruct my Speech, that I cou'd see it moved others to Tears that heard me.
>
> MF, 224

Thick with verbs of asking, speaking, representing, telling, saying and hearing, particulars of tone and gesture, Moll's narration foregrounds the oral and theatrical nature of this very public occasion. At first silent, she is prompted to speak up by that mysterious 'some Body' who reminds us of the presence of a participatory public, some of whom would have sympathised with the convicted, and perhaps been better informed than the accused about judges' roles in reprieving and obtaining pardons. Addressing the bench but conscious of her wider audience, Moll takes the hint and pleads her case clearly and fluently, yet with pathos strong enough to move her hearers to tears. First come circumstances that we know to be true, ones which absolve her of any violence, 'putting in fear' or actual theft: she had 'broken no Doors, had carried nothing off ... [and] no Body had lost any thing'. Defoe then has her pull out of the hat Johnson's petition for mercy, thus reminding us of his initial hesitation about prosecuting and his wife's opposition to formal process.[34] Moll's statement that this had been her 'first Offence' we know to be untrue except in the technical sense that she 'had never been before any Court of Justice before'.

It is a brilliant rhetorical performance, yet is it more so than any put on by actual convicts? Is Defoe giving his readers a chance to hear, through his first fictional convict, voices that the *Old Bailey Proceedings* occludes? Did he mean them to share the sympathetic response of her weeping audience? They would surely have understood why Moll is so intimidated by the polite, stony silence observed by the judges, and why, when they pronounce her fate, she is for once unable to speak, or even make the traditional gesture imploring divine mercy:

> THE Judges sat Grave and Mute, gave me an easy Hearing, and time to say all that I would, but saying neither Yes, or No to it, Pronounc'd the Sentence of Death upon me; a Sentence that was to me like Death itself, which after it was read confounded me; I had no more Spirit left in me, I had no Tongue to speak, or Eyes to look up either to God or Man.
>
> MF, 224

---

34 According to Hay (1975, 40), prosecutors were often the first to plead for mercy to be shown to the person they had indicted.

Early 1720s readers familiar with the sentences currently being handed down on thieves acquitted of burglary would not have expected such severity from the bench. As we shall see in the next chapter, Moll will in the end avoid the rope, but only by going through a pardoning procedure which by the early 1720s was out of date. If Defoe diverges from verisimilitude in having Moll sentenced to death for larceny, it was surely so that he will be able to present alienation from family and community, a hazardous journey across the Atlantic and grinding labour on the plantations as the merciful alternative to death rather than as the dreaded alternative to short, sharper forms of correction for which many petitioners pleaded.[35] Neither to Moll nor to his early readers would transportation have been perceived as an act of benign clemency had he not first had the fear of God put into her by the 'dreadful Sentence' which brings her trial to a close.

6   Conclusion

For the most part, Defoe's narrative of the trial of Moll Flanders keeps within the bounds of what early 1720s readers of the *Proceedings* would have found credible in terms of the procedure followed at the Old Bailey. The point of view from which the trial is narrated is, however, that of a defendant, and perhaps more exclusively Moll's than in episodes where 'other subjectivities' come more to the fore. It is certainly not the point of view of the journalists and printers who were licensed by the City of London to produce the semi-official *Proceedings*, and who selected so drastically, especially in these early years before verbatim reporting became the norm, and did so in such a way as to present verdicts and sentences as the logical and inevitable outcomes of hearings. It is possible, however, that Londoners who actually attended trials at the Old Bailey would have found the strong defence Moll puts up truer to what was said in court than the at best meagre versions offered in the reports.[36] The same could be said of Defoe's inclusion of the judge's jeering interruption of Moll's testimony, of the helpful advice from a knowledgeable member of the public which stimulates Moll into making her plea at *allocutus*,

---

35   Morgan (1989, 112) concludes from his study of petitions addressed to the Lord Mayor between 1725 and 1735 that they 'testify, simply but eloquently, to a popular dread of transportation as an alternative to physical corrections such as whipping, branding, or burning in the hand'; see also Ekirch 1987, 40–42.

36   I am grateful to Robert Shoemaker for pointing this out.

and of the speech itself; as we have already noticed, at least some of her actual equivalents must have given some reason why sentence should not be passed, but none is reported in the *Proceedings*. By the early 1720s neither readers nor attenders would have expected a capital sentence for a conviction for 'Felony only'. As the next chapter will show, however, this was the sentence Defoe was obliged to have his judges pass if he was to represent transportation as conceded as a condition of pardoning rather than handed down as a punishment.

CHAPTER 10

Punishing and Pardoning

1   Introduction

On 14 November 1715, after two days of fighting on the streets of Preston in Lancashire, a besieged Jacobite force surrendered unconditionally to government troops. Defoe's Colonel Jack explains what happened to the 'Miserable People' taken prisoner: 'some were executed for Examples, as in such Cases is usual; and the Government extending Mercy to the Multitude, they were kept in *Chester* Castle, and other places a considerable time, till they were disposed of, some one Way, some another, as we shall hear' (*CJ*, 301). We are not told how those 'executed for Examples' were selected, the practice being supposedly so 'usual in such Cases' that the reader is not expected to be curious. The memory of their grisly deaths will, however, later return to terrify Jack. The death sentence is in any case embedded in the 'extending [of] Mercy': 'Benevolence … was not a simple positive act; it contained within it the ever present threat of malice' (Hay 2011, 62). In Defoe's criminal fictions the threat of the gallows is ever present, not least in his thieves' managing to avoid the rope for so long, and in the alternative ways the authorities find of dealing with those they do not wish to kill. As Jack intimates, 'the Multitude' may be kept somewhere or other 'a considerable time', but sooner or later they will somehow have to be 'disposed of'.

As with traitors, so with the huge numbers of common property offenders whom the 'Bloody Code' had brought within the executioner's reach. We have already seen that in his criminal fictions Defoe makes transportation the main alternative to the gallows, even though within the time schemes of both novels most of those actually convicted would have incurred lighter punishments. Coming onto the market so soon after the passing of the Transportation Acts of 1718 and 1720, it is not surprising that *Moll Flanders* (but also *Colonel Jack*) 'is intensely interested in the laws and processes that enabled felons to escape execution by way of exile … it certainly occludes some hard facts about transatlantic life … but it also captures subtle features of an expanding judicial world which we can only with difficulty reconstruct' (Cervantes 2011, 316). The section that follows builds on Cervantes's reconstruction of those laws and processes, while subsequent sections discuss the multiple, often contradictory and ambivalent ways in which Defoe imagined their application.

2   Pardoning Procedures

Like justice itself, mercy was conceived of in early modern England as emanating from the reigning monarch. 'Special pardons', issued on parchment under the great seal, could be obtained directly from the crown (Beattie 1986, 288) but only at great expense and with help from influential intercessors. Maximillian Novak (2001, 85) has suggested that, to obtain indemnity for his part in the Monmouth rebellion of 1685, Defoe himself bought one for £60. More commonly issued were the 'administrative pardons' which, until the early 1690s, were throughout England controlled by the bench. At the end of every sessions, the judges would respite those they wished to save and recommend them, via the secretary of state, to the monarch, who would invariably assent.

This was the procedure followed throughout the provinces for the whole of the eighteenth century, but sometime soon after the Glorious Revolution a new practice was adopted for London. From then on, the Recorder for the City would report orally on each of those condemned at the Old Bailey to a committee of the privy council presided over by the king himself when he was in England. After a brief discussion, this 'hanging cabinet' or 'hanging council' would communicate to the sheriff of Newgate, in a document known as the 'dead warrant', the names of those to be executed. If there was time before hanging day, these unfortunates could still appeal to the monarch via the secretary of state for their sentences to be overturned or reduced (Beattie 2001, 290).

Endorsed by family members, neighbours, employers, community worthies, often the prosecutors themselves, these petitions have been described by V.A.C. Gatrell as occupying 'the centre ground of a judicial system whose very basis was the discretionary application or mitigation of penal pain' (1994, 197). They would have been submitted for their comments to the judges who had passed sentence. Some resisted what were in effect requests to allow their initial decisions to be reversed, but most responded neutrally or outlined plausible grounds for clemency. As for the reasons why some succeeded and others failed, Peter King has analysed a large number of late eighteenth-century petitions and ranked according to their effectiveness the mitigating 'factors' cited in them: the non-violent nature of the offence, youth, old age, need, the 'respectable' character of both petitioners and of their supporters. Douglas Hay, on the other hand, insists on the prime importance of 'connection', arguing that the higher the social status of a patron the greater the likelihood of success, and that success reinforced patrons' influence by allowing them to share in the ideology of benevolence (2011, 51; see also Hay 2006).

To obtain absolute, free pardons must have required strong backing: most remissions came with conditions attached. During wartime, men could volunteer for service in the armed forces, and a few saved themselves by undergoing medical experiments.[1] The majority of those reprieved, however, were assigned whippings, branding, spells in a house of correction or several years' hard labour in the colonies. The last of these options had been resorted to increasingly from the 1650s on but was beset by financial problems. Some prisoners undertook to pay for their own passages, but there were complaints about failures to honour such undertakings. Many were taken for free by merchants who would recoup their costs and more by selling them to labour-hungry planters, but those harder to sell – women, older or infirm men, and the very young – tended to get left behind. In 1697, faced with severe overcrowding of gaols, the government paid £8 a head to send fifty convicted women to the Windward Islands. Another crisis, that of disposing of the 1,468 taken prisoner at Preston in 1715, transformed transportation 'from a haphazard local practice to a national policy': 'The new Hanoverian régime, sufficiently anxious about its own security to experiment with penalties that had never before been deployed at the level of state, sent captured Jacobite rebels *en masse* to America, some at their own request' (O'Brien 1998, 72). Less than three years later came the Act that allowed all of those convicted of clergyable offences except receiving to be sentenced directly to transportation, and two years after that the Treasury was authorised to pay £3 a head to merchants agreeing to take all of those sentenced across the Atlantic.

While this legislation streamlined procedure and facilitated logistics, it created a new ideological problem by rendering obsolete the legal fiction that had been worked out as a way of legitimating banishment, a practice contrary to belief in the rights of free-born Englishmen inherited from the ancient con-

---

1 When a warrant was issued for his arrest for seditious libel in 1703 Defoe himself appealed to the secretary of state, offering to raise and lead a troop of horse for the Queen. During the much publicised, controversial and politically sensitive 'Newgate Smallpox Experiment' of the summer of 1721, seven inmates of Newgate had their sentences remitted on condition of undergoing inoculation; Weinreich, 2020. Shoplifter Richard Evans (*OBO*, t17200115-34), pickpocket Anne Tompion (*OBO*, t17200112-5, s17201012-1), Elizabeth Harrison, convicted of stealing 62 guineas from her employer (*OBO* t17210419-42) and Mary North, condemned for returning from transportation (*OBO* t17200303-10), had been sentenced to death, while shop-lifters John Alcock (*OBO* s17211206-1), Ruth Jones (*OBO* t17210525-14) and John Cauthrey (*OBO* t17210525-28; Cawthery in Weinreich) had been sentenced directly to transportation, so their consenting to undergo medical experimentation shows how deep was their dread of exile.

stitution (Atkinson 1994). A loophole had been provided by the Act of Habeas Corpus of 1679, which allowed for the possibility that 'if any person or persons, lawfully convicted of any felony, shall in open Court, pray to be transported beyond the seas, and the Court shall think fit to leave him or them in prison for that purpose, such person or persons may be transported into any parts beyond the seas'. Transportation had thus been framed not as a punishment, but as a remission of punishment, a favour or grant for which those condemned to death had to beg on their knees in a show of humble petitioning. Recalling the ancient custom by which offenders claimed sanctuary in holy places and promised to voluntarily abjure the realm, the ceremony embodied 'claims to penitence, repentance, and pleading for mercy as religious apparatuses' (Cervantes 2011, 329). In allowing courts to sentence offenders directly, making no provision for pardoning and eliminating the pretence that convicts had any choice in the matter, the Act of 1718 invalidated those claims. It thus effected a 'fundamental alteration' in the conception of transportation. Convicts whose offences were not clergyable and who had been sentenced to death continued to be sent off under the old procedure, but these made up a minority of those transported: most 'were no longer exercising their freedom as British subjects by accepting a pardon; they were merely acceding to the penalty now stipulated under the law' (O'Brien 1998, 72).[2]

Nevertheless, according to Alan Atkinson (1994, 94), for most of the eighteenth century

> a belief persisted – a deeply ingrained collective wishful thinking – to the effect that the new system was in line with the ancient virtues of the constitution, that it somehow preserved the element of consent; or in other words, that the typical convict was, as before, the man or woman who had been spared the gallows by conditional pardon.

Whether one thinks of this continuing belief as wishful thinking, or as O'Brien prefers to call it, a product of 'amnesia', 'a strategic forgetting of many of the Act's key provisions', Defoe seems to have shared in and helped perpetuate it. As we shall now see, in *Moll Flanders* and *Colonel Jack* he consistently repre-

---

2 G.A. Starr (1976, 404) explained the difference between the two conceptions of transportation, but O'Brien and more recently, Dennis Todd (for whose approach, see below), are rare among Defoe scholars in having taken notice of this and suggested some of the implications for the novels. Rather misleadingly, however, O'Brien refers to transportation as a 'penalty' even in the seventeenth century context, and writes of Moll Flanders as having been 'sentenced to transportation in lieu of hanging for theft', something she most definitely is not.

sents transportation as a 'Grant' or 'Favour' obtained through pardoning in remission of a death sentence, and not as what it had become – or been revealed to be – by the 1720s:[3] a punishment that could for some felonies be directly assigned by a court. Yet, as we shall see, his protagonists, especially Moll, show little sense of gratitude for the mercy bestowed on them.

3 Avoiding the Rope in *Moll Flanders*

3.1 *The Favour of Being Transported*

There are moments in *The Life ... of Moll Flanders* when we must take seriously its last words, which claim that it was 'Written in the Year 1683', for all of those transported in the novel go through the pardoning procedure allowed by Habeas Corpus.[4] Taken while 'borrowing three Pieces of fine Holland, of a certain Draper in Cheapside', Moll's mother is first condemned to death, then respited for pregnancy and only after giving birth obtains 'the Favour of being Transported to the Plantations' (*MF*, 10). In Virginia many years later, she generalises her experience, revealing to her daughter-in-law/daughter how most of the inhabitants of the colony came to be there: either as indentured servants,[5] or, like herself, 'Transported from *Newgate* and other Prisons, after having been found guilty of Felony and other Crimes punishable with Death' (*MF*, 70).[6] When Moll's teacher and a fellow pupil are taken they too are sentenced to death and respited for pregnancy (*MF*, 161), even though, Moll interposes

---

[3] Todd (2010, 11) recognises that the 1718 Act 'created a new class of non-capital felons who could be sentenced to transportation, not as an act of mercy but as a punishment' but sees this as having 'thus articulated explicitly what was understood implicitly and experienced viscerally; transportation as both a punishment *and* an act of mercy'–i.e. as exposing the 'twofold nature of transportation'. It seems to me that Defoe tried to keep the two conceptions distinct, and needed to do so if he was to represent transportation as providential.

[4] Loveman (2023, 424–425) draws attention to the difficulty of assessing Defoe's representation of crime and the law given the chronologies of *Moll Flanders* and *Colonel Jack,* which are far from clear or consistent (see Sertoli, 1991). On the whole, this study treats the novels as concerned with issues that were alive and topical in the 1720s, but collective memories of the events of the previous century are sometimes called upon to help deal with those issues.

[5] A phenomenon with which Defoe was familiar, for in 1688 he had paid the passage to Maryland of several such servants and received a healthy profit from their sale; Backscheider 1989, 482–483, 487–488; Todd 2010, 6.

[6] She herself 'came away openly' (*MF*, 71), she specifies in what may be a cryptic allusion to the ritual of having, as foreseen under Habeas Corpus, 'in open Court pray[ed] to be Transported'. This would fit Linda Bree's glossing of 'openly' as 'voluntarily' in her note (Defoe 2011, 299).

sardonically, 'my Tutress was no more with Child than I was'. The ruse is presumably discovered, for 'my Comerade having the Brand of an Old Offender, was Executed', while by contrast 'the young Offender was spar'd, having obtained a Reprieve; but lay starving a long while in Prison, till at last she got her Name into what they call a Circuit Pardon, and so came off' (*MF*, 161).[7] We may imagine the young woman to have been an active agent in 'getting' her name onto that pardon, perhaps by petitioning for remission in view of her youth and susceptibility to the bad influence of her teacher.[8]

By the time Moll comes to the Old Bailey she is no novice and, although she has not been branded, is widely known to be an 'old Offender'. Back in Newgate after sentencing,

> IT is rather to be thought of, than express'd what was now my Condition; I had nothing before me but present Death, and as I had no Friends to assist me, or to stir for me, I expected nothing but to find my Name in the Dead Warrant, which was to come down for the Execution the *Friday* afterward, of five more and myself.
>
> *MF*, 225

Sure enough, twelve days later, 'the Dead Warrant, *as they call it*, came down, and I found my Name was among them' (*MF*, 227). Readers familiar with the London pardoning procedure would have inferred that Moll's plea at *allocutus* had been ignored, and that the Recorder has not used his power to 'represent favourably' her case to the hanging cabinet. They would also have understood that if she had had 'Friends to assist me, or stir for me', she might be saved yet. She has none, she tells us for the umpteenth time, but is proved wrong when help comes from an unlikely source. Overcome by remorse at having corrupted and caused the deaths of so many, her Governess has turned to a minister, 'a serious pious good Man, and apply'd herself with such earnestness by his assistance to the Work of a sincere Repentance' (*MF*, 225). Anxious to help her protégé undertake the same task, she sends Moll a minister. Whether or not he is the same clergyman as has assisted the Governess, he evidently has not only excellent moral and spiritual qualities but also contacts in judicial circles, for he tells Moll that she must renounce

---

7 G.A. Starr (1976, 389) suggests that the printer mistakenly expanded 'Ct.' to 'Circuit' whereas Defoe meant 'Court', but it is just as likely that he is referring to the kind of administrative pardon which in the provinces was initiated by judges riding the assize circuits.
8 These are among the factors mentioned in many successful petitions; King 2000, Chapter 9.

all 'hopes of Life, which he said, he was inform'd there was no room to expect' (*MF*, 225). Invited to 'disburthen my own Mind', she tells us she 'unravell'd all the Wickedness of my Life to him: in a word, I gave him an Abridgement of this whole History; I gave him the picture of my Conduct for 50 Years in Miniature' (*MF*, 226); next morning, amidst tears of shame for things past, she comes to experience 'a secret surprising Joy at the Prospect of being a true Penitent ... casting my Soul entirely into the Arms of infinite Mercy as a Penitent' (*MF*, 227).[9]

As Gladfelder notes (2001, 126), '[t]here is no reason 'to question the authenticity of Moll's Newgate conversion ... yet if Moll is repentant, she is not cripplingly repentant'. That she is not wholly reconciled to casting herself into the Arms of Mercy becomes evident when, on learning on the Wednesday that she is to die on the Friday, she falls – twice – into a swoon. The minster also seems to be of two minds: having done 'what he could to comfort me with the same Arguments, and the same moving Eloquence that he did before', he spends the critical Thursday 'employ'd on my account', and late that evening comes to the prison with the news that he has 'obtain'd a favourable Report from the Recorder to the Secretary of State in my particular Case, and in short that he had brought me a Reprieve' (*MF*, 228). Since the Recorder must have previously reported on Moll *un*favourably, we may assume that he had been persuaded to change his mind on hearing of her penitence (Cervantes 2011, 326).[10] Yet it seems that neither the minister nor Moll can be sure that he will allow a reprieve to be transformed into a pardon:

> I had some just Apprehensions that I should be included on the next dead Warrant at the ensuing Sessions; and it was not without great difficulty, and at last an humble Petition for Transportation, that I avoided it, so ill was I beholding to Fame and so prevailing was the fatal Report of being an old Offender, tho' in that they did not do me

---

[9] Kietzman (1999, 699) places great importance on Moll's telling the minister her 'whole History': 'In the course of her previous life, Moll had serialized herself in fictions aimed to secure material ends; it is only when she proves herself able to contain and read these serializations in a continuous history that she is considered a true convert and eventually pardoned'. But what has she left out in reducing the story we have been reading to the 'Abridgement' or 'Miniature' offered the minister?

[10] The explanation Moll gives Jemy, however, makes no reference to penitence: 'the Judges having been made sensible of the hardship of my Circumstances, had obtain'd leave to remit the Sentence upon my consenting to be transported' (234).

> strict Justice, for I was not in the Sense of the Law an old Offender, whatever I was in the Eye of the Judge; or I had never been before them in a judicial way before, so the Judges could not Charge me with being an old Offender, but the Recorder was pleas'd to represent my Case as he thought fit.
>
> MF, 230

Gabriel Cervantes (2011, 330) describes the legal fiction of petitioning for transportation in terms of an 'interplay of religious and legal forces ... [signifying] both a general sense of God's mercy while also connoting Royal Mercy', one which intertwines 'spiritual concerns and those of the criminal justice system ... in the service of an expanding Empire'. This convincingly explains the ideology embodied in the ceremony, but not why Defoe makes so little of it here. Moll's 'humble Petition for Transportation' is mentioned casually and left sandwiched between her apprehensions and her resentment at having been being unjustly considered 'an old Offender'. To make sense of this resentment we must take it as referring back to the Recorder's first, negative judgement of her case, which is recalled in terms that suggests subtle criticism of a judicial process that leaves it up to one powerful man to decide whether a woman should live or die as he 'was pleas'd' and 'thought fit'. Informed Londoners among Defoe's early readers might have taken this as reflecting on the man whose 'attitudes and ideas shaped the pattern of execution at Tyburn' during the quarter century of his recordership. Sir William Thomson, whom we have already met in his role as architect of the transportation policy, also took an active part in applying it in practice. Both in reporting to the hanging cabinet and in reviewing petitions for pardons he discriminated clearly and consistently between those he judged to be 'settled into a life of crime' and those he deemed to have been unfortunate or convicted on weak evidence (Beattie 2001, 442–444, 454–455).

However indignantly Moll insists on her not being, 'an old Offender ... in the Sense of the Law', there is no doubt about which of Thomson's categories she fits into, so she is fortunate in being offered the chance to make 'humble Petition for Transportation'. Yet she does not come over as very humble in telling us of it, or as very grateful for the remission of her death sentence:

> I HAD now a certainty of Life indeed, but with the hard Conditions of being order'd for Transportation, which indeed was a hard Condition in it self, but not when comparatively considered; and therefore I shall make no Comments upon the Sentence, nor upon the Choice I was put to; we shall all choose any thing rather than Death, especially

when 'tis attended with an uncomfortable prospect beyond it, which was my Case.

MF, 230

In having Moll refer to 'Conditions' and being 'put to' a choice, Defoe makes it clear that we are to understand her as having received a conditional pardon under the pre-1718 dispensation, and to 'strategically forget' current practice at the Old Bailey, where those receiving verdicts like hers would have had no option and no need to petition to be transported – although many petitioned *not* to be.

Defoe comes very near to making Moll do just that, for he does not see her off to America without dangling before her – and us – other possible outcomes. The minister, fearing the bad influence of convict company, tries 'very hard ... to prevent my being Transported also, but he was answer'd, that indeed my Life had been given me at his first Solicitations, and therefore he ought to ask no more' (*MF*, 240). From this we infer that he has petitioned the secretary of state for a free pardon, but had exhausted his credit in high places. Moll's Governess, as usual, has her own ideas about how to fix things: 'ways and means might be found out to dispose of me in a particular way', she hints, intimating that pardons can be bought: 'Why, *you have Money, have you not?* did you ever know one in your Life that was Transported, and had a Hundred Pound in his Pocket, I'll warrant you Child, *says she*' (*MF*, 231). Moll is content to 'leave all that' to her Governess, who is optimistic: '*we will try what can be done*'. If nothing comes of her efforts, it is not because the system proves impervious to bribery, but because, Moll tells us, 'it could not be done unless with an Expence too heavy for my Purse' (*MF*, 240).

Even now, all is not lost.[11] After more than a year in Newgate, Moll is taken with thirteen other convicts on board a ship which makes its way down the Thames to a point from where it is supposedly harder to escape: harder, but not impossible, for a helpful boatswain offers, for a mere £50, to get her ashore. If Moll refuses, it is because she has in the meantime come to see in America not a chance to reform, but a chance to make a new and better life for herself and her recently re-acquired *'Lancashire* husband'. We now turn to the even more complicated stop/start process by which Defoe gets him too out of Newgate and onto his wife's Virginia-bound ship.

---

[11] As Loveman remarks (2023, 433), 'for determined players such as Moll and the Governess, with verbal facility, money, and some connections, each stage of the legal process becomes the start of a negotiation, not a conclusion'.

3.2 Jemy and Friends

We last left Moll and Jemy catching up on their lives since parting in Dunstable several years earlier. She then enquires into

> the Circumstances of his present Case at that time, and what it was he expected when he came to be try'd; he told me that they had no Evidence against him, or but very little, for that of the three Robberies which they [he and his comrades] were all Charg'd with, it was his good Fortune, that he was but in one of them, and that there was but one Witness to be had for that Fact, which was not sufficient; but that it was expected some others would come in against him; that he thought indeed, when he first see me, that I had been one that came of that Errand; but that if no Body came in against him, he hop'd he should be clear'd, that he had had some intimation, that if he would submit to Transport himself, he might be admitted to it without a Tryal, but that he could not think of it with any Temper, and thought he could much easier submit to be Hang'd.
>
> MF, 236

Jemy's hopes of being cleared – which would have entailed being discharged by the magistrate who had committed him – rest on a very big 'if' for, as he later admits, 'one hard mouth'd Countryman swore home to him, and they were like to have others come in according to the Publication they had made' (MF, 239).[12] From the 'intimation' he has received we infer that some well-connected patron thinks Jemy had better not risk going before an Old Bailey jury. Readers familiar with the *Proceedings* and Ordinary's *Accounts* of the time would have agreed: of the one hundred and eleven trials for highway robbery celebrated between 1720 and 1722, fifty-four ended with death sentences.

Jemy seems intent on joining the condemned. Modelling himself on the stereotype of the gentleman-highwayman, he declares that death is preferable to 'the Woods and Wildernesses of *America*' and above all to 'Servitude and hard Labour ... things Gentlemen could never stoop to' (MF, 236).[13] Defoe here attributes to Moll's husband a snobbish and 'unproductive' position which she

---

12 On the numbers of witnesses needed to prove guilt, see above p.168, n. 22.
13 Ekirch (1987, 63–64) cites several actual prisoners as preferring death to banishment, 'bondage' and 'slavery', but not for Jemy's reasons. For convicts preferring to undergo medical experiment, see above, note 1.

sets about talking him out of and replacing with a 'more pragmatic alternative' (Cervantes 2011, 324):

> I told him the infamy of a publick Execution was certainly a greater Pressure upon the Spirits of a Gentleman, than any of the Mortifications that he could meet with Abroad could be; that he had at least in the other a Chance for his Life, whereas here he had none at all; that it was the easiest thing in the World for him to manage the Captain of the Ship ... especially if there was Money to be had ... to buy himself off, when he came to *Virginia*.
>
> *MF*, 236–237

Piling on the arguments, Moll promises to add her own stock of money to his, enabling him to 'not only avoid the Servitude, suppos'd to be Consequences of Transportation; but begin the World upon a new Foundation', and to show that she is 'fully acquainted with the Method' of doing this, she will 'deliver ... [herself] from the Necessity of going over at all, and then ... go with him freely, and of my own Choice ... and that we should live as new People in a new World'. Jemy gives in, but still hopes 'that there might be some way to get off, before he went' – whatever that means – and Moll promises to do her 'utmost in that Part too' (*MF*, 238).

Fortunately, she is not called upon to fulfil these over-generous promises.[14] A definite offer of exile is made 'upon the intercession of some great Person who press'd him hard to accept of it before a Tryal', and faced with the danger of more witnesses coming in against him, Jemy grudgingly consents, 'his great Friend, who was his Intercessor for the Favour of that Grant having given Security for him that he should Transport himself, and not return within Term' (*MF*, 239). The option of leaving the country at one's own expense 'had always been an option for convicts who could mobilise powerful support'

---

14   Why is Moll ready to go to such lengths to have Jemy accompany her? Zomchick (1989, 551) sees her reunion with her only true love after the elder brother at Colchester as 'reintroducing normative gender traits designed to restrain her unbounded acquisitive appetites. In short, Moll is softened by affection ... The *quid pro quo* that has governed Moll's behaviour throughout the novel ceases momentarily, for she has nothing to gain by her compassion for Jemy.' However, as Zomchick also mentions, 'her aggressive productivity can henceforth prosper because it is nominally under *coverture*. *Coverture* brings with it the luxury of indulging "natural" feelings ...'. It also enables her to assume a genteel position in society, to negotiate successfully for her freedom and, incidentally, would provide immunity if she were ever again in trouble with the law.

PUNISHING AND PARDONING

(Beattie 2001, 295) and Defoe clearly appreciated the importance of 'connection' in judicial matters.[15] He also, however, finds a place for the role of bribery. When Jemy and Moll compare the assets with which they are to leave England, he can produce little more than a hundred pounds: 'for his Stock was pretty good when he came into the Prison, but the living there as he did in a Figure like a Gentleman, *and which was ten times as much*, the making of Friends, and soliciting his Case, had been very expensive' (*MF*, 244).

Perhaps not expensive enough, for at one point it begins to look as if Jemy will not be discharged from prison in time to cross the Atlantic on the same ship as his wife, and although the Governess does manage to get him out of prison in time, the promised voluntary status is not forthcoming. When Moll finally sees her husband come on board, he is

> drag'd along with three Keepers of *Newgate,* and put in board like a Convict, when he was not so much as been brought to a Tryal; he made loud complaints of it by his Friends, for it seems he had some interest; but his Friends got some Cheque in their Application, and were told he had had *Favour enough* and that they receiv'd such an Account of him since the last Grant of his Transportation that he ought to think of himself very well treated that he was not prosecuted a new.
>
> *MF,* 243

Defeated by this barely veiled threat, Jemy curses the 'Hell-hounds' who have let him down but takes consolation in the arms of his affectionate wife (*MF*, 244).[16]

The minister, the Recorder, the great persons and 'Friends' who have effectively manipulated the couple into more or less resentfully leaving their native

---

15   In eighteenth-century Scotland It seems to have been common for accused men and women to be allowed transport themselves before coming to trial. At the High Court of Judiciary in Edinburgh between 1736 and 1775, 108 men and women indicted on capital charges asked to be banished to America before their cases came on; Ekirch 1987, 61.

16   Defoe seems to have had some difficulty with deciding on the legal status of Jemy at this stage. The first edition of *Moll Flanders* contained two, mutually contradictory passages, one of which stated that 'we were both on Board, actually bound to *Virginia*, in the despicable Quality of Transported Convicts destin'd to be sold as Slaves', the other that 'he was not order'd to be sold when he came there, as we were, and for that Reason he was obliged to pay for his Passage to the Captain, which we were not'. In his edition of the novel Albert J. Rivero (2004, 269) explains the compositor's error behind this textual problem.

country disappear from their lives at this point, and they set about making a new and vitally important alliance – with the ship's captain. The helpful boatswain acts as conduit, representing the captain as 'one of the best humour'd Gentlemen in the World' (*MF*, 245), and giving the captain 'so good a Character of me, and of my Husband, as to our civil Behaviour' that even before meeting they are offered a choice of deck cabins and an invitation to dine at his table (*MF*, 246–247). When the captain comes aboard, Jemy's – presumably gentlemanly – conversation gains them an even better cabin and, for a mere fifteen guineas, their passage, provisions and handsome entertainment for the whole voyage (*MF*, 246–247).

More important in the long run is the Captain's advice as to how the couple may obtain their freedom and set up as planters. As he explains to the Governess, they

> in the first Place must procure some Body to buy them as Servants, in Conformity to the Conditions of their Transportation, and then in the Name of that Person, they may go about as they will, they may either Purchase some Plantations already begun, or they may purchase Land of the Government of the Country, and begin where they please, and both will be done reasonably.
>
> *MF*, 248

The Captain has clearly acted as intermediary for wealthy transportees before; as the ship nears the shore,

> he brought a Planter to treat with him, as it were for the Purchase of these two Servants, my Husband and me, and there we were formally sold to him, and went a Shore with him: The Captain went with us, and carried us to a certain House whether it was to be call'd a Tavern or not, I know not, but we had a Bowl of Punch there made of Rum, &c. and were very Merry. After some time the Planter gave us a Certificate of Discharge, and an Acknowledgement of having serv'd him faithfully, and we were free from him the next Morning, to go whither we would.
>
> *MF*, 250

For this 'Peice of Service', which makes a mockery of 'the Conditions of their Transportation', the Captain asks 6,000 weight of tobacco and is given in addition 'a present of 20 Guineas, besides with which he was abundantly satisfy'd'. If one could estimate how much Moll and Jemy have spent between them on lodgings and provisions in Newgate and on board ship, on the tools and supplies they buy in order to set up as planters, in bribing Jemy's way out of a trial and both their ways out of servitude, it is a wonder that enough is left over from the profits of their thieving careers to rent – as they do – a warehouse and lodging, and to purchase two plantations and servants to work them.[17]

Defoe may have felt that in telling how Moll and Jemy avoid the rope and make their improbably easy transition to a new life, he had allowed the theme of penitence and pardoning – which in any case has no place in Jemy's story and only a small one in Moll's – to be overshadowed by a series of business deals and moves in the game of influence and interest. In *Colonel Jack* he was to place the topic within the novel's 'overarching theme of gratitude' (Novak 2001, 608), and attempt 'a complex reworking of the vision of transportation that appears in Moll Flanders – one that remakes the transport's story into a narrative model of reform applicable to convicts and non-convicts alike' (Cervantes 2011, 331n).

4   Avoiding the Rope in *Colonel Jack*

4.1   *The Value of a Pardon*

Like Jemy, a figure Colonel Jack resembles in name, in gentlemanly pretentions, in a tendency to depend on powerful men and indeed on powerful women (Gregg 2009, Chapter 6), the protagonist of Defoe's second criminal fiction is never brought to justice for his own crimes, but as we saw earlier, he risks being punished for those of his various doubles. As a boy he longs to join Major Jack's pickpocketing gang, follows in the footsteps of Will as he progresses to street robbery, and profits from his brother the Captain's marauding on their journey from London to Edinburgh. The Major, as well as at least one of his Rosemary Lane 'Society', Will and the Captain all come to a ghastly end without our glimpsing any possibility of respite or remission.

The Colonel, on the other hand, discovers in America, 'a more satisfying model … a model that leads eventually, he believes, somewhere better: freedom, employment, and innocence' (Cervantes and Sill, 2016, 31). The path to this utopian condition lies through direct and indirect experiences of receiving and bestowing clemency. Kidnapped, shipped to Virginia/Maryland and sold as a servant to a rich planter, he looks forward to eventually being

---

[17]   David Wallace Spielman (2012, 76–81) notes that in turning to agriculture she at last attains a settled income.

given land to cultivate and to living without stealing (*CJ*, 164). Configuring his slave-like condition as having been imposed by a 'strange directing Power, as a Punishment for the Wickedness of my younger Years' (*CJ*, 165), Jack begins to develop 'the vision of himself as a pardoned criminal – not unlike his more famous counterpart, Moll Flanders – [that] kills off other possible doubles and proves the most accommodating for a narrative driven by and towards moral and spiritual recalibrations' (Cervantes and Sill, 2016, 34).

The first big step towards those recalibrations comes in a long scene in which his master, Smith, comes down to his plantation to receive convicts off a transport ship. Jack has been chosen to form part of the guard that is to take them into custody and is thus able to observe an elaborate ritual:

> WHEN his Worship had read over the Warrants, he call'd them over by their Names, One by One, and having let them know by his reading the Warrants over again to each Man respectively, that he knew for what offences they were Transported; he talk'd to each one separately very gravely, let them know how much Favour they had receiv'd in being sav'd from the Gallows, which the Law had appointed for their Crimes, that they were not Sentenced to be Transported, but to be hang'd, and that Transportation was granted them upon their own Request and humble Petition.
>
> *CJ*, 166–167

According to the time scheme of *Colonel Jack*, this inset episode takes place in the 1680s, so Justice Smith's purchases could *only* have ended up in chains on his plantation 'upon their own Request and humble Petition'. In calling attention to what has *not* happened to these felons, Defoe reminds the reader of the current, very different framing of transportation as a punishment.

This collective message is illustrated and brought home by the story of one of the convicts, a lad who strongly reminds Jack of his own, younger self. Although 'not above 17 or 18 Years of Age', this 'incorrigible Pick-pocket' had specialised in stealing just those merchants' pocket-books that Will and the young Colonel had targeted, but proved less canny than they at getting away with them. He has been 'several times Condemn'd, but ... Respited or Pardon'd', 'Whipt two or three times, and several times punish'd by Imprisonment, and once burnt in the Hand', corporal punishments that have no lasting deterrent effect. Like the early episode in which the Captain is beaten bloody in Bridewell but soon reverts to kidnapping, these failures prepare the reader to see transportation as a more effective alternative (Cervantes 2011–2012,

264–265). Finally taken while trying to cash a large bill, he had been sentenced to death but reprieved when 'the Merchant upon his earnest Application … obtained that he should be Transported, on Condition that he restor'd all the rest of the Bills' (*CJ*, 168).

Cervantes and Sill (2016, 33) see in this boy an alternative to the models followed earlier, 'a crucial one as it gives Jack another (extremely persuasive) narrative model for understanding what has happened to him and what he has done', one that comes 'within the purview of penitence, repentance, and God's providence'. But does it? The condition imposed on the pickpocket is not that he repent, but that he make good the prosecutor's financial loss, and although while talking 'mighty religiously to this Boy' Justice Smith represents his reprieve as having been orchestrated by God, no one suggests that transportation offers an opportunity to reform – it merely removes the opportunity to steal (O'Brien, 1998, 71). It is true that Jack identifies completely with the boy; he is so moved by his master's discourse that he is convinced that it had been addressed to him, and when called into his master's parlour Jack enters 'like a Malefactor indeed … like one just taken in the Fact' (*CJ*, 169). Yet when questioned about his past, he omits any mention of his early life and disingenuously denies any resemblance to the young transport: 'that Boy is a Thief, and condemn'd to be hang'd, I never was before a Court of Justice in my Life'. Deploying a combination of half-truths and legalistic equivocation similar to that which he had used when examined by the London magistrate, Jack convinces his Virginia equivalent to refrain from asking awkward questions, and indeed to 'do something' for him. The interview ends with Smith offering to help negotiate the £94 bill Jack has saved out of his (ill-gotten) gains, bestowing on him the rank of overseer and having him fitted out as a gentleman.

This new status opens up yet another perspective on punishment and pardoning, for in being raised up the chain of command Jack at once incurs a debt of gratitude and obedience and finds himself judge, executioner and dispenser of mercy. As part of his gentleman's costume Jack is given a horsewhip so that he will be able to 'correct and lash the Slaves and Servants when they proved Negligent, or Quarrelsome, or in short were guilty of any Offence' (174). Finding himself unable to wield it effectively, he discovers that 'the brutal Temper of the *Negroes*' may be better 'manag'd' by inducing gratitude, a method he convinces his master to adopt by means of an elaborate piece of play acting. First, he leads him past two terrified, manacled slaves 'making pitiful Signs … for Mercy', explains that they have been condemned to a series of probably fatal beatings and argues 'the Necessity of making Examples' (176–177). He then reveals that all this is merely a piece of theatre. By passing a 'cruel Sentence' on a rebellious slave and leaving him in a simulacrum of Newgate's 'Condemn'd Hole', Jack argues,

> first, Sir, he remains under the terrible Apprehensions of a Punishment, so Severe, as no *Negro* ever had before; this Fellow, with your leave, I intended to Release to Morrow, without any Whipping at all, after Talking to him in my way about his Offence, and raising in his Mind a Sense of the value of Pardon; and if this makes him a better Servant than the severest Whipping will do, then I presume you would allow, I have gain'd a Point.
> *CJ*, 180

In accordance with accepted opinion in the colony, Smith objects that 'these Fellows have no Sense of Gratitude', but Jack corrects this 'Publick and National Mistake':

> That is, Sir, because they are never Pardoned, if they Offend they never know what Mercy is, And what then have they to be Grateful for? ... Besides, Sir, if they have at any time been let go, which is very seldom, they are not told what the Case is; they take no pains with them to imprint Principles of Gratitude on their Minds, to tell them what Kindness is shewn them, and what they are Indebted for it, and what they might Gain in the End by it.
> *CJ*, 180

Defoe's early readers would have seen how this reproof could apply to Old Bailey trial procedure, which 'let go' offenders without taking 'pains ... to imprint Principles of Gratitude on their Minds'.

The recipients of mercy are not the only ones to gain by the 'Kindness' shown them, as Jack illustrates by the story of his dealings with the slave Mouffat. By means of threats, a couple of cruel lashes, much talking and a pardon for which he pretends to have interceded, Jack had tamed this drunk, thief and abuser of women into a state of such abject gratitude that he is willing to lay down his life for his benefactor. More usefully, in terms of plantation management, Mouffat readily agrees to convince his fellow slaves to 'shew themselves grateful, for kind usage', and to work harder (*CJ*, 185). It is only after Jack himself becomes a planter and owner of slaves that he comes to see the spiritual benefits of clemency, but even then, the practical advantages never disappear from view.

4.2 The Wonders of Providence

The bringer of new light is one of Jack's purchases, a clever transported highwayman to whom he turns in search of an education. This 'Tutor' tells him how he had been taken not for any of his hundred robberies but for 'for a Triffle, a peice of Sport', and therefore 'privately Hurried into a Country Goal, under a wrong Name; try'd for a small Fact within Benefit of Clergy, and in which ... [he]was not principally Guilty, and by this means obtained the favour of being Transported' (CJ, 208). The lucky accidents and judicial blunders that enabled the Tutor to obtain this favour he perceives as one of 'the Wonders of that merciful Providence', the means by which God had wrought a 'blessed Change ... in my Soul'. The 'sparing Thieves from the Gallows certainly makes more Penitents than the Gallows it self', he declares, enthusiastically explaining to Jack the difference between the horror which overtakes men facing death and is mistaken for repentance, and the true 'Sense of mercy' which

> Seizes all the Passions, and all the Affections, and Works a sincere Unfeigned Abhorrence of the Crime, as a Crime; as an Offence against our Benefactor, as an Act of Baseness and Ingratitude to him, who has given us Life, and all the Blessings and Comforts of Life; and who has Conquer'd us by continuing to do us good, when he has been Provok'd to destroy us.
>
> CJ, 209

Jack is much affected by hearing yet another life history which 'in so many ways suited my own Case' but, with his Tutor as with Justice Smith, he is reticent about his own past and careful to let him know that he 'did not come over to *Virginia* in the Capacity of a Criminal' (CJ, 210). As for the 'religious Inference' drawn by the man, 'it struck into my Thoughts like a Bullet from a Gun', but while his tutor praises God for having delivered him from the temptation to sin, Jack is grateful for the 'good Circumstances' he enjoys, and not to God but to his 'old Master, who had rais'd me from my low Condition ... I had not so much as once thought of any higher obligation' (CJ, 213). Some thoughts of providence begin to dawn, and a course of scripture reading 'almost' persuades him to be a Christian, but not quite: 'as to commencing Penitent, as this Man had done, I cannot say, I had any Convictions upon me sufficient to bring it on, nor had I Fund of religious Knowledge to support me in it; so it wore off again Gradually, as such things generally do, where the first Impressions are not deep enough' (CJ, 214)

The study of modern history, on the other hand, arouses 'an unquenchable Thirst in ... [him], after seeing something that was doing in the World', a thirst that takes Jack back to Europe and entangles him in attempts to restore the Stuarts to the British throne. About his Jacobite activities he is less than candid with the reader. He first tells us that his sensible third wife, Moggy, had persuaded him not to join the Pretender's supporters at Preston (*CJ*, 287), a story he later overlays with a version in which he goes 'secretly' to the field, senses defeat and flees back across the Atlantic (*CJ*, 299). Nemesis follows when a number of Scots prisoners who have been 'at their own Request transported' (*CJ*, 301) arrive at plantations near his own and force him into hiding:

> I was now reduced from a great Man, a Magistrate, a Governor, or Master of three great Plantations, and having three or four Hundred Servants at my Command, to be a poor self condemn'd Rebel ... the Danger was come Home to me, even to my very Door, and I expected nothing, but to be inform'd against every Day, to be taken up, and sent to *England* in Irons, and have all my Plantations seiz'd on, as a forfeited Estate to the Crown.
>
> *CJ*, 302

If Jack is not 'discover'd, betray'd, carried to *England*, hang'd, quarter'd and all that was terrible' (*CJ*, 303), it is by the good management of yet another grateful, pardoned criminal. A convict bought by Jack reveals herself to be his discarded, adulterous first wife, and tells how she had joined a gang of thieves but had fortunately been – like the Tutor – taken 'for a very triffling Attempt, in which she was not Principal, but accidentally concern'd ... [and] sent to this Place' (*CJ*, 294). Jack forgives this 'sincerely Penitent' woman, reinstates her as his wife and when disaster strikes is rewarded by her offer to go to England and 'endeavour to obtain the King's Pardon whatever it cost' (*CJ*, 303). Ever ready to discover in himself gentlemanly virtues, Jack now finds that he had all along harboured loyalties to the monarch who alone has the power to forgive his treasonable actions:

> tho' I was unhappily Prejudic'd in favour of the wrong Interest, yet I had always a Secret, and right Notion of the Clemency, and merciful Disposition of his Majesty, and had I been in *England*, should I believe have been easily perswaded to have thrown myself at his Foot.
>
> *CJ*, 303

This hypothetical scenario of penitent rebel prostrate before a merciful monarch remains unrealised, as does the more prosaic one in which his Majesty's clemency is purchased in the form of an expensive special pardon. Jack's wife proposes to write to 'her Particular Friend at *London*' to discover whether a pardon is possible and how much it will cost, and he urges her to tell her correspondent

> that if he saw the way clear, and that he was sure to obtain it, he should go thorough Stitch with it, if within the Expence of two, or three, or four Hundred Pounds, and that upon Advice of its being practicable, he should, have Bills payable by such a Person on Delivery of the Warrant for the thing.
>
> *CJ*, 306

In the event Jack is saved from making this huge outlay, for news arrives from his wife's contact that a general pardon is imminent and 'Private Sollicitation' no longer needed. When copies of the Act of Grace of 1717 arrive and reveal that Jack is not among those excluded, he declares himself 'a generous Convert' and launches into a fulsome effusion:

> I became sincerely given in to the Interest of King GEORGE, and this from a Principle of Gratitude, and a Sense of my Obligation to his Majesty for my Life ... to those who graciously give us our Lives, when it is in their Power to take them away; those Lives are a Debt ever after ... I can never pay the Debt fully, unless such a Circumstance as this should happen, that the Prince's Life should be in my Power, and I as generously preserv'd it; and yet neither would the Obligation be paid then, because the Cases would differ; thus, that my preserving the Life of my Prince was my natural Duty, whereas the Prince on his Side (my Life being forfeited to him) had no Motive but meer Clemency and Beneficence.
>
> *CJ*, 310–311

Maximillian Novak (2001, 610) sees in this speech 'the culminating moment of his [Jack's] education', the point at which he attains 'some comprehension that true gentility lies in an understanding of the system of benefits, obligation and gratitude'. That system, however, is deeply ambiguous, relying as it does on shared knowledge of unrealised acts of cruelty. Far from having 'no

Motive but meer Clemency and Beneficence', the new, unpopular Hanoverian king had had good political motives for *not* taking away the lives of (too many) defeated rebels, thus avoiding raising Jacobite sympathies to danger levels and putting his precarious claim to sovereignty at risk. In this sense the Act of Indemnity, David Blewett (1979, Chapter 4) remarks, serves in *Colonel Jack* as an analogue for all the 'various acts of clemency intended to produce obedience'. Jack had brought his fellow slaves to gratefully serve their owner by first threatening and then waiving punishment; Lincoln Faller (1993, 195) imagines 'Somewhere in Whitehall, the king's ministers … "managing" Jack and other restive Britons … by the same techniques'.

5   Conclusion

The network of reprieves, remissions, pardons, favours and grants of mercy in *Colonel Jack* is just one of the several sets of analogies, comparisons and contrasts which Faller (1993, 198), drawing on the theoretical work of Pierre Macherey, sees as binding this 'jumpy' novel together at the level of the signifier, while exposing ideological chaos at the level of the signified:

> the more impressed we are by Defoe's efforts to make *Colonel Jack* seem 'all of a piece' (Macherey's phrase), the more aware we become that 'it is fissured, unmade even in its making' by the ideology out of which it is formed and which it seeks to transform: 'the disorder that permeates the work is related to the disorder of ideology (which cannot be organized as a system).'

The 'confusions and contradictions' that mainly interest Faller have to do with social class and early capitalism: the ways in which thieves, gentlemen and merchants are 'alike and yet opposite' (195). But much the same could be said of Defoe's fictional representations of law enforcement, especially as regards judicial punishment and acts of mercy. In *Moll Flanders*, respite from death is obtained by pregnancies false and real, pardons by humility and penitence but also by bribery and influence, with help from good minsters, but also from the Governess and great persons operating behind the scenes. In any case, Moll shows little sense of humility or of gratitude either to God or to the powers that be in accepting 'the favour of transportation'. In *Colonel Jack*, on the other hand, gratitude for remission of punishment is a central theme. Yet the overseer, master, husband or king who refrains from exercising his authorised legal power to oppress and take away life bestows a kindness on his subjects which they fulsomely acknowledge, but at the same time reveals the malice contained in that benevolence. By pardoning, Defoe has his protagonists show us, the bestower of mercy increases his own wealth, standing and power, and reinforces the power of the law itself.

Epilogue

This book proposes readings of *Moll Flanders* and *Colonel Jack* that focus more on enforcing the law than on breaking it. The protagonists of both novels are thieves who for the most part get away with their loot, but the possibility that they may be detected and caught, dragged before a justice and pursued by their prosecutors to the foot of the gallows, is always present. The 'thief-taker's story' is transmitted by way of a series of sophisticated narrative techniques. Numerous references to and anecdotes about mothers and brothers, partners and other doubles who are taken, tried and punished repeatedly remind Moll and Jack what may happen to them. Dialogues and 'trialogues' between thieves, victims, constables and justices set the principals' points of view off against what Faller (1993, 61) labels as the more 'normal' ones of those who abide by and uphold the law. And by incorporating into narrators' accounts of what actually happens imaginings of how things could or should have gone differently, Defoe has them enter into 'other subjectivities' and conjure up alternative scenarios which culminate in their being detected, taken and brought to justice.

In narrating what did or suggesting what might have taken place at the scene of a crime and after, and in writing fictions that (more or less) claimed to be true, Defoe inevitably took account of his readers' assumptions about what was possible or likely, assumptions that would have been very different from our own. If we are to read the criminal phases in the histories of Moll Flanders and Colonel Jack without too many anachronistic expectations, we need to foreground the now obsolete givens embedded in them. That law enforcement was 'everybody's business' and not that of trained professionals is the most basic of these. Those from whom Moll, Jack and their kind steal, those we now call 'victims', would for eighteenth-century readers have been potentially active detectives and apprehenders of thieves, perhaps participants in a beating, ducking or other form of street justice, perhaps exacting an apology and/or some form of compensation, perhaps seeking out criminals by advertising or through brokers and compounding for the return of the goods stolen, perhaps undertaking the expensive, time-consuming and problematic business of organising a formal prosecution. In eighteenth-century England even this last option depended largely on the agency of ordinary people, and was 'at every stage of the trial and in the administration of punishment shot through with discretionary powers' (Beattie 1986, 406). Those who caught thieves would have had to decide whether to call in a constable, which – if any – justice of the peace to go before, how severely to frame an indictment for vetting by a grand jury, whether or not to turn up in court and with which witnesses, how to testify convincingly and, if they obtained a guilty verdict from the petty jury, whether to petition for the convict to be pardoned. Most of those with whom prosecutors would interact as they harried their suspects along this tortuous path would also have been amateurs untrained in the law, themselves expected to make choices and apply personal or group preferences that their modern equivalents – if they exist – are forbidden. Noticeably absent from the whole process, up to and including the 1720s, are those that now dominate law enforcement and the administration of justice: a professional police force with detective functions, public prosecutors and lawyers.

Defoe's criminal fictions have not until recently been read with close reference to the work of the social and cultural historians who have brought to life the peculiar justice system of early modern England, and this study is the first to read them alongside the largest printed source of pertinent information dating from Defoe's time. The *Old Bailey Proceedings* are invaluable as bases for informed guesses about the expectations of early readers and how those expectations may have influenced their responses to *Moll Flanders* and *Colonel Jack*. The crucial role played by two maidservants in the capture of Moll, for example, would have surprised early readers less than it does us, although the entrusting to plebeian women of all the testimony for the prosecution may have puzzled them. They would have expected the 'Felony only' verdict on Moll but not, perhaps, the death sentence that follows. There is also, however, a great deal of judicial matter in the novels for which there is little or no trace in the reports. Apart from a number of passing references to thieves 'not yet taken', the *Proceedings* by definition tell us only about offenders caught and brought to trial; Moll Flanders steals successfully for many years without coming to the Old Bailey, while Colonel Jack never does. Their success in avoiding capture and arguing their way out of arrests makes them representative of the actual thieves – probably a large majority – who escaped formal process of law. In this sense the novels throw light on real experiences which are not illuminated by the journalism of Defoe's day.

In so doing, however, they expose weaknesses in the system, what de Certeau calls 'cracks ... in ... surveillance' (1988, 37) which do not show up in the uncritical *Proceedings*. In the novels it is not only sex and drink that can distract attention and render people inept at detecting and taking thieves, but also poor health and business worries. It is not only via rag fairs and professional receivers that thieves are able to dispose of stolen goods; the willingness of wealthy victims of the middling and upper sort to treat for the return of their valuables, behaviours that amount to collusion with theft, is just as prominent. Will's and Jack's street robbery phase supports current fears that against superior numbers night travellers on the outskirts of London were only safe if they hired armed bodyguards, and that even a posse of neighbours may not manage to fight off a gang of determined burglars without losing life. Defoe's picture of Moll's time in Newgate on the one hand confirms the already commonly-held view that the promiscuous gaols only degraded their inmates further, on the other shows the grand jury phase as offering opportunities to tamper with witnesses and jurors. When Moll is finally brought to trial it is on a burglary charge for which no evidence is offered, and her own defence against the larceny charge is demolished by interference from a judge who in theory was supposed to supply the defendant's lack of legal counsel. Nowhere does the discretionary nature of the English judicial system have more potentially fatal consequences than during the final phase, when the condemned seek remission of death and transportation sentences by petitioning, bribing or bringing influence to bear behind the scenes. Years of penal servitude may emerge from the novels as a golden opportunity to reform and make a new life, but none of the main characters actually serve time on a plantation as a condition of pardoning. The only felons we see actually doing so, Jack's highwayman tutor and his cast off wife, have been enabled to do so by providential interference; in human terms that interference manifests itself as a series of accidents and judicial blunders.

Some of the features of the English law enforcement system which Defoe takes for granted were already on their way out by the time *Moll Flanders* and *Colonel Jack* were published in 1722. Did the novels indirectly help to naturalise change? As we have seen, the humble petitioning procedure Defoe assumes in both novels had been rendered obsolete by the 1718 Transportation Act: in anachronistically prolonging the association of banishment with pardoning he encouraged acceptance of exile as a secondary punishment for lesser crimes, but at an ideological price. By the 1720s the office of constable was already being *de facto* professionalised as more and more of those selected by parish vestries paid deputies to serve in their place; already nearly one third of London's constables were paid deputies. Defoe's episodes featuring officers at work would have done nothing to slow down the process, and might have prepared the ground for the formation of a paid, trained detective force by Henry and John Fielding in the 1750s. Episodes in which thieves run rings round justices may not have encouraged J.P.s to make themselves more available to complainants: the lack of active ones was to spur the City of London into establishing the first regular magistrates court in 1737. *Moll Flanders* and *Colonel Jack* may have helped promote these and the other 'piecemeal, incremental, *ad hoc*' changes taking place well before the reform debate really got under way (Beattie, 2001, 464). At the very least, they offered the middling sort of people – the sort who could have afforded to buy them and who would have been most likely to find themselves acting as prosecutors, constables and jurors – a chance to experience vicariously and imaginatively the conflicts, compromises and difficult decision-making involved in dealing with crime and with the machinery of justice, and to think about ways in which current strategies of law enforcement could be improved.

It is also possible that these fictions played a part in changing the way in which 'actual' law enforcement was narrated. In the early 1720s the *Old Bailey Proceedings* were still meagre publications of four to nine pages from which the words of defendants and witnesses are almost wholly absent. By the end of the decade they had become

> much longer and more accessible and interesting to the public. The December 1729 issue of the Sessions Papers was very different indeed from its predecessors. It was reduced slightly in size, but increased from eight to twenty-four pages, printed on better paper, with larger type and a much more generous layout that made it easier to read and more attractive to collect.
>
> BEATTIE 2001, 373

The intention was, the printer explained, 'to enlarge upon Trials ... with respect to the Crime, the Evidence, and the Prisoner's Defence' (cited in Beattie 2001, 374). Defoe's narrators are ahead of their time in anticipating the verbatim transcriptions and dramatised presentations of evidence that came to be included in trial reports from the 1730s on. Did his first-person accounts of plebeian thieves fighting for their lives, and of ordinary people seeking justice, help bring about that development and stimulate the growth of critical interest in testimony, its value and reliability? My enquiry started from the hypothesis that the *Proceedings* journalist was of help to a master of fictions, but that master of fictions may also have been of help to the journalist, and to the long line of his successors in the narrating of true crime, its detection, prosecution and punishment.

Bibliography

Primary Sources

Statutes

1 & 2 *Phil. & Mar.*, c. 13 (1554-5) [Marian bail statute]
2 & 3 *Phil. & Mar.*, c. 10 (1555) [Marian bail statute]
31 *Car.* II c. 2. (1679) [Habeas Corpus Act]
3 & 4 *Wm. & M.*, c. 9 (1691) [Benefit of Clergy Act]
4 & 5 *Wm. & M.*, c. 8 (1692) [Apprehending of Highwaymen Act]
10 & 11 *Wm. & M.*, c. 23 (1699 [Shoplifting Act]
1 *Anne*, stat. 2, c. 9 (1702) [Accessories & Receivers Act]
5 *Anne*, c. 31 (1706) [Apprehending of Housebreakers & Burglars Act]
12 *Anne*, c. 7 (1713) [Theft from Houses Act]
3 *Geo.* I, c. 19 (1717) [Act of Grace & Free Pardon/Indemnity Act]
4 *Geo.* I, c. 11 (1718) [First Transportation Act]
6 *Geo.* I, c. 23 (1720) [Second Transportation Act]

Websites

British History Online (www.history.ac.uk) last accessed 24 April 2025.
Christie's (wwww.christies.com) last accessed 24 April 2025.
Hitchcock Tim, Robert Shoemaker, Sharon Howard and Jamie McLaughlin, *et al.*, *London Lives, 1690–1800* (*www.londonlives.org, versions 1,1, 24 April 2012*), last accessed 16 January 2025.
Hitchcock Tim, Robert Shoemaker, Clive Emsley, Sharon Howard and Jamie McLaughlin, *et al.*, *The Old Bailey Proceedings Online, 1674–1913* (www.oldbaileyonline.org,version9.0,Autumn2023), last accessed 16 January 2025.
Law Dictionary (https://thelawdictionary.org/allocutus/) last accessed 24 April 2025
Oxford English Dictionary (2024), 'Mistake, verb'. DOI: 10.1093/OED/1561370541>, last accessed 1 March 2024.
Wikipedia (www.wikipedia.org) last accessed 24 April 2025.

Published Primary Sources

Anon. (1682), *A Guide to English Juries: Setting forth their Antiquity, Power and Duty, from the Common Law and Statutes. With a Table. By a Person of Quality. Also a Letter to the Author upon the same Subject*, London, printed for Thomas Cockerill.
Anon. (1699?) *The Great Grievance of Traders and Shopkeepers, by the Notorious Practice of Stealing Their Goods Out of Their Shops and Warehouses, by Persons Com-*

monly Called Shoplifters: Humbly Represented to the Consideration of the Honourable House of Commons*, London.

Anon. (1728), *Directions for Prosecuting Thieves without the Help of those False Guides, the Newgate Sollicitors, with a great deal of Ease, and little Expense: wherein is laid down the Manner of Indicting a FELON at Guild-Hall, Hick's-Hall, or the Old Bailey. To which is added A Lesson, very Necessary to be perus'd by those Gentlemen who serve as Jurors in any of His Majesty's Courts of Judicature*, London, printed for the author.

Anon. (1701), *Hanging not punishment enough FOR Murtherers, High-way Men, and House-Breakers. Offered to the Consideration of the Two HOUSES of PARLIAMENT*, London, printed for A. Baldwin.

Anon. (1717), *The History of the Press-Yard: Or, a Brief Account ...*, London, T. Moor.

Anon. (1742), *Select Trials at the Sessions-House in the Old-Bailey, For Murder, Robberies, Rapes, Sodomy, Coining Frauds, Bigamy, and Other Offences: To Which Are Added Genuine Accounts of the Lives, Behaviour, Confessions and Dying Speeches of the Most Eminent Convicts: In Four Volumes from the Year 1720 to This Time*, London, printed by J. Applebee for George Strahan, 4 vols.

Bohun Edmund (1693), *The Justice of Peace, His Calling and Qualifications ...*, London, printed for T. Salusbury.

Bray Thomas (1850), 'An Essay Towards ye Reformation of Newgate and Other Prisons in and about London', in W.H. Dixon, *John Howard and the Prison-World of Europe*, New York, Robert Carter & Brothers, 36–44.

Bullock Christopher (1717), *The Per-Juror. As it is acted at the Theatre in Lincoln's-Inn-Fields*, London, printed for William Mears, Jonas Brown and F. Clay.

Care Henry (1703), *English Liberties: or, The Free-born Subject's Inheritance. Being a Help to Justices as well as a Guide to Constables*, London, printed for B. Harris.

Coke Sir Edward (2003), *The Selected Writings and Speeches of Sir Edward Coke*, vol. 1, ed. by S. Sheppard, Indianapolis, Liberty Fund, 3 vols., <https://oll.libertyfund.org/titles/911>, accessed 1 March 2024.

Dalton Michael (1715), *The Country Justice: Containing the Practice of the Justices of the Peace As well IN, as Out of Their Sessions, Gathered for the Better Help of Such Justices of Peace as have not been much conversant in the Study of the Laws of this Realm*, Stafford printed for John Walthoe.

Defoe Daniel (1727), *Parochial Tyranny: or, the Housekeepers Complaint ...*, London, printed by J. Roberts.

Defoe Daniel (1750) *The Fortunes and Misfortunes of Moll Flanders, Who Was Born in Newgate, And during a Life of Continued Variety for Sixty Years, Was 17 Times a Whore, 5 Times a Wife, Once to Her Own Brother, 12 Years a Thief, 11 Times in Bridewell, 9 Times in New-Prison, 11 Times in Wood-Street Compter, 6 Times in the Poultry Compter, 14 Times in the Gate-House, 25 Times in Newgate, 15 Times Whipt at*

BIBLIOGRAPHY

the Cart's Arse 4 Times Burnt in the Hand, Once Condemned for Life, and ... Years a Transport in Virginia. At Last ... Rich, Lived Honest and Died a Penitent, London, printed in Aldermary Church-Yard.

Defoe Daniel (1976 [1722]), *The Fortunes and Misfortunes of the Famous, Moll Flanders, &*, ed. by G.A. Starr, London and Oxford, Oxford University Press.

Defoe, Daniel (2004 [1722]), *Moll Flanders: An Authoritative Text, Contexts, Criticism*, ed. by A. J. Rivero. New York, W.W. Norton.

Defoe, Daniel (2011 [1722]), *Moll Flanders*, ed. by G. A. Starr and Linda Bree. Oxford, Oxford University Press.

Defoe Daniel (2004 [1725]), *Defoe on Sheppard and Wild: The History of the Remarkable Life oof John Sheppard, A Narrative of All the Robberies, Escapes &c of John Sheppard, The True and Genuine Account of the Life and Actions of the Late Jonathan Wild*, ed. by Richard Holmes, London, Harper Perennial.

Defoe Daniel (2016 [1722]), *Colonel Jack*, ed. by G. Cervantes and G. M. Sill, Peterborough, Broadview Press.

De Veil Thomas (1747), *Observations on the Practice of a Justice of the Peace: Intended for Such Gentlemen as Design to Act for Middlelex* [sic] *or Westminster*, London, printed for Edward Withers.

Fielding Henry (1751), *An Enquiry into the Causes of the Late Increase of Robbers, &c ...*, London, printed for A. Millar.

Gardiner Robert (1710 [1692]), *The Compleat Constable ...*, London, printed for Tho. Beever.

Jacob Giles (1720 [1718]), *The Compleat Parish-Officer ...*, London, printed by Eliz Nutt and R. Gosling.

Jacob Giles (1729), *New Law Dictionary ...*, London, printed by E. and R. Nutt and R. Gosling.

Kettlewell John (1697), *An Office for Prisoners for Crimes, Together with Another for Prisoners for Debt Containing Both Proper Directions, and Proper Prayers and Devotions, for Each of Their Needs and Circumstances ...*, London, printed by A. and J. Churchill.

Meriton George (1682 [1669]), *A Guide for Constables ...*, London, printed for H. Herringman, H. Sawbridge, F. Tyton, J Starky, T. Baffet, R. Pawlet, S. Heyrick, W.R. Place and W. Leak.

P.S. Gent. (1721 [1705]), *A Help to Magistrates and Ministers of Justice: Also A Guide to Parish and Ward-Officers ...*, London, printed by Eliz. Nutt and R. Gosling.

Smith Sir Thomas (1982 [1583]), *De Republica Anglorum*, ed. by M. Dewar, Cambridge, Cambridge University Press.

T.H. (1705), *A Glimpse of Hell: Or a Short Description, of the Common Side of Newgate*, London, np.

Welch Saunders (1754), *Observations on the Office of Constable. With Cautions for the More Safe Execution of that Duty. Drawn from Experience*, London, printed for A. Millar.

Secondary Sources

Books

Backscheider P.R. (1989), *Daniel Defoe: His Life*, Baltimore and London, The Johns Hopkins University Press.

Backscheider P.R. (1990), *Moll Flanders: The Making of a Criminal Mind*, Boston, Twayne Publishers.

Bardotti Marta (1990), *Times of Pain and Distress*: A Journal of the Plague Year *di Daniel Defoe*, Pisa, E.T.S.

Beattie J.M. (1986), *Crime and the Courts in England 1660–1800*, Oxford and Princeton, Clarendon Press and Princeton University Press.

Beattie J. M. (2001), *Policing and Punishment in London 1660–1750: Urban Crime and the Limits of Terror*, Oxford, Oxford University Press.

Bell I.A. (2020 [1991]), *Literature and Crime in Augustan England*, London and New York, Taylor Francis, Kindle Edition.

Bender John (1987), *Imagining the Penitentiary, Fiction and the Architecture of Mind in Eighteenth-Century England*, Chicago and London, The University of Chicago Press.

Blewett David (1979), *Defoe's Art of Fiction*: Robinson Crusoe, Moll Flanders, Colonel Jack *and* Roxana, Toronto, Toronto University Press.

Chartier Roger (1987), *The Cultural Uses of Print in Early Modern France*, trans. by L.G. Cochran, Princeton, Princeton University Press.

Cox Pamela, R.B. Shoemaker and Heather Shore (2023), *Victims and Criminal Justice: A History*, Oxford, Oxford University Press.

Davis Lennard J (1996 [1983]), *Factual Fictions: The Origins of the English Novel*, Philadelphia, University of Pennsylvania Press.

de Certeau Michel (1988 [1984]), *The Practice of Everyday Life*, trans. by S. Rendall, Berkeley, Los Angeles and London, University of California Press.

Durston Gregory (2007),*Victims and Viragos: Metropolitan Women, Crime and the Eighteenth-Century Justice System*, Bury St Edmonds, Arima Publishing.

Durston, Gregory (2014 [2012]). *Whores and Highwaymen: Crime and Justice in the Eighteenth-Century Metropolis*, Hook, Hampshire, Waterside Press.

Ekirch A.R. (1987), *Bound for America: The Transportation of British Convicts to the Colonies, 1718–1775*, Oxford, Clarendon Press.

BIBLIOGRAPHY 231

Emsley Clive (2021), *A Short History of Police and Policing*, Oxford, Oxford University Press.

Faller L.B. (1987), *Turned to Account: The Forms and Functions of Criminal Biography in Late Seventeenth- and Early Eighteenth-Century England*, Cambridge, New York and Melbourne, Cambridge University Press.

Faller L.B. (1993), *Crime and Defoe: A New Kind of Writing*, Cambridge and New York, Cambridge University Press.

Foucault Michel (1991 [1979]), *Discipline and Punish: The Birth of the Prison*, trans. by A. Sheridan, London, Penguin Books.

Furbank P.N. and W.R. Owens (1988), *The Canonisation of Daniel Defoe*, New Haven and London, Yale University Press.

Furbank P.N. and W.R. Owens (1994), *Defoe De-Attributions: A Critique of J. R Moore's Checklist.*, London, The Hambledon Press.

Gatrell V.A.C (1994), *The Hanging Tree: Execution and the English People, 1770–1868*, Oxford, Oxford University Press.

Gladfelder Hal (2001), *Criminality and Narrative in Eighteenth-Century England: Beyond the Law*, Baltimore, The Johns Hopkins University Press.

Gregg S.H. (2009), *Defoe's Writings and Manliness: Contrary Men*, Farnham and Burlington, Ashgate.

Green T. A. (1985), *Verdict According to Conscience: Perspectives on the English Criminal Trial Jury 1200–1800*, Chicago and London, University of Chicago Press.

Grovier Kelly (2008), *The Gaol: The Story of Newgate, London's most Notorious Prison*, London, John Murray.

Herrup C.B. (1989 [1987]), *The Common Peace: Participation and the Criminal Law in Seventeenth-Century England*, Cambridge and New York, Cambridge University Press.

Halliday Stephen (2007 [2006]), *Newgate: London's Prototype of Hell*, Stroud, Sutton Publishing.

Hitchcock Tim and R.B. Shoemaker (2015), *London Lives: Poverty, Crime and the Making of a Modern City, 1690–1800*, Cambridge, Cambridge University Press.

Hitchcock Tim (2004), *Down and Out in Eighteenth-Century London*, London, Hambledon Continuum.

Howson Gerald (1970), *Thief-Taker General: The Rise and Fall of Jonathan Wild*, London, *Hutchinson*.

Humfrey Paula (2016 [2011]), *The Experience of Domestic Service for Women in Early Modern London*, London, Routledge.

Hunter J.P. (1990), *Before Novels: The Cultural Contexts of Eighteenth-Century English Fiction*, New York and London, W.W. Norton & Company.

Hurl-Eamon Jennine (2005), *Gender and Petty Violence in London, 1680–1720*, Columbus, Ohio State University Press.

Kayman M.A. (1992), *From Bow Street to Baker Street: Mystery, Detection and Narrative*, New York, St Martin's Press.

King Peter (2000), *Crime, Justice and Discretion in England, 1740–1820*, Oxford, Oxford University Press.

Lamoine Georges, ed. (1992), *Charges to the Grand Jury, 1689–1803*, London, Offices of the Royal Historical Society.

Landau Norma (1984), *The Justices of the Peace, 1679–1760*, Berkeley, Los Angeles and London, University of California Press.

Landau Norma and J.M. Beattie, eds. (2002a), *Law, Crime and English Society, 1660–1830*, Cambridge, Cambridge University Press.

Langbein J.H. (1974), *Prosecuting Crime in the Renaissance: England, Germany, France*, Cambridge, Harvard University Press.

Langbein J.H. (2005 [2003]), *The Origins of Adversary Criminal Trial*, Oxford, Oxford University Press.

Lemmings David, ed. (2012), *Crime, Courtrooms and the Public Sphere in Britain, 1700–1850*, Farnham and Burlington, Ashgate.

Lemmings David (2015 [2011], *Law and Government in England in the long Eighteenth Century: From Consent to Command*, Houndmills, Basingstoke.

Linebaugh Peter (2006 [1991]), *The London Hanged: Crime and Civil Society in the Eighteenth Century*, London, Verso Books.

Loretelli Rosamaria and Roberto De Romanis, eds. *Narrating Transgression: Representations of the Criminal in Early Modern England*, Frankfurt am Main, Berlin, Bern, New York, Paris, Wien, Peter Lang.

McKenzie Andrea (2007), T*yburn's Martyrs: Execution in England, 1675–1775*, London, Hambledon Continuum.

Morgan Gwenda and Peter Rushton (1998), *Rogues, Thieves and the Rule of law: The Problem of Law Enforcement in North-East England, 1718–1800*. London, UCL Press.

Morgan Gwenda and Peter Rushton eds. (2000), *The Justicing Notebook (1750–64) of Edmund Tew, Rector of Boldon*, Surtees Society Publications, Woodbridge, Boydell Press.

Mui Hoh-cheung and L.H Mui (1989), *Shops and Shopkeeping in Eighteenth-Century England*, Kingston, Montreal and London, McGill-Queen's University Press and Routledge.

Novak M.E (2001), *Daniel Defoe Master of Fictions: his Life and Ideas*, Oxford and New York, Oxford University Press.

Paley Ruth (1991), *Justice in Eighteenth-Century Hackney: The Justicing Notebook of Henry Norris and the Hackney Petty Sessions Book*, London, London Record Society.

Palk Deirdre (2006), *Gender, Crime and Judicial Discretion 1780–1823*, Woodbridge, Royal Historical Society and Boydell Press

Ray William (1990), *Story and History: Narrative Authority and Social Identity in the Eighteenth-Century French and English Novel*, Oxford, Blackwell.

Rabin D. Y. (2004), *Identity, Crime, and Legal Responsibility in Eighteenth-Century England*, Houndmills, Basingstoke, Palgrave Macmillan.

Rawlings Philip (2002), *Policing: A Short History*, Collompton, Willan Publishing.

Rawlings Philip (1992), *Drunks, Whores and Idle Apprentices*: *Criminal Biographies of the Eighteenth Century*, London, Routledge.

Reynolds E.A. (1998), *Before the Bobbies: The Night Watch and Police Reform in Metropolitan London, 1720–1830*, London and Basingstoke, Palgrave Macmillan.

Richetti John (1999), *The English Novel in History 1700–1780*, London, Routledge.

Richetti John (2005), *The Life of Daniel Defoe*, Oxford, Blackwell Publishing.

Robson Robert (1959), *The Attorney in Eighteenth-Century England*, Cambridge, Cambridge University Press.

Schramm Jan-Melissa (2000), *Testimony and Advocacy in Victorian Law, Literature and Theology*, Cambridge, Cambridge University Press.

Sharpe J.A. (1999 [1984]), *Crime in Early Modern England 1550–1750*, London and New York, Longman.

Shoemaker R.B. (2004), *The London Mob: Violence and Disorder in Eighteenth-Century England*, London and New York, Hambledon Continuum

Shoemaker R.B. (2008b [1991]), *Prosecution and Punishment: Petty Crime and the Law in London and Rural Middlesex, c. 1660–1725*, Cambridge, New York and Melbourne, Cambridge University Press.

Spraggs Gillian (2001), *Outlaws and Highwaymen: The Cult of the Robber in England from the Middle Ages to the Nineteenth Century*, London, Pimlico.

Starr G.A. (1971), *Defoe and Casuistry*, Princeton, Princeton University Press.

Swan Beth (1997), *Fictions of Law: An Investigation of the Law in Eighteenth-Century English Fiction*, Frankfurt am Main, Berlin, Bern, New York, Paris, Wien Peter Lang.

Thompson E.P. (1977 [1975]) *Whigs and Hunters: The Origin of the Black Act*, Harmondsworth, Middlesex, Penguin Books.

Tickell Shelley (2018), *Shoplifting in Eighteenth-Century England*, Woodridge, The Boydell Press.

Todd Dennis (2010), *Defoe's America*, Cambridge, Cambridge University Press.

Welsh Alexander (1992), *Strong Representations: Narrative and Circumstantial Evidence in England*, Baltimore, The Johns Hopkins University Press.

Ward R.M. (2014), *Print Culture, Crime and Justice in 18th-Century London*, London, Bloomsbury Academic.

Journal Articles and Chapters in Books

Andrew D.T. (1998), 'The Press and Public Apologies in Eighteenth-Century London, in *Law, Crime and Society: England 1660–1830*, ed. by Norma Landau and J. M. Beattie, Cambridge, Cambridge University Press, 208–229.

Ascari Maurizio (2016), 'The Shades of a Shadow: Crime as the Dark Projection of Authority in Early Modern England', *Critical Survey* 28 (1), 78–92.

Atkinson Alan (1994), 'The Free-Born Englishman Transported: Convict Rights as a Measure of Eighteenth- Century Empire', *Past & Present*, 144, 88–115.

Baker J. H. (1977), 'Criminal Courts and Procedure at Common Law 1550–1800', in *Crime in England 1550–1800*, ed. by J.S. Cockburn, Princeton, Princeton University Press.

Bauer W. A. (1982), 'Defoe's *Review* and the Reformation of Manners Movement', *Neophilologus*, 66, 149–159.

Blair Ann (2003), 'Reading Strategies for Coping with Information Overload ca.1550–1700', *Journal of the History of Ideas* 64 (1), 11–28. DOI.: 10.2307/3654293.

Bond C.S. (1971), '*Street-Robberies, Consider'd* and the Canon of Daniel Defoe', *Texas Studies in Literature and Language* 13 (3), 431–445.

Boulukos, G. E. (2001), 'Daniel Defoe's *Colonel Jack*, Grateful Slaves, and Racial Difference', ELH, 68 (3), 615–631. DOI: 10.1353/elh.2001.0021

Campbell Ann (2019), 'The Trial of the (Eighteenth) Century: Active Learning and *Moll Flanders*', *Digital Defoe*, 11.1.

Cecconi Elisabetta (2019), 'The Popularisation of Trial Discourse in 18th-century Periodicals: A Corpus-based Study of the Old Bailey Trial Proceedings and Newspaper Trial Reports (1710–1779)', *Lingue e Linguaggi* 30, 65–85 <http://siba-ese.unisalento.it/index.php/linguelinguaggi/article/view/19293>.

Cervantes Gabriel (2011), 'Convict Transportation and Penitence in *Moll Flanders*', ELH 78 (2), 315–336.

Cervantes Gabriel (2011–2012), 'Episodic or Novelistic? Law in the Atlantic and the Form of Daniel Defoe's *Colonel Jack*', *Eighteenth-Century Fiction* 24 (2), 247–277. Project Muse, DOI: 10.1353/ecf.2011.0046.

Cervantes Gabriel and G.M Sill (2016), 'Introduction', in D. Defoe, *Colonel Jack*, ed. by Gabriel Cervantes and G.M. Sill, Peterborough, Broadview Press, 11–56.

Chaber L.A. (1982), 'Matriarchal Mirror: Women and Capital in *Moll Flanders*', PMLA, 97 (2), 212–226. DOI: 10.2307/462188.

Clayton Mary and R.B. Shoemaker (2022), 'Blood Money and the Bloody Code: The Impact of Financial Rewards on Criminal Justice in Eighteenth-Century England', *Continuity and Change* 37, 97–125. DOI:10.1017/S0268416022000078.

Clegg Jeanne (1998), 'Evidence and Eye-Witness in Defoe', *Textus* 11 (2), 261–288.

Clegg Jeanne (2003), 'Inventing Organised Crime: Daniel Defoe's *Jonathan Wild*', *Many Voicéd fountains: Studi di anglistica e comparatistica in onore di Elsa Linguanti*, ed. by M. Curreli and F. Ciompi, Pisa, ETS, 214–234.

Clegg Jeanne (2004a), 'Reforming Informing in the Long 18th Century', *Textus* 19, 337–356.

Clegg Jeanne (2004b), 'Swift on False Witness', in *SEL: Studies in English Literature 1500–1900*, 44 (3), 461–485.

Clegg Jeanne (2008), 'Popular Law Enforcement in *Moll Flanders*', *Textus* 21, 525–548

Clegg Jeanne (2013), 'Criminal Genres in Early Eighteenth-Century England: *Moll Flanders*, the Ordinary's *Accounts* and the *Old Bailey Proceedings*', in *Liminal Discourses. Subliminal Tensions in Law and Literature*, ed. by D. Carpi and J. Gaakeer, Berlin and Boston, De Gruyter, 95–112.

Clegg Jeanne (2015), 'The Prosecution and Trial of Moll Flanders', *Digital Defoe: Studies in Defoe & His Contemporaries*, 7 (1). <https://digitaldefoe.org/2015/10/28/the-prosecution-and-trial-of-moll-flanders/>, accessed 1 March 2024.

Clegg Jeanne (2016), '"Quite Another Vein of Wickedness": Making Sense of Highway Robbery in Defoe's *Colonel Jack*', *Annali di Ca' Foscari. Serie occidentale* 50, 219–237. DOI: 10.14277/2499-1562/AnnOc-50-16-11.

Clegg Jeanne (2019a), '"Piecemeal, Incremental, *ad hoc*": "Beccarian" Experiments in Law Enforcement in Late Seventeenth- and Early Eighteenth-Century England,' *Diciottesimo Secolo* 4, 85–94. DOI: 10.13128/ds-25441.

Clegg Jeanne (2019b), 'De l'arrestion au procès: le parcors judiciare de Moll Flanders' in *Témoigner à l'âge classique et moderne: de sens au sens*, ed. by D. Berton-Charriè and M.Vénuat, Paris, Honoré Champion.

Clegg, Jeanne (2021), 'The Intricacies of Office: Constables, Thieves and the Uses of Literacy in *Moll Flanders* and *Colonel Jack*', *Journal of Early Modern Studies*, 10, 193–209. DOI: 10.13128/jems-2279-7149-12547.

Curtis L.A. (1993), 'A Rhetorical Approach to the Prose of Daniel Defoe', *Rhetorica: A Journal of the History of Rhetoric*, 11 (3). 293–319. DOI: 10.1525/rh.1993.11.3.293

Curtis T.C. and W.A. Speck (1976), 'The Societies for the Reformation of Manners: A Case Study in the Theory and Practice of Moral Reform', *Literature & History* 3, 45–64.

Dabhoiwala Faramerz (2006), 'Summary Justice in Early Modern London', *The English Historical Review* 121 (492), 796–822.

Damrosch Jr, Leopold (1973), 'Defoe as Ambiguous Impersonator', *Modern Philology* 71 (2), 153–159.

Davies Owen (2007), 'Talk of the Devil: Crime and Satanic Inspiration Eighteenth-Century England', University of Hertfordshire. http://herts.academia.edu/Owen Davies.

Ellison, Katherine (2023), 'Defoe and the Chatbot: The Emotional Avoidance of Predictive Prose,' *Digital Defoe*, 15 (1). DOI: 10.70213/1948-1802.1000.

Fleming Catherine (2019), '"My Fellow-Servants": Othering and Identification in Daniel Defoe's *Colonel Jack*', *Digital Defoe: Studies in Defoe & His Contemporaries* 11, 1, 17-35, <https://digitaldefoe.org/2019/12/04/my-fellow-servants-othering-and-identification-in-daniel-defoes-colonel-jack/,> accessed 1 March 2024.

Fludernik Monica (2023), 'The Penal System' in *Daniel Defoe in Context*, ed. A. J. Rivero and George Justice, Cambridge, Cambridge University Press, 189-196. DOI: 10.1017/9781108872140

Foyster Elizabeth (2007), 'Introduction: Newspaper Reporting of Crime and Justice', *Continuity and Change* 22, (1), 9-12. DOI: 10.1017/S0268416007006224.

Franks Rachel (2016), 'Stealing Stories: Punishment, Profit and the Ordinary of Newgate', in *Authorised Theft: Refereed Conference Papers of the 21st Annual AAWP Conference, 2016*, ed. by N. Fanaiyan, R. Franks and J. Seymour, Canberra University, Canberra, 1-11.

Furbank P.N. and W.R. Owens (2010), 'On the Attribution of Novels to Daniel Defoe', *Philological Quarterly* 89 (2-3), 243-253.

Gallanis, T. P. (2009), 'Reasonable Doubt and the History of the Criminal Trial' (reviewing *The Origins of Reasonable Doubt: Theological Roots of the Criminal Trial* by James Q. Whitman), *University of Chicago Law Review*, 76 (2), 941-964. Available at: https://chicagounbound.uchicago.edu/uclrev/vol76/iss2/7

Gladfelder Hal (2008), 'Defoe and Criminal Fiction', in *The Cambridge Companion to Daniel Defoe*, ed. by John Richetti, Cambridge University Press, 64-83

Gladfelder Hal (2018), 'Theatre of Blood: On the Criminal Trial as Tale of Terror', in *Criminal Justice During the Long Eighteenth Century*, ed. by David Lemmings and A. N. May, New York and London, Routledge.

Gollapudi, Aparna (2017), 'Criminal Children in the Eighteenth Century and Daniel Defoe's *Colonel Jack*', *Philological Quarterly*, 96 (1), 27-53.

Green T. A. (1988), 'A Retrospective on the Criminal Trial Jury, 1200-1800', in *Twelve Good Men and True: The Criminal Trial Jury in England, 1200-1800*, ed. by J.S. Cockburn and T.A. Green, Princeton, Princeton University Press, 358-399.

Harris Michael (1982), 'Trials and Criminal Biographies: A Case Study in Distribution', in *Sale and Distribution of Books from 1700*, ed. by Robin Myers and Michael Harris, Oxford, Oxford Polytechnic Press, 1-36.

Hay Douglas (1989), 'Prosecution and Power: Malicious Prosecution in the English Courts, 1750-1850', in *Policing and Prosecution in Britain, 1750-1850*, ed. by Douglas Hay and F. G. Snyder, Oxford, Clarendon Press, 345-395.

Hay Douglas, (2011 [1975]), 'Property, Authority and the Criminal Law', in *Albion's Fatal Tree: Crime and Society in Eighteenth-Century England*, ed. by Douglas Hay,

Peter Linebaugh, J. G. Rule, E.P. Thompson and Cal Winslow. London and New York, Verso.

Higdon, D. L. (1975). 'The Chronology of *Moll Flanders*', *English Studies*, 56(4), 316–319. DOI: 10.1080/00138387508597704.

Hollingshead, David (2017), Daniel Defoe and Abandoned Life, *Studies in the Novel*, 49 (1), 1–23. DOI: https://doi.org/10.131353/sdn.2017.0000.

Hurl-Eamon Jennine (2005), 'The Westminster Impostors: Impersonating Law Enforcement in Early Eighteenth-Century London', *Eighteenth-Century Studies* 38 (3), 461–483.

Kahan Lee (2009), '"A Thousand Little Things": The Dangers of Seriality in *The Spectator* and *Moll Flanders*', *Digital Defoe* 1 (1), 25–44.

Kalman H.D. (1969), 'Newgate Prison', *Architectural History* 12, 50–61. DOI:10.2307/1568336

Kent Joan (1981), 'The English Village Constable, 1580–1642: The Nature and Dilemmas of the Office', *Journal of British Studies* 20, (2), 26–49, DOI: 10.1086/385771.

King Peter (2009), 'Making Crime News: Newspapers, Violent Crime and the Selective Reporting of Old Bailey Trials in the Late Eighteenth Century', *Crime, Histoire et Socieétés/Crime, History and Societies* 13 (1), 91–116. DOI: 10.4000/chs.695.

King Peter and R. Ward (2015), 'Rethinking the Bloody Code in Eighteenth-Century Britain: Capital Punishment at the Centre and on the Periphery', *Past and Present* 228 (1), 159–205. DOI: 10.1093/pastj/gtv026.

Kietzman M. J. (1999), 'Defoe Masters the Serial Subject', *ELH* 66 (3), 677–705.

Landau Norma (1999), 'Indictment for Fun and Profit: A Prosecutor's Reward at Eighteenth-Century Quarter Sessions', *Law and History Review* 17 (3), 507–536. DOI: 10.2307/744380.

Lamb Jonathan (2004), 'The Crying of Lost Things', *ELH* 72, 949–967.

Landau Norma (2002), 'The Trading Justice's Trade', in *Law, Crime and English Society, 1660–1830*, ed. by N. Landau and J.M. Beattie, Cambridge, Cambridge University Press, 46–70.

Langbein J.H. (1978), 'The Criminal Trial before the Lawyers', *The University of Chicago Law Review* 45 (2), 263–316. DOI: 10.2307/1599166.

Lemire Beverly (1988), 'Consumerism in Preindustrial and Early Industrial England: The Trade in Second-hand Clothes', *Journal of British Studies* 27 (1), 1–24.

Lemire Beverly (1990), 'The Theft of Clothes and Popular Consumerism in Early Modern England', *Journal of Social History* 24 (2), 255–276.

Lemmings David (2017), 'Emotions, Power and Popular Opinion about the Administration of Justice: The English Experience, from Coke's 'Artificial Reason' to the Sensibility of 'True Crime Stories', *Emotions: History, Culture, Society*, 1 (1), 59–90.

Liebe Lauren (2021), 'Mary Frith, Moll Cutpurse, and the Development of an Early Modern Criminal Celebrity', *Journal of Early Modern Studies* 10, 233–248. DOI: 10.13128/jems-2279-7149-12549. http://dx.doi.org/

Linebaugh Peter (1977), 'The Ordinary of Newgate and His Account', in *Crime in England 1550–1800*, ed. by J.S. Cockburn, Princeton, Princeton University Press, 246–269.

Loveman Kate (2013), '"A Life of Continu'd Variety": Crime, Readers, and the Structure of Defoe's *Moll Flanders*', *Eighteenth-Century Fiction*, 26 (1), 1–32. DOI: 10.3138/ecf.26.1.1.

Loveman Kate (2023), '*Crime and the Law in Defoe's Works*', in *The Oxford Handbook of Daniel Defoe*, ed. by Nicholas Seager and J. A. Downie, Oxford Handbooks,online edn, Oxford Academic, 18, 417–436, DOI: 10.1093/oxfordhb/9780198827177.001.0001.

Mack Ruth (2011–12), '"Seeing Something that was Doing in the World": The Form of History in *Colonel Jack*', *Eighteenth-Century Fiction*, 24 (2), 227–245. Project Muse, DOI: 10.1353/ecf.2011.0043.

Marshall Ashley (2010), 'Did Defoe Write *Moll Flanders* and *Roxana?*', *Philological Quarterly* 89 (2–3), 209–241.

McBurney W.H. (1962), '*Colonel Jacque*: Defoe's Definition of the Complete English Gentleman', *Studies in English Literature, 1500–1900* 2 (3), 321–336. DOI: 10.2307/449482.

McKenzie Andrea (1998), 'Making Crime Pay: Motives, Marketing Strategies, and the Printed Literature of Crime in England 1670–1770', in *Criminal Justice in the Old World and the New: Essays in Honour of J.M.Beattie*, ed. by G. T. Smith, A.N. May and Simon Devereaux, Toronto, University of Toronto Press.

Michael S.C. (1996), "Thinking Parables: What *Moll Flanders* does not Say," *ELH* 63 (2), 367–395.

Moore J.R. (1939), 'Defoe's Use of Personal Experience in *Colonel Jack*', *Modern Language Notes* 54, (5), 362–363.

Morgan Gwenda and Peter Rushton (2007), 'Print Culture, Crime and Transportation in the Criminal Atlantic', *Continuity and Change* 22 (1), 49–71. DOI: 10.1017/S0268416006006175.

Morgan Kenneth (1989), 'Petitions against Convict Transportation, 1725–1735', *English Historical Review*, 104 (410), 110–113.

Novak M.E. (1970), 'Defoe's "Indifferent Monitor": The Complexity of *Moll Flanders*', *Eighteenth-Century Studies* 3 (3), 351–365. DOI: 10.2307/2737876.

Novak M.E. (1996), 'The Defoe Canon: Attribution and De-Attribution', *Huntington Library Quarterly* 59 (1), 83–104.

Novak M.E. (2012), 'Daniel Defoe and *Applebee's Original Weekly Journal*: An Attempt at Re-attribution', *Eighteenth-Century Studies* 45 (4), 585–608.

O'Brien John (1998), 'Union Jack: Amnesia and the Law in Daniel Defoe's *Colonel Jack*', *Eighteenth-Century Studies* 32 (1), 65–82

Parrinder Patrick (2001), 'Highway Robbery and Property Circulation in Eighteenth-Century English Narratives', *Eighteenth-Century Fiction* 13 (4), 509–528. DOI: 10.1353/ecf.2001.0023.

Punter David (1982), 'Fictional Representation of the Law in the Eighteenth Century,' *Eighteenth-Century Studies* 16 (1), 47–74. DOI: 10.2307/2738000.

Rabin D. Y. (2003), 'Searching for the Self in Eighteenth-Century English Criminal Trials, 1730–1800', *Eighteenth-Century Life*, 27 (1), 85–106.

Rogers Nicholas (1992), 'Confronting the Crime Wave: The Debate over Social Reform and Regulation, 1749–53', in *Stilling the Grumbling Hive: The Response to Social and Economic Problems in England, 1689–1750*, ed. by Lee Davison, Tim Hitchcock, T. Keirn and R.B. Shoemaker, Stroud, Alan Sutton, 82–87.

Rothwell Molly (2022), *Blackman Street. The Map of Early Modern London*, <mapoflondon.uvic.ca/edition/7.0/BLAC22.htm>, accessed 1 March 2024. ???'

Rubin A.T. (2012), 'The Unintended Consequences of Penal Reform: A Case Study of Penal Transportation in Eighteenth-Century London', *Law and Society Review*, 46 (4), 815–851. DOI: 10.1111/j.1540-5893.2012.00518.x

Rudolph Julia (2008), 'That "Blunderbuss of Law": Giles Jacob, Abridgment, and Print Culture', *Studies in Eighteenth-Century Culture* 37, 197–215. DOI: 10.1353/sec.0.0022.

Schneider C.E. (1979), 'The Rise of Prisons and the Origins of the Rehabilitative Ideal', *Michigan Law Review* 77 (3), 707–746, <https://repository.law.umich.edu/mlr/vol77/iss3/27>, accessed 1 March 2023.

Sertoli Giuseppe (1999), 'Cronologia e veridicità in Defoe (con alcune ipotesi su *Colonel Jack*)' in *L'invenzione del vero: Forme dell'autenticazione nel romanzo inglese del '70* ed. by Loretta Innocenti, Pisa, Pacini, 49–76.

Sheehan W.J. (1977), 'Finding Solace in Eighteenth-Century Newgate', in *Crime in England, 1550–1800*, ed by J.S. Cockburn, London, Routledge, 229–245.

Shoemaker, R. B. (2006). The Street Robber and the Gentleman Highwayman: Changing Representations and Perceptions of Robbery in London, 1690–1800, *Cultural and Social History*, *3* (4), 381–405. DOI: 10.1191/1478003806cso78o.

Shoemaker R.B. (2008a), '*The Old Bailey Proceedings* and the Representation of Crime and Criminal Justice in Eighteenth-Century London', *Journal of British Studies* 47 (3), 559–580. DOI: 10.1086/587722

Shoemaker R.B (2009), 'Print Culture and the Creation of Public Knowledge about Crime in 18th-Century London' in *Urban Crime Prevention, Surveillance, and Restorative Justice: Effects of Social Technologies*, ed. by Paul Knepper, Jonathan Doak and Joanna Shapland London and New York, Routledge, 1–21.

Shoemaker R.B. (2010), 'Print and the Female Voice: Representations of Women's Crime in London, 1690–1735', *Gender & History* 22 (1), 75–91. DOI: 10.1111/j.1468-0424.2009.01579.x.

Shoemaker R.B (2017), 'Worrying About Crime: Experience, Moral Panics and Public Opinion in London, 1660–1800', *Past & Present* 234 (1), 71–100. DOI: 10.1093/pastj/gtw046.

Shore Heather (2003), 'Crimes, Criminal Networks and the Survival Strategies of the Poor in Early Eighteenth-Century London', in *The Poor in England, 1700–1850: An Economy of Makeshifts* ed. by Steven King and Alannah Tomkins, Manchester and New York, Manchester University Press, 137–165.

Shore Heather (2009), '"The Reckoning": Disorderly Women, Informing Constables and the Westminster Justices, 1727–33', *Social History* 34 (4), 409–427. DOI: 10.1080/03071020903256994.

Sill G.M. (1976), 'Rogues, Strumpets and Vagabonds: Defoe on Crime in the City', *Eighteenth-Century Life* 2 (4), 74–78.

Sill G.M. (1983), 'Defoe's Two Versions of the Outlaw', *English Studies* 64 (2), 122–128. https://DOI.org/10.1080/00138388308598240.

Sill G.M.(2014), "Daniel Defoe and the Sentimental Novel," *Topographies of the Imagination: New Approaches to Daniel Defoe*, ed. by Katherine Ellison, Kit Kincade, and Holly Faith Nelson New York, AMS, 3–13.

Singleton R.R. (1976), 'Defoe, Moll Flanders, and the Ordinary of Newgate', *Harvard Library Bulletin* 24 (4), 407–413, <https://nrs.harvard.edu/URN-3:HUL.INSTREPOS:37363964>, accessed 1 March 2024.

Snell Esther (2005), 'Representations of Criminality and Victimisation in Provincial Newspapers: The Kentish Post 1717 to 1768', *Southern History*, 27, 48–75.

Snell Esther (2007), 'Discourses of Criminality in the Eighteenth-Century Press: The Presentation of Crime in *The Kentish Post*, 1717–1768', *Continuity and Change* 22 (1), 13–47. DOI:10.1017/S0268416007006236

Spielman D. W. (2012), 'The Value of Money in *Robinson Crusoe, Moll Flanders*, and *Roxana*' *The Modern Language Review*, 107 (1), 65–87. https://DOI.org/10.5699/modelangrevi.107.1.0065.

Starr G.A. (1976 [1971]), Introduction and notes to Defoe, *Moll Flanders*, London and Oxford, vii–xxix, 344–408.

Styles John (1989), 'Print and Policing: Crime Advertising in Eighteenth-Century England', in *Policing and Prosecution in Britain, 1750–1850* ed. by Douglas Hay and Francis Snyder, Oxford, Clarendon Press, 55–101.

Styles John (1987), 'The Emergence of the Police – Explaining Police Reform in Eighteenth and Nineteenth Century England', *British Journal of Criminology* 27 (1), 15–22.

Swan Beth (1998), 'Moll Flanders: The Felon as Lawyer', *Eighteenth-Century Fiction* 11(1), 33–48. DOI: 10.1353/ecf.1998.0031

Swarninathan Srividhya (2003), 'Defoe's Alternative Conduct Manual: Survival Strategies and Female Networks in *Moll Flanders*', *Eighteenth-Century Fiction*, 15 (2), 185–206. DOI: 10.1353/ecf.2003.0032

Wales Tim (2000), 'Thief-Takers and their Clients in Later Stuart London', in *Londinopolis: Essays in the Cultural and Social History of Early Modern* London, ed. by Paul Griffiths and M.S.R. Jenner, Manchester and New York, Manchester University Press, 67–84.

Weinreich S. J. (2020), 'Unaccountable Subjects: Contracting Legal and Medical Authority in the Newgate Smallpox Experiment (1721), *History Workshop Journal* 89, 22–44. DOI: 10.1093/hwj/dbz047

Wrightson Keith (1980), 'Two Concepts of Order: Justices, Constables and Jurymen in Seventeenth-Century England' in *An Ungovernable People: the English and their Law in the Seventeenth and Eighteenth Centuries*, ed. by John Brewer and John Styles, London, Hutchinson, 21–46.

Zomchick. J.P. (1989), '"A Penetration Which Nothing Can Deceive": Gender and Juridical Discourse in Some Eighteenth-Century Narratives', *Studies in English Literature, 1500–1900* 29 (3). 535–561. DOI: 10.2307/450654.

Index of Participants in Old Bailey Trials, J.P.s' Hearings and Related Names

—, alias Foster (defendant)   43
—, Sir John (prosecutor)   177

Ackersly, Thomas (prosecutor)   55
Adams, Thomas (defendant)   109
Addis, Samuel (defendant)   188n23, 190
Alcock, John (defendant)   202n
Alexander, Ann, Elizabeth and Mary (defendants)   57
Allen, James (defendant)   57
Alston, John (defendant)   28
Anderson, Luke (witness)   79
Appleton, James, alias Appleby, alias John Doe (defendant)   177, 178n, 188n22, 189
Armstrong, Samuel, alias Welshman (defendant)   79, 80n
Arnold, Edward (prosecutor)   158
Arnold, Richard (prosecutor)   78, 158
Ashworth, Elizabeth (witness)   159
Askew, Elizabeth (witness)   58
Atkinson, Christopher (defendant)   137n
Austin, Joseph (witness)   43

Baine, Jane (defendant)   57
Baker, Elizabeth (defendant)   194
Baker, Mr. (witness)   55
Barber, James (prosecutor)   27
Barr, Thomas (prosecutor)   27
Barrow, William (witness, constable?)   41n
Barry or Berry, Roger (witness)   82
Barter, John (defendant)   149n21
Barton, William (defendant)   81–82
Bartram, Thomas (defendant)   194
Bates, Thomas (defendant)   132n8
Baylis, Henry (prosecutor)   43
Bays, Richard (witness, constable)   108–109
Beal, George (defendant)   66
Beaul, Thomas, alias Handy (defendant)   79
Beachcroft or Beachcrest, Mr. (accused)   55
Becket, Henry (witness, constable)   107
Bedford, Thomas (prosecutor)   28
Behn, Jane, alias Macopny (defendant)   106

Bennet, Catherine (defendant)   11n
Best, John (defendant)   178
Biew, Charles (witness)   132 & n7
Biggs, Henry (witness)   40
Bird, James (defendant)   79
Bishop, Henry (witness)   58
Bishop, Thomas (defendant)   81, 159
Blackstone, John (defendant)   182–183, 188n24, 194
Blewit, William (defendant)   28
Boat, John (defendant)   177n, 189n
Body, John (prosecutor)   56, 177
Boice, Samuel (defendant)   173n7, 177n, 188n24
Boon, Charles (witness)   134
Boon, John (witness)   81, 159
Boon, Michael (witness)   159
Booth, Joseph (defendant)   28
Bonner, John (broker)   66
Bostock, Mary (defendant)   193n31
Bostock, Thomas (defendant)   28
Bow, George (prosecutor)   79
Bowman, Isaac (witness)   56
Bowyer, William (witness)   57
Braithwait, John (witness)   56
Brocas, Sir Richard (J.P., Lord Mayor)   130, 137
Brocken, John (defendant)   180, 188n23, 189
Brook, Thomas (prosecutor)   27
Browne, Richard (defendant)   158
Bryan, Joseph (defendant)   28, 194
Bull, William (witness)   29
Bun, Mary (defendant)   106
Burgess, Jonah (defendant)   176n12, 188n22, 189
Burridge, William, alias Berridge (defendant)   83, 159
Burridge, William (witness)   29
Burton, Joseph (witness)   42
Burton, Sir Charles (defendant)   40–41 & n
Bury, Joseph (defendant)   78
Busby, Edward (defendant)   194

INDEX OF PARTICIPANTS

Butler, Rebecca, alias Neal (defendant) 106
Butler, Thomas, alias Clark, alias Smith (defendant) 133*n*
Buxton, Francis (defendant) 158

Caldicut, Samuel (prosecutor) 166*n*19
Camfield, Sarah (witness) 56–57
Carl, William (defendant) 42
Carrick, James (defendant) 80–81
Carrol, Daniel (defendant) 80
Carter, John, alias Whalebone (defendant) 149*n*21
Carter, Elizabeth (prosecutor) 66
Cauthrey, John (defendant) 55, 202*n*
Cawderoy, Ann (defendant) 188*n*23, 190
Cecil, Richard (defendant) 157*n*8, 188*n*22, 189
Champman or Chapman, Mrs. (broker) 64–65
Cheston, Matthew (defendant) 109
Child William, alias Giles (defendant) 194
Clare, John (defendant) 28
Clark, Francis (guarantor) 135
Clark, Nathaniel (prosecutor) 40*n*
Clemenson, Joseph (prosecutor) 106
Clifford, Dr. (accused) 54
Coates, Mary (defendant) 136
Coats or Court, Susan or Susannah, alias Barret, alias Winter (defendant) 57, 134, 135 & *n*10
Cobidge, John (defendant) 81
Codner, James (defendant) 55, 107
Cole, Elizabeth (defendant) 26*n*
Cole, Elizabeth (prosecutor) 82
Colthorp, Robert (defendant) 28
Colthouse, William (defendant) 83
Conner, Hannah (defendant) 56, 61, 135
Constable, Philip (prosecutor) 180–181
Cook, Thomas (prosecutor) 27
Cooper, James (prosecutor) 27
Cope, Mary (defendant) 173*n*7, 177*n*, 189*n*24
Corder, Edward (defendant) 40
Cotterel Edward (defendant) 79
Courland, John (witness) 79
Courtney, William (defendant) 176*n*12, 182*n*18, 188*n*22
Coxsell, Richard (prosecutor) 27

Creech, James (prosecutor) 176
Crib, Thomas (defendant) 176*n*12, 181–182, 188*n*23
Crompton, Katherine (defendant) 42
Cross, Charles, alias Williams (defendant) 194
Crouch, Mr. (witness) 56–57
Cryer, William (defendant) 188*n*22

D'arbieau, Mary (defendant) 58, 189*n*24
Dace, John (prosecutor) 27
Daffey, John, alias Mosely (defendant) 188*n*23, 190*n*27
Dakins, Flaxmore (prosecutor) 109
Deard, William (prosecutor) 55
De La Mee, Isaac (witness) 183
Delforce, Stephen (defendant) 179*n*15, 188*n*23, 190*n*27
Dely, Samuel, alias Deling (defendant) 176*n*12, 177*n*, 182*n*18, 188*n*24, 189*n*25
de Plosh, Peter (defendant) 133–134
Dexter, Samuel (defendant) 177*n*
Dickens, Samuel (prosecutor) 55
Dickinson, Richard (accused) 81
Dickman, John (witness) 108*n*3
Dikes, John (witness) 83
Dixon, Barnard (prosecutor) 28
Dormy, Joseph (prosecutor) 107
Dorton, John (defendant) 109
Dower, Martha (defendant) 26*n*
Downing, William (witness) 178, 183 & *n*19, 191
Drew, Isaac (witness) 82–83
Drumman, Robert or Robin (defendant) 79, 80*n*
Dunkley, William (witness) 44
Dye, Penelope (defendant) 106, 194
Dyer, Susan (defendant) 177, 189*n*24, 196

Eades, Thomas, alias Eaves (witness) 82
Earl, John Bartholomew (defendant) 158
Earnly, Mrs. Ann (prosecutor) 24
East, Robert (prosecutor) 192
Edwards, John (defendant) 29
Elliot, Susannah (defendant) 179*n*16, 188*n*24
Elliot, William (prosecutor) 28

INDEX OF PARTICIPANTS

Ellis, Tabitha (accused)   20
Elson, Mrs. (witness)   40–41
Elson, Samuel (prosecutor)   40
Emmery, Henry (defendant)   131–133
England, Richard (defendant)   81
Evans, Richard (defendant)   194, 202n
Evans, Sarah (defendant)   26n
Everingham or Evveringham, John (prosecutor)   56–57, 136
Eves, Elizabeth (defendant)   56–57, 61, 135n

Faires, John, alias Robert Smith (accused)   58
Falkner, William (witness)   81, 178
Farmer, Daniel (broker)   136
Farren, Henry (prosecutor)   27
Feast, Richard (defendant)   188n23
Felton, John (watchman, witness)   80
Fen, Oliver (witness)   81
Fenwick, Robert (prosecutor)   40
Festrop, Ann (defendant)   106
Field, William (witness)   83, 178
Fielding, Henry (J.P.)   6, 103, 130, 224
Fielding, John (J.P.)   103, 224
Flemming, Eleanor (defendant)   106
Fletcher, Thomas (prosecutor)   42
Floyd, Sarah (defendant)   106
Folwell, John (prosecutor)   58–59
Forster, Thomas (witness)   43–44
Forward, Benjamin (prosecutor)   28
Fox, Butler (defendant)   83
Fox, Sarah (defendant)   28
Freeman, Mary (defendant)   178–179
Fryer, Sir John (J.P., Lord Mayor)   55, 133n, 135n12, 136

Gambol, John (defendant)   188n23
Garrard, Robert (witness)   132
Gascoign, Philip (prosecutor)   28
Gerrard, Isaac (defendant)   188n23, 190
Gilbert, Elizabeth (defendant)   20
Giles, William, alias Charles Saunders (defendant)   81, 188n24
Glanister, Nathaniel and Thomas (defendants)   58, 61, 63
Glover, James (prosecutor)   27
Glover, John (defendant)   29
Godfrey, Sarah (witness)   191

Goodchild, John (prosecutor)   42
Goodman, William (prosecutor)   44
Graham, Hannah (defendant)   56, 61
Granger, Mary (defendant)   31n, 106
Gray, Arthur (defendant)   173n5
Green John (defendant)   28
Greenhill, Arthur (prosecutor)   40
Greening, Richard (witness)   29
Greenland, John (defendant)   178n, 189n24, 191
Griffin, Jane (defendant)   194
Griffith, Francis (defendant)   173n6, 188n22
Griffith, Thomas (defendant)   179n15, 188n23, 190n27
Gush, James (witness)   78

Hacker, Gustavus (prosecutor)   55
Hains, Sarah (defendant)   178n, 189n24
Halfpenny, Robert (witness)   78–79
Hall, James (defendant)   4n4
Hall, Mr. (broker)   56–57
Hansel, Simon (prosecutor)   79
Hargrove, Elizabeth (defendant)   106
Harris, John (defendant)   178 & n, 188n22
Harrison, Elizabeth (defendant)   202n
Harrison, Joseph (defendant)   176 & n11, 177, 182, 188n24
Hart, John (prosecutor)   41n6, 54
Harvey, Mary (defendant)   106
Harvey, James (defendant)   178, 183n19, 188n24
Hatchet, Elizabeth (prosecutor)   66
Hawes, Nathaniel (witness)   82–83
Hawkins, John (defendant)   81, 83–84, 110
Hawkins, William (witness)   81, 84
Hawks, Henry (defendant)   182
Heater, William (defendant)   110
Hedgly, Richard (defendant)   40
Hellom, Dorothy (defendant)   166n19
Helson, Mary (defendant)   194
Hemyn, Jeremiah (prosecutor)   29
Herbert, Sarah (defendant)   56, 61
Herbert, Walter (defendant)   177n, 183, 188n22, 189
Hewet, Richard (prosecutor)   43
Higgs, John (prosecutor)   28
Hill, Mr. (witness, constable)   110
Hilliard, Richard (prosecutor)   27, 64

INDEX OF PARTICIPANTS

Hillior, Edward (prosecutor)   42
Hilton, William (defendant)   55
Hipsly, Mary (defendant)   188*n*23
Hitchen, Charles (thief taker, broker)   65–66
Hobbs, William (defendant)   179*n*15, 188*n*23, 190*n*27
Hoe, Robert (prosecutor)   20
Holden, Thomas (witness)   43
Holland, Mr. (witness)   29
Holloway, Humphrey (witness)   28
Holloway, John (prosecutor)   27
Holms, Jane (defendant)   42
Holstock, Hannah (defendant)   194
Holt, Chief Justice (judge)   116
Homer, John (witness)   83
Hopkins, James (defendant)   79
Hornby, John (defendant)   66
Howard, William (prosecutor)   27, 133–134
Huggins, Bartholomew (prosecutor)   19
Hughes, Mary (defendant)   40, 194
Hullerton. Arthur (defendant)   43
Humphris, Joan (dealer)   54
Hunt, Richard (defendant)   189*n*24
Hunter, Robert (defendant)   159
Hurst, Christian (defendant)   64
Husbands, Thomas (witness)   28
Hutton, Mary (witness)   41

Illidge, Samuel (prosecutor)   27
Illidge, Samuel (defendant)   42
Isaac, William (defendant)   178*n*, 192

Jackson, Elizabeth (witness)   40
Jackson, Francis (accused)   135*n*10
Jackson, James (defendant)   188*n*23
Jackson, John (prosecutor)   40
Jacobs, Simon (defendant)   176*n*12, 178*n*, 183, 189–190
James, John (witness)   81
James, John of Ealing (defendant)   82
Jersey, Philip (defendant)   27
Jesson, Elizabeth (accused)   20
Johnson, Isaac (witness)   44
Jones, Alice (defendant)   42
Jones, Alice or Elenor, alias Evans (defendant)   56, 136
Jones, Griffith (defendant)   135

Jones, Mary (defendant)   182, 194
Jones, Mr. (witness, constable)   176
Jones, Richard (witness)   177
Jones, Ruth (defendant)   40, 202*n*
Jones, Susanna (defendant)   28
Josephs, Isaac (defendant)   179*n*15, 188*n*23, 190*n*27
Justus, Thomas (defendant)   176*n*12, 182, 188*n*23

Katharine, Edward (defendant)   179*n*15, 188*n*23, 190*n*27
Kean, Gilbert (prosecutor)   19–20
Kelley, Hugh (defendant)   82
Kelley, Mary (defendant)   173*n*7, 177*n*, 188*n*24
Kidgell, Jane (defendant)   194
King, Moll (celebrity criminal)   20*n*
Kirby, William (prosecutor)   65
Kirton, Susan (witness)   40–41
Knight, Thomas (defendant)   39*n*, 55–56
Knight, William (defendant)   55
Knowles, Elizabeth (prosecutor)   82

Lade, John (J.P.)   54, 134–135, 176*n*11
Lanman, James (defendant)   79, 80*n*
Lawson, Sarah (defendant)   106
Lazenby, David (defendant)   178, 182–183 & *n*21 188*n*22, 189
Leak, Mary (defendant)   26*n*
Leaky, Alice (defendant)   173*n*7, 177*n*, 178*n*, 188*n*24, 192, 196
Lee, Edward (prosecutor)   109
Lee, John (defendant)   182, 188*n*24
Leighton, Mary (witness)   41
Leonard, Christopher (witness)   58–59
Lewellin, William (witness)   107
Lloyd, Susannah (defendant)   40*n*
Lock, Joseph (witness)   42, 107
Lock, William (witness)   183
Lockwood, Elizabeth, alias Logwood (defendant)   64
Lorrain, Paul (Ordinary of Newgate)   158*n*9

Macdonnel, Barbara (witness)   180, 189
Manson, Anne (defendant)   54–55, 57
Manwaring (witness)   57
Margaret, Paul (J.P.)   135*n*12

Marriot, William (prosecutor) 42
Matthews, George (defendant) 179*n*15, 188*n*23
Mattison, Hugh (defendant) 57
Mawhood, Collet (prosecutor) 82
May, Sarah (defendant) 194
Mayo, Robert (defendant) 178*n*, 188*n*24, 196
Merritt, John (witness, thief-taker?) 110
Metcalf, John (prosecutor) 71*n*
Michel, D'Oyley (J.P.) 129 & *n*, 132
Mills, Richard (witness) 110
Mills, William (prosecutor) 166*n*19
Mires, Samuel (defendant) 54, 57
Mitten, Mr. (prosecutor) 27
Mob, Elizabeth (defendant) 106
Moittier, Mr. (witness) 56
Moll Cutpurse (celebrity criminal) 62–63 & *n*
Molony, John (defendant) 80
Morgan, John (defendant) 81
Motherby, Charles (defendant) 66
Murrel (witness) 110
Murrel, Mr. and Mrs. (thief-takers) 82

Neal, Edmund (defendant) 107–109
Neal, Mr. (witness, constable?) 43
Newman, Charles (witness) 82*n*
Nichols or Nicholls, Ann, alias Ireland (defendant) 54–55, 135*n*12, 194
Nichols, Solomon (prosecutor) 108 & *n*3
Norris, Henry (J.P.) 126, 128–130, 137, 150
Norris, Margaret (defendant) 194
North, Mary (defendant) 43, 202*n*

Palmer, Charles (defendant) 176–177, 178*n*, 188*n*22, 189
Parish, Alexander (defendant) 58
Parker, Ann (defendant) 106
Parker, Mr. (defendant) 159
Parry, Benjamin (prosecutor) 55
Pars, Katharine, alias Smith (defendant) 58
Parsons, Simon (witness) 176
Parthyday, Ann (prosecutor) 109
Partington, Mrs. (witness) 176
Partington, Thomas (prosecutor) 176
Peacock, Thomas (witness) 57
Peak, Alice (defendant) 137
Pearce, Thomas (defendant) 43

Perry, Samil (J.P) 132*n*8
Peterson, Phebe (witness) 109
Phillips, Elizabeth (defendant) 194
Phillips, John (witness) 176
Phillips, Thomas, alias Cross (defendant) 110
Pidgeon, R. (clerk) 132 & *n*8
Pincher, William (defendant) 107–109
Pinkly, Mark (witness) 177
Pitway, William (defendant) 54, 57
Plummer, William (defendant) 109
Polock, Zachary (prosecutor) 27
Pomeroy, John (defendant) 28
Pool, Elizabeth (defendant) 55, 194
Pool, Sarah (defendant) 177, 189*n*24, 196
Porter, Mercia (prosecutor) 82
Post, George (defendant) 159
Powel, John (prosecutor) 11*n*
Preston, Edward (defendant) 55
Price, Ann (witness) 176
Prior, John (prosecutor) 29
Pritchard, John (witness) 110
Pritchard, David (defendant) 44
Pritchard, Owen (defendant) 41*n*6
Pritchet, David (accused) 81
Purdue or Purdew, Martha defendant) 31*n*, 64
Purney, Thomas (Ordinary of Newgate) 24*n*, 83–84

Radwell, Johanna (defendant) 194
Rainbow, Sarah (prosecutor) 28
Rand, Jeremy (defendant) 81
Ranse, Susan (defendant) 188*n*24
Rawlinstone or Rowlscone, Christian (witness) 56–57, 136
Raymund or Raymond, Edward (defendant) 55
Read, John (defendant) 65
Reading, James (witness, defendant) 81, 82*n*, 83
Reed, Sarah (prosecutor) 81, 159
Reeves, Joseph (defendant) 107, 136
Reynolds, William (defendant) 57, 107, 135*n*12
Rice, Thomas (defendant) 40
Rider, Katherine (witness) 79
Rigby, Elizabeth (defendant) 194

INDEX OF PARTICIPANTS 247

Robinson, William of Fulham (defendant) 178–179, 188n24
Robinson, William of Wapping (defendant) 178 & n, 188n24
Rogers, Thomas, alias Cane (defendant) 31n
Room, Richard (witness, constable) 110
Rowe, Richard (defendant) 194
Rowlet, John (witness) 110

Sands, James (defendant) 179n15, 188n23, 190n27
Saunders, William (defendant) 158
Scipiers, Evan (prosecutor) 137
Scoon, John (defendant) 42, 107, 136
Selby, Mary (defendant) 194
Shaw, James, alias Smith (defendant) 81–82
Shelton, Walter (defendant) 78, 178–179, 189n24
Shephard, Richard (accused) 191
Shepherd, James (defendant) 81
Short, Jane (defendant) 41
Siddal, John (prosecutor) 78
Simpson, George (defendant) 81, 83, 110
Smalwood, John (prosecutor) 40
Smart, Francis (prosecutor) 131–133
Smith, Ann (defendant) 178n, 189n24
Smith, Edward (witness) 182n18
Smith, Elizabeth, alias Burchley (defendant) 194
Smith, John (defendant) 188n23, 194
Smith, Joseph, alias Smithson, alias Horton (defendant) 158, 176n12, 178, 183, 188n22, 189
Smith, Mary (defendant) 178, 188n23, 189, 191
Smith Mr. (prosecutor) 159
Smith, Samuel (defendant) 188n23
Smith, Sarah (witness) 134, 135 & n10, 136
Smith, Thomas, alias Newcomb (defendant) 178, 188n22
Smith, William (defendant) 178, 182, 188n24, 189, 191
Smithers, John, alias Smithurst (defendant) 42
Socket, Sarah (defendant) 26n
Sparry, James (defendant) 55
Spavin, Joseph (defendant) 194
Speerman, Mary (defendant) 106

Spencer, William (defendant) 43
Spigget or Spiggot, William (defendant) 110
Stanborough, Richard, alias Hall (defendant) 189n24
Stanly, John (witness) 55
Stevens, John (prosecutor) 28
Stewart, Sir William (J.P., Lord Mayor) 135
Stockwell, Richard (prosecutor) 28
Storey, Richard (prosecutor) 28
Story, Philip (defendant) 24n
Stratton, James (defendant) 133n
Street, Robert (prosecutor) 28
Streight, George (prosecutor) 40n
Strickland, William (witness) 159
Strut (defendant) 82n
Sturges, John (witness) 42
Sutton, Robert (defendant) 28
Syddal or Siddal, John (prosecutor) 54, 134–135

Tapping, Thomas (prosecutor) 149n21
Taylor, John (defendant) 179n15, 188n23, 190n27
Tew, Reverend Edmund (J.P.) 129
Thatcher, Ann and Mary (defendants) 136
Thatcher, William (witness) 43
Thompson, John, alias Williams (defendant) 66–67
Thompson, John (prosecutor) 109
Thomson, Sir William (Recorder) 165n17, 194, 195 & n32, 196, 207
Thorn, William (prosecutor) 40
Thornton, Mary (witness) 136
Thorp, Henry (defendant) 79
Tillard, Isaac (J.P.) 129, 133–134
Tilliard, Isaac (prosecutor) 29
Tinsly, Thomas (defendant) 43
Tinsty, Thomas (defendant) 179n15, 188n23, 190n27
Tomlinson, Joseph (defendant) 173n7, 188n24, 189, 193n31, 196
Tompion, Ann (defendant) 82, 202n
Tompion, Thomas (defendant) 82
Townley Margaret (defendant) 41
Trantrum, John (defendant) 173n6, 188n22
Trantum, Richard (defendant) 58, 178n, 188n24
Turner, John (prosecutor) 110

INDEX OF PARTICIPANTS

Tyler, Mary & William (witnesses)   133–134

Useley, Barbara (defendant)   19

Vaughan, John (defendant)   78, 178–179, 189*n*24
Vine, Michael (defendant)   27

Wade, William (defendant)   81, 82*n*
Wafer, Samuel (defendant)   179*n*15, 188*n*23, 190*n*27
Wager, Sir Charles (prosecutor)   182
Wagland, William (witness)   82*n*
Waldren, Laurence (defendant)   188*n*24
Walker, Joseph (prosecutor)   58
Walker, Mrs. (witness)   43
Ward, John (prosecutor)   43
Wass, Mr. (witness)   57, 135
Waters, Katherine (defendant)   137
Waterson or Waters, John (prosecutor)   135
Watkins, John (prosecutor)   110
Watson, George (defendant)   4*n*4
Wattson, Dll. (victim refusing to prosecute)   136
Wayland, Elizabeth (defendant)   177, 189*n*24, 196
Weaver, Mrs. (prosecutor)   107
Webb or Web, John or Thomas (defendant)   173*n*7, 176*n*12, 178*n*, 181, 189*n*24
Wedhal, Thomas (prosecutor)   177, 192
Wellbone, John (defendant)   188*n*23
Wells, Sarah, alias Calicoe Sarah (defendant)   20, 24, 106, 194
Werrey (witness, constable)   133
Whalebone, John (defendant)   179*n*15, 188*n*23, 190*n*27
White, John (defendant)   194
White, John of St Botolph without Bishopsgate (defendant)   178*n*, 183, 188*n*23, 190*n*27
White, John of St Katherine Coleman (defendant)   178*n*, 188*n*24
Wigley, James (defendant)   83, 87
Wild, Abel (defendant)   28
Wild, Jonathan (witness, thief taker, broker)   9, 38*n*, 59, 63, 65–66, 77, 82–83, 89, 178, 189
Wilkinson, Anne (defendant)   40
Williams, Ann (prosecutor)   109
Williams, John, alias Williamson (defendant)   188*n*23, 190
Williams, Mary (defendant)   179*n*15, 188*n*23, 190*n*27
Williams, Thomas (defendant)   28–29, 78–79
Williams, William (defendant)   178*n*, 188*n*24
Williamson, Anne (murder victim)   11*n*
Willis (witness, constable)   107
Wilson, James (witness)   83
Wilson, John (defendant)   180–181, 188*n*23
Wilson, Margaret (defendant)   106, 194
Wilson, Ralph or Richard (witness)   81, 83–84, 110
Wilson, Samuel (prosecutor)   42
Wilson, Thomas (defendant)   83
Windel or Windell, Charles (prosecutor)   189
Winckworth, Charles (prosecutor)   28
Winship or Winshipp, John (defendant, witness)   24*n*, 81
Winter, Reynolds (defendant)   54, 78, 80*n*, 134–136
Withall, William, alias Harris (defendant)   176*n*12, 182, 188*n*22
Witherel, William (defendant)   27
Withers, Sir William (J.P.)   136
Wood, John (defendant)   29
Wooton, Edward (defendant)   66
Wright, Edward (defendant)   58
Wright, James (defendant)   81, 83–84
Wright, Mary (defendant)   57–58
Wyser, Thomas (witness)   28

Yeomans, Mary (defendant)   40
Yeomans, Thomas (witness)   54, 78, 134, 135 & *n*10–11, 136
Young, William (prosecutor)   80

Author and Subject Index

accomplices 8, 76–95, 140–141, 158–159, 178, 183 & *n* 19, 20
advertisements 56, 71 & *n*, 112, 158, 168
allocutus 193–198, 205
America 122, 153, 202, 209, 213
Andrew, Donna *143n*
Applebee, John 11*n*, 108*n*2
Appleby's Original Weekly Journal (Defoe) 9, 163 & *n*15
apprehending 5, 17–95, 106–107
apprentices 1, 90–91, 181–182
arraignment 173–175. *See also* indictments
Ascari, Maurizio 103, 110, 123
Atkinson, Alan 202–203
attorneys 8, 11, 123, 127, 132 & *n*8, 143, 158

Backscheider, P. R. 8, 204*n*5
Bardotti, Marta 154
Bauer, W.A. 149*n*23
Beattie, J. M. 7–8, 18, 32, 36*n*, 38, 46 & *n*, 54, 56, 58–59, 64–66, 77 & *n*, 78–79*n*, 86, 92, 103, 105, 126–127, 129–130, 137, 140, 145, 156, 159–162, 166, 171–174, 178–179, 183–184, 187–188, 190*n*28, 192, 195, 207, 210–211, 222, 225
Beccaria, Cesare 7
Bell, Ian 32*n*
Bender, John 156*n*3
benefit of clergy 8, 18, 36, 3, 59, 63, 66, 161, 192, 194–5, 217
Blackstone, William 166
Blewett, David 91*n*, 220
Bloomsbury 141
'Bloody Code' 8, 36, 95 & *n*, 191, 200
Bludworth, Sir Thomas 145. 147
Bohun, Edmund 138
Bond, C. S. 9
Bray, Dr. Thomas 156*n*3
Bree, Linda 4*n*6, 204*n*6
Bridewell. *See* punishments: houses of correction
Bullock, Christopher 103, 149

Campbell, Ann 172*n*2
Care, Henry 105, 123
Cecconi, Elisabetta 160

Cervantes, Gabriel 2*n*, 9, 31, 73*n*, 200, 203, 207, 209–210, 213–215
Chaber, Lois 156*n*5
Child thieves 26–31, 58, 79, 173*n*7, 188*n*24, 189. *See also* defendants, witnesses in Index of Participants
City of London 1, 33, 144, 160
    aldermen 50, 136, 145–147, 150
    Guildhall 27, 64, 131, 135, 140, 144, 159, 165
    Lord Mayors 73*n*, 86–87, 130–131, 135, 139–141, 150, 156, 171, 198*n*35
    Recorder 63, 110, 165*n*17, 195*n*33, 201, 205–206
    royal proclamation 77, 82, 94
Clayton, Mary 8, 78*n*, 95, 167*n*
clerks 5, 70–71, 128*n*2, 131–132, 134, 160*n*12, 161–162, 165, 167, 169, 171, 174
Coke, Sir Edward 113
Colonel Jack (Defoe) 2–4, 9–10, 29–35, 69–75, 79*n*, 89–95, 99–100, 108*n*2, 118–123, 149, 195*n*32, 203, 204*n*4, 213–225. *See also* narrative and rhetorical techniques
    advertised 11*n*, 108*n*2
    chronology of 204*n*4
Complete English Tradesman (Defoe) 46
conduct books 9–11, 101, 103–105, 112, 123 & *n*, 128 & *n*2. *See also* individual authors
confessions 34, 37, 55, 57, 59, 70, 80, 93, 107, 123, 132–136, 138, 140, 157–158, 173 &*n*7, 181, 189
constables 5, 10, 20, 29, 41*n*6, 42–43, 48–49, 51–52, 55, 77*n*, 81*n*5, 82*n*, 99–124, 132–134, 140–145, 150, 162, 164, 176 & *n*12, 222, 224–225
    deputy constables 7, 105, 108–109, 117, 224
    headboroughs 5, 102, 108
corruption 103, 123, 158–159, 162–165, 168, 169*n*, 219
Covent Garden 48, 107, 114, 141, 144
coverture 189 & *n*26, 210*n*14
Cox, Pamela 4*n*4
crimes 129. *See also* defendants, prosecutors in Index of Participants
    accessory to felony 38, 57, 59, 138, 158

crimes (*cont.*)
   assault   28*n*, 76, 80, 82, 89, 93, 104, 107, 109, 126, 141–143, 158, 161, 174*n*
   breach of the peace   117, 143
   burglary   58, 76, 81, 92, 119, 166–167, 173, 175–193
   compounding for return of stolen goods   37, 53–54, 63–75, 94, 128–129, 157*n*7
   grand larceny   39*n*, 161, 166, 191–192, 195, 198, 224
   highway robbery   9, 76–77, 80–84, 89–95, 107–109, 111, 150, 160–161, 167–169, 195, 209, 213, 224
   horse-stealing   8, 130
   housebreaking   36, 59,-60, 76–77, 148–149 & *n*21, 166, 195
   kidnapping   32, 149, 213–214
   murder   11*n*, 82, 94, 122, 137*n*, 149
   perjury   134, 138–139 & *n*, 159
   petty larceny   191, 195
   pickpocketing   9, 13, 17–36, 39, 64–66, 81–82, 91, 94, 106–107, 133, 137, 161. 202, 213, 215
   receiving stolen goods   53, 57, 59–60, 63–65, 69, 72, 74–75, 107, 135*n*10, 136
   shoplifting   13, 17, 36–52, 55, 59–60, 63, 77*n*–80, 106–107, 118, 131–132, 134–137, 158, 202*n*
   stealing from a specified place   161, 192–193 & *n*31
crowds   24–26, 30–31, 33, 45, 48–50, 103, 109, 113–114, 118, 144, 171, 175, 183
Curtis, L.A.   190*n*28

Dabhoiwala, Faramez   128*n*3
Dalton, Michael   128*n*2, 129, 138
Davies, Owen   61*n*
de Certeau, Michel   100–101, 112–113, 123, 170–171, 223
defences   34, 122, 138, 146, 179–182, 185. *See also* defendants in Index of Participants
Defoe, Daniel. *See also* narrative and rhetorical techniques, titles of ndividual works
   experience of law   8
   frequenting Newgate   84

indentured servants   204*n*5
pardon   201
De Veil, Sir Thomas   127–128
Directions for Prosecuting Thieves   158, 190–191
drapers   46, 85, 90, 204
drunkenness   21–22, 27, 92

Ekirch, A.R.   198*n*35, 209*n*13, 211*n*13
Ellison Katherine   3*n*
Essay on Projects (Defoe)   9
Evans, Sir Stephen   69
evidence   121, 147

Faller, L. B.   3, 47–48, 72, 114, 119, 144, 155, 164, 220, 222
false arrest   49, 104, 115–116, 120–121, 141
Fludernick, Monica   157*n*6
Franks, Rachel   158*n*9
Foucault, Michel   156*n*3
'Friends'   1, 87, 165, 167, 169, 185, 201, 205, 211, 219

'gangs'   17, 38, 63, 72, 77, 79 & *n*, 81, 83, 90–94, 161, 168
Gardiner, Robert   105, 111, 113, 123
Furbank, F.N.   9*n*8, 163*n*15
Gallanis, T.P.   172*n*4
Gatrell, V.A.C.   201
gender   17–20, 26–27, 34, 139, 150, 210*n*
George I, King   183, 218–219
Gladfelder, Hal   12–13, 30, 74, 90, 165 & *n*18, 206
Gollapudi, Aparna   29
goldsmiths   55–56, 69–70, 73*n*, 144
grand juries   131, 159–163, 165–167, 190, 223
Great Grievance of Traders and Shopkeepers   36 & *n*, 37, 63, 158
Great Law of Subordination (Defoe)   42*n*
Green, T. A.   191
Gregg, Stephen   91, 213
Grovier, Kelly   156
Guide to English Juries   162, 167
Guildhall. *See* City of London

Halliday, Stephen   156*n*3
Hanging, Not Punishment Enough   63
'hanging cabinet'   201, 205, 207

AUTHOR AND SUBJECT INDEX 251

Hay, Douglas   104, 107, 197*n*, 200–201
Herrup, Cynthia   5–6, 102, 112
Hicks Hall   143, 159, 161
History of the Press-Yard   157
Hitchcock, Tim   101, 104, 107, 110, 114
Hollingshead, David   115*n*
Howson, Gerald   20*n*, 81
hue and cry   110–112
Humfrey, Paula   42*n*
Hunt, Margaret   22*n*, 33*n*15
Hunter, J.P.   9, 61, 122–123
Hurl-Eamon, Jennine   103, 120–121

immunity from prosecution   76–95, 134, 140, 177, 210*n*14
impeachment   76–89
indictments   5, 39*n*, 140, 159–163, 173–175, 190–191

Jacob, Giles   104 & *n*, 112, 117*n*, 121, 123
Jacobites   91*n*, 200, 202, 218–220
journeyman   44, 48–49, 52, 116–118, 141–144
judges   18, 39, 43, 133, 171, 173, 184, 186–187, 190–193, 196–199, 201, 205*n*7, 224
juries. *See* grand juries, petty juries
justices of the peace   5, 8, 20, 34, 49, 51–55, 59, 80, 86–88, 99–100, 106–107, 112, 115, 117–122, 125–150, 173, 177 & *n*, 186, 190, 214, 222, 224. *See also* J.P.s in Index of Participants
justice system   4*n*, 5–6
   participatory   4–7, 28–29, 80–81, 90, 222
   changes in practice   7–8, 22, 36, 38, 95*n*, 102, 105, 125–129, 224–225

Kahan, Lee   26
Kalman, H.D.   156 & *n*
Kent, Joan   102
Kietzman, Mary Jo   160*n*12, 165*n*18, 206*n*9
King, Peter   5, 6, 13*n*, 17*n*, 164*n*, 175*n*, 190, 201, 205*n*8

Lamb, Jonathan   65, 74*n*
Lambarde, William   103–104, 123, 128*n*2
Landau, Norma   125 & *n*, 127, 128*n*2, 143
Langbein, John   5–6, 8, 76, 112, 121, 148*n*, 172*n*4, 173, 179
lawsuits   49, 107, 115, 120

lawyers   5, 8, 147*n*, 172 & *n*3, 184, 189
Lemmings, David   8, 172*n*3
Liebe, Lauren   63*n*
Linebaugh, Peter   123, 158*n*9
London Lives   56–57, 130–136, 176*n*11
Lorrain, Paul   158*n*9
Lord Mayors. *See* City of London: Lord Mayors. *See also* Index of Participants
Loveman, Kate   4*n*6, 145 & *n*, 149, 169*n*, 204*n*4, 208*n*

Macherey, Pierre   220
magistrates. *See* justices of the peace
makeshift economy   32, 38, 54, 61
Marshall, Ashley   9*n*8
McBurney, W.H.   91*n*
McKenzie, Andrea   13*n*11, 91
mercers   45–49, 88, 114–118, 141–144
merchants   32, 63, 69–75, 127, 175, 214
mercy   13, 51, 148, 193, 196–197, 200–201, 203 – 204, 206, 216–217, 219–220
Meriton, George   104
misdemeanours   59, 66, 107, 112–113, 126, 128, 148–149 & *n*21
Moll Flanders (Defoe)   1–4, 13, 20–26, 84–89, 99–100, 111–118, 137–150, 153–155, 163–169, 174–175, 183–187, 192–193, 196–199, 204–213, 220, 222–225. *See also* narrative & rhetorical techniques
   advertised   11*n*
   chapbook editions   149*n*22, 195*n*32
   chronology of   204
Morgan, Gwenda   129
Morgan, Kenneth   198*n*35
Much Ado about Nothing (Shakespeare)   103
Mui, Hoh-cheung & L.H.   36

narrative & rhetorical techniques   2–3 & *n*, 7, 12–13, 23, 25, 67, 85, 138, 146, 155*n*, 187, 197–198, 213, 220, 222, 225
Nelson, William   128*n*2
Newgate prison   2, 30, 62, 83–86, 88, 93, 100, 118–119, 134–135, 139–140, 143, 153–170, 178, 204–206, 210
Novak, M. E.   8–9, 84–85, 163, 201, 213, 219

O'Brien, John   202–203 & *n*, 215
Old Bailey   92, 143, 171–199, 205. *See also* defendants, prosecutors, witnesses in Index of Participants
    courthouse   171
    procedures   171–173, 175, 187
    Proceedings   11 & *n*, 12–13, 19–20, 40 & *n*, 41–42 & *n*, 43–44, 54–58, 78–79, 80–81 & *n*5, 82 & *n*, 83–84, 93, 105–108 & *n*3, 109–110, 131–132, 135 & *n*10–11, 136–137, 158–159, 166 & *n*19, 171–173 & *n*5–7, 176 & *n*2, 177 & *n*, 178 & *n*, 179 & *n*15 &16, 180–181, 182 & *n*18, 183 & *n*19–21, 184, 187, 191–193, 197–199, 209, 223, 225
Ordinary of Newgate   24*n*, 83, 157 & *n*8, 158*n*9. *See also* defendants, witnesses in Index of Participants
    Account   4*n*4, 11*n*, 24*n*, 31*n*, 80*n*, 83–84, 108*n*2, 123, 133, 157 & *n*8, 183 *n*19, 189, 209
Owens, W.R   9*n*8, 163*n*15
Oxford English Dictionary   47

Paley, Ruth   126–128 & *n*2, 129–131
Palk, Dierdre   17–19, 21
pardons   6, 13, 31*n*, 38, 76, 80*n*, 85, 88, 94, 127, 169, 183 & *n*19, 193, 198–221
Parochial Tyranny (Defoe)   101–102, 104, 124
Parrinder, Patrick   91
pawnbrokers   54–55, 61, 132, 177
petitions   6, 197–198 & *n*35, 201–205 & *n*8, 214
petty juries   6, 31, 39, 106, 161, 171–172, 178, 183*n*20, 184, 186–192, 223.
    See also verdicts
Poor Man's Plea (Defoe)   9
prosecutors   4, 6, 14, 18, 21–22, 27–29, 76, 106–110, 137–139, 148, 159 & *n*, 160–162, 164 & *n*, 166, 168, 176, 178.
    See also prosecutors in Index of Participants
prosecutions   4–5, 35–38, 52, 63, 191
    entrepreneurial   143
    malicious   109, 127
prostitution   18–20, 106
P.S. Gent.   104, 113, 118, 120, 123
punishments   5–8, 195 & *n*32–33. *See also* statutes
    branding   37–39, 46, 194–196, 202, 205
    capital   31, 39, 46, 56–58, 80–81, 85, 89, 133 & *n*, 135, 165, 192, 196, 199–200
    houses of correction   34, 128 & *n*3, 129, 133, 149, 194, 202, 214
    informal   5, 30–31, 222
    transportation   31–32, 37, 80, 89, 134, 194–196, 198–199, 202–204, 206–215, 217–218, 220, 224
    whipping   31, 37, 39, 149*n*22, 195*n*32, 202

Rabin, D.Y.   6*n*, 193
Ray, William   146*n*
recognisances   5, 86, 128*n*2, 134–135, 139, 142, 148, 159*n*, 160, 164–165, 190
Recorder. *See* City of London, Recorder
Reformation of Manners (Defoe)   9, 149 & *n*23
Reformation of Manners movement   19*n*, 107
repentance   2, 83, 193, 203, 205–206, 213, 215, 217
rewards   8, 38, 43, 65, 70–71 & *n*, 76–78, 80–82, 89, 94–95&*n*, 103, 110, 127, 157*n*7, 162–163, 167, 178, 183*n*19
Reynolds, E.A.   105
Richetti, John   155*n*
Rivero, Albert J.   1*n*, 211*n*16
Rosemary Lane   20, 118–119, 121, 213
Rubin, Ashley   7, 195
Rudolph, Julia   104 & *n*
Rushton, Peter   129

Satanic inspiration   1, 32, 61*n*, 193
Schramm, Jan-Melissa   148*n*
searches   13, 26–29, 41–42, 48, 106–107, 113–114, 116, 123, 176
Select Trials   41*n*5
Sentencing. *See allocutus see also* punishments
Sertoli, Giuseppe   119*n*, 204*n*4
Sheehan, W.J.   123*n*, 156*n*4, 158
Shoemaker, R.B.   4*n*4, 5, 8, 12, 78, 79*n*, 82, 91–92, 95*n*, 101–104, 106–107, 110, 112, 114, 116, 123, 126, 128–129*n*, 133, 142, 167*n*, 179–180, 182*n*, 183–184, 193, 198*n*

AUTHOR AND SUBJECT INDEX

Shore, Heather   4*n*4, 32, 61, 104, 107
servants   1–3, 11*n*, 14, 37, 40–43, 48–52, 55, 57, 59, 63, 91–92, 117–118, 141–142, 149, 163–164, 177 & *n*, 182*n*18, 185–188, 192, 212–213, 215–217
 indentured servants   204 & *n*5
Sharpe, James   160 & *n*12
Sill, Geoffrey   2*n*, 9, 18*n*, 73*n*, 79*n*, 91, 213–214
Singleton, R. R.   158*n*9
smallpox experiment   202 & *n*
Smith, Alexander   52
Snell, Esther   8
Solicitors. *See* attorneys
Spraggs, Gillian   81*n*6, 91
Starr, G. A.   4*n*6, 13*n*12, 21*n*, 45–46*n*, 139*n*, 148, 158, 162–163*n*, 168*n*, 174*n*, 203*n*, 205*n*7
statutes. *See also* City of London: royal proclamation
 1 & 2 *Phil. & Mar.*, c. 13 (1554–5) [Marian bail statute]   5, 129, 149–150, 190
 2 & 3 *Phil. & Mar.*, c. 10 (1555) [Marian bail statute]   5, 129, 149–150, 190
 31 *Car.* II, c. 2. (1679) [Habeas Corpus Act]   115 & *n*, 203, 204*n*6
 3 & 4 *Wm. & M.*, c. 9 (1691) [Benefit of Clergy Act]   59
 4 & 5 *Wm. & M.*, c. 8 (1692) [Apprehending of Highwaymen Act]   76
 10 & 11 *Wm. & M.*, c. 23 (1699 [Shoplifting Act]   36, 39*n*, 59, 77, 140, 166*n*20
 1 *Anne*, stat. 2, c. 9 (1702) [Accessories and Receivers Act]   59
 5 *Anne*, c. 31 (1706) [Apprehending of Housebreakers & Burglars Act]   59, 77
 12 *Anne*, c. 7 (1713) [Theft from Houses Act]   59, 77
 3, *Geo.* I, c. 19 (1717) [Act of Grace and Free Pardon/ Indemnity Act]   218–218
 4 *Geo.* I, c. 11 (1718) [First Transportation Act]   7, 31, 59, 66 & *n*, 75, 77, 194–196, 200, 202–203 & *n*
 6 *Geo.* I, c. 23 (1720) [Second Transportation Act]   7, 66, 75, 200

stolen goods   21, 23, 27 & *n*9, 29–30, 32, 37–38, 53–57, 60, 63–64, 69–70, 74–75, 106, 113, 182, 223. *See also* crimes: compounding, receiving stolen goods
Styles, John   56, 112, 158, 168
Swan, Beth   4*n*5, 100, 147*n*, 174*n*8
testimony   12, 19, 27, 30, 43–44, 58, 78–79, 81–84, 106, 112, 130, 136–138, 165, 168 & *n*, 169, 175–183, 192, 209. *See also* witnesses in Index of Participants
thief-taking   19*n*, 29, 44, 65–66, 76–78, 82–83, 94–95, 103, 105, 108*n*3, 110, 157*n*7, 158, 178, 189. *See also* thief-takers in Index of Participants
Tickell, Shelley   27*n*9, 36–40*n*3, 41*n*, 43, 48*n*, 51, 54, 58, 166*n*20, 175
Todd, Dennis   203*n*, 204*n*3
Tour through the Whole Island of Great Britain (Defoe)   145
trial formats   6, 8, 187. *See also* justice system; Old Bailey: procedures
True and Genuine Account ... Jonathan Wild (Defoe)   59–60, 63, 66*n*
'Tyburn ticket'   38, 43, 77*n*, 80, 105

verdicts   175, 178–179, 182, 187–192, 198, 208
violence   42, 76, 80–81, 89–94, 104, 106, 108, 137*n*, 189*n*25

Wales, Tim   8, 18*n*, 19*n*, 63, 65
Ward, R.M   10
warrants   34, 100, 105, 107, 110, 112, 118–122, 128*n*, 131, 150, 176, 202*n*, 213
 'dead warrant'   201, 205–206
watchmen   20, 48, 80–81*n*5, 99, 106, 140, 176*n*12, 181–182
Weinreich, S.J.   201*n*
Welch, Saunders   103, 112
Welsh, Alexander   30*n*, 147
Whittington, Richard   156
Wikipedia   104*n*, 189–190*n*26
Wrightson, Keith   102

Zomchick, J.P.   210*n*

Printed in the United States
by Baker & Taylor Publisher Services